Learning ServiceNow
Second Edition

Administration and development on the Now platform, for powerful IT automation

Tim Woodruff

BIRMINGHAM - MUMBAI

Learning ServiceNow
Second Edition

Commissioning Editor: Vijin Boricha
Acquisition Editor: Rahul Nair
Content Development Editor: Devika Battike
Technical Editor: Mohd Riyan Khan
Project Coordinator: Judie Jose
Indexer: Tejal Daruwale Soni
Graphics: Tom Scaria
Production Coordinator: Shantanu Zagade

First published: March 2017

Second edition: June 2018

Production reference: 1180618

Published by Packt Publishing Ltd.
Livery Place
35 Livery Street
Birmingham B3 2PB, UK.

ISBN 978-1-78883-704-0

www.packtpub.com

`mapt.io`

Mapt is an online digital library that gives you full access to over 5,000 books and videos, as well as industry leading tools to help you plan your personal development and advance your career. For more information, please visit our website.

Why subscribe?

- Spend less time learning and more time coding with practical eBooks and Videos from over 4,000 industry professionals
- Learn better with Skill Plans built especially for you
- Get a free eBook or video every month
- Mapt is fully searchable
- Copy and paste, print, and bookmark content

PacktPub.com

Did you know that Packt offers eBook versions of every book published, with PDF and ePub files available? You can upgrade to the eBook version at `www.PacktPub.com` and as a print book customer, you are entitled to a discount on the eBook copy. Get in touch with us at `service@packtpub.com` for more details.

At `www.PacktPub.com`, you can also read a collection of free technical articles, sign up for a range of free newsletters, and receive exclusive discounts and offers on Packt books and eBooks.

Contributors

About the author

Tim Woodruff is a ServiceNow architect and developer who has spent his entire adult life working in IT systems and development, with over a decade of experience in both. Tim has written several books on ServiceNow, and runs a ServiceNow development blog called SN Pro Tips.

Tim writes ServiceNow apps which he gives away through his development blog. When he's not working, Tim can be found researching obscure and arcane programming trivia and studying physics. You can find Tim on Twitter at @ TheTimWoodruff.

Thanks to Kim, Roger, Ciel, Chuck, and Genie, for their support and general awesomeness.

Thanks to Gary and Georgia for their inspiration and total radness.

Thanks to Seven for being a good dog.

Special thanks to John Helebrant and Mike Hade for their invaluable contributions, technical expertise, and content editing.

About the reviewers

John Helebrant has been in the IT industry for over 20 years. He started a small computer business in his hometown of Austin, MN, and eventually moved to the Twin Cities to continue his career in technology. He worked as an Application Developer and an IT Service Management expert while earning several certifications and a BA in Professional Writing. He now works as a ServiceNow Developer and Administrator after discovering what an exciting set of challenges and opportunities ServiceNow has to offer.

In his spare time, he enjoys playing bass, writing and editing, walking his dogs, watching movies, continuing to evolve as a developer, and spending time with his better half: Jen.

Michael Hade is a Senior ServiceNow Architect with over 9 years of development experience on the platform. He specializes in designing and creating dynamic and efficient ServiceNow solutions. He has worked on over 100 different ServiceNow instances including both commercial and government clients. Mike designed and created the Best Practice Engine app available on the ServiceNow Store which validates that all developers on the platform are following ServiceNow best practices and company standards.

Mike lives in Fort Wayne, IN with his wife Trisha and his two boys, Danny and Jacob.

Packt is Searching for Authors Like You

If you're interested in becoming an author for Packt, please visit authors.packtpub. com and apply today. We have worked with thousands of developers and tech professionals, just like you, to help them share their insight with the global tech community. You can make a general application, apply for a specific hot topic that we are recruiting an author for, or submit your own idea.

Table of Contents

Preface

ServiceNow is a powerful and versatile cloud-based IT Service Management (ITSM) platform that supports Incident, Problem, Change, and Knowledge management, as well as a great many other IT processes. With Information Technology Infrastructure Library (ITIL) processes baked right in, powerful workflow-driven processes, and a robust scripting engine for both client-side and server-side customizations, ServiceNow can provide fairly comprehensive ITSM functionality right out of the box, or it can be extensively customized to suit the needs of any business.

If you're reading this, then there's a good chance you are, or aim to be, a ServiceNow administrator or developer. This means that it'll be your responsibility to extend and modify ServiceNow's existing functionality to meet the needs of your business' users. This book will help get you up to speed on how ServiceNow works, what its capabilities are, and how to customize its functionality and appearance!

Who this book is for

While expert ServiceNow developers, administrators, and architects can expect to learn much from this book, it is geared toward people with less than 2 years of experience as ServiceNow developers/administrators.

Whether you're getting the hang of things, are just starting out, or even if you haven't yet begun your ServiceNow career, this book is for you.

What this book covers

Chapter 1, The Interface, learn about the different interfaces of ServiceNow (including UI15 and UI16), and pick up pro tips on how to fly around the interface like a seasoned pro.

Chapter 2, Lists and Forms, see the differences between the new and old style of lists (both of which are present in ServiceNow), and learn how to customize them as well as the form view and related lists.

Chapter 3, UI Customization, customize your ServiceNow instance's user interface, using themes, System Properties, UI Properties, and custom CSS.

Chapter 4, Understanding Data and Relationships, understand table inheritance, and the different types of relationships that go into the underlying ServiceNow relational database structure; including one-to-one, one-to-many, and many-to-many relationships.

Chapter 5, Tasks and Workflows, expanding on the data relationship concepts we learned in the previous chapter, this chapter teaches specifically about Tasks in ServiceNow, and best practices surrounding their use. Herein, we also learn about workflows - closely tied with the Task table - and how to leverage them effectively.

Chapter 6, UI and Data Policies, learn about UI Policies, Data Policies, and best practice guidelines surrounding them. Pick up "Pro Tips" from industry experts, and learn how to debug potential issues.

Chapter 7, User Administration and Security, ServiceNow's security and access rights are determined by Access Control Lists (ACLs) also known as Security Rules. Learn to utilize these rules to define permissions for your users in your instance.

Chapter 8, Introduction to Scripting, scripting in ServiceNow has its own quirks and best practices. In this chapter, learn how (and when) to use custom scripted functionality.

Chapter 9, The Server-Side Glide API, learn about the server-side ServiceNow API, also known as the Glide API, built on top of Mozilla Rhino: a Java-based implementation of JavaScript.

Chapter 10, The Client-Side Glide API, see real-world examples while learning about the client-side Glide API, including how to avoid the major performance pitfalls using AJAX and asynchronous scripting.

Chapter 11, Server-Side Scripting, now that you understand the server-side Glide API, learn about scripting best practices, how and when to use server-side scripts, and what types of scripts are available.

Chapter 12, Client-Side Scripting, learn all about client-side script types and best practices, including how to access server-side data and functionality asynchronously, while preserving client-side performance.

Chapter 13, Service Portal Scripting, learn how to write and interact with scripts in the Service Portal, including some of the pitfalls to avoid in Service Portal code.

Chapter 14, Debugging, now that you know enough to be dangerous, this chapter teaches you how to debug your scripts to make sure they'll run without error, and handle potential issues as, or even before, they arise.

Chapter 15, Pro Tips, get tips and advice on how to avoid common pitfalls. Learn advanced tips, and what industry pros wish they'd known when they were first starting out as ServiceNow administrators and developers.

To get the most out of this book

There are a couple of things you'll need, before you set off on your journey toward becoming a ServiceNow developer:

Basic knowledge of JavaScript

JavaScript is the language that's used to interact with ServiceNow on both the client, and the server. While an administrator can do a lot of customization within ServiceNow without any code at all, any scripting you do will be done in JavaScript.

 There's a common saying: "'Java' is to 'JavaScript', as 'Car' is to 'Carpet'". The two are effectively unrelated. The language you need to know for ServiceNow development, is JavaScript.

A free developer instance of ServiceNow

ServiceNow is kind enough to provide a free development instance to anyone who wants one.

To request an instance, simply register for an account on `www.developer.servicenow.com`, and then click the **Request Instance** link on your account page.

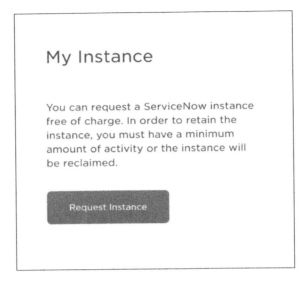

When requesting an instance, you may select which version of ServiceNow you'd like. You can change this at any time down the road, but it often takes a few hours to do so.

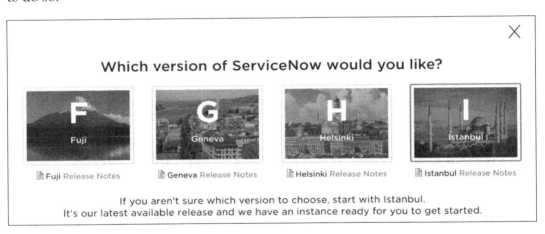

This book deals primarily with the **Jakarta**, **Kingston**, and **London** versions of ServiceNow. If you're going to follow along in your own instance, we recommend doing so in either **Jakarta**, **Kingston**, or **London**.

Download the color images

We also provide a PDF file that has color images of the screenshots/diagrams used in this book. You can download it here: `https://www.packtpub.com/sites/default/files/downloads/LearningServiceNowSecondEdition_ColorImages.pdf`.

Conventions used

There are a number of text conventions used throughout this book.

`CodeInText`: Indicates code words in text, database table names, folder names, filenames, file extensions, pathnames, dummy URLs, user input, and Twitter handles. For example; " Here is an example of a scripted condition field using `gs.hasRole()`"

A block of code is set as follows:

```
var GetPropertyAjax = Class.create();
GetPropertyAjax.prototype = Object.extendsObject(AbstractAjaxProcessor, {
    getProp: function() {
        var propName = this.getParameter('sysparm_prop_name');
        return(gs.getProperty(propName));
    },
    type: 'GetPropertyAjax'
});
```

When we wish to draw your attention to a particular part of a code block, the relevant lines or items are set in bold:

```
var GetPropertyAjax = Class.create();
GetPropertyAjax.prototype = Object.extendsObject(AbstractAjaxProcessor, {
    getProp: function() {
        var propName = this.getParameter('sysparm_prop_name');
        return(gs.getProperty(propName));
    },
    type: 'GetPropertyAjax'
});
```

Bold: Indicates a new term, an important word, or words that you see on the screen, for example, in menus or dialog boxes, also appear in the text like this. For example: "Select **System info** from the **Administration** panel."

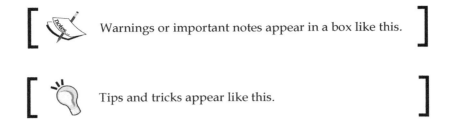

Warnings or important notes appear in a box like this.

Tips and tricks appear like this.

Get in touch

Feedback from our readers is always welcome.

General feedback: Email feedback@packtpub.com, and mention the book's title in the subject of your message. If you have questions about any aspect of this book, please email us at questions@packtpub.com.

Errata: Although we have taken every care to ensure the accuracy of our content, mistakes do happen. If you have found a mistake in this book we would be grateful if you would report this to us. Please visit, http://www.packtpub.com/submit-errata, selecting your book, clicking on the Errata Submission Form link, and entering the details.

Piracy: If you come across any illegal copies of our works in any form on the Internet, we would be grateful if you would provide us with the location address or website name. Please contact us at copyright@packtpub.com with a link to the material.

If you are interested in becoming an author: If there is a topic that you have expertise in and you are interested in either writing or contributing to a book, please visit http://authors.packtpub.com.

Reviews

Please leave a review. Once you have read and used this book, why not leave a review on the site that you purchased it from? Potential readers can then see and use your unbiased opinion to make purchase decisions, we at Packt can understand what you think about our products, and our authors can see your feedback on their book. Thank you!

For more information about Packt, please visit packtpub.com.

1
The Interface

ServiceNow is a very robust IT service management tool and has an interface to match. It's designed to be both easy to use, and to support a multitude of business processes and applications (including the unforeseen variety). It must be able to bend to the will of the business and be putty in the hands of a capable developer like you! Don't worry if you don't consider yourself a *capable ServiceNow developer* just yet; read on!

Regardless of what software system you're interested in learning about, understanding the interface is likely to be the first step toward success. In this chapter, you'll learn all the major components of the **user interface (UI)**, and how to manipulate them to suit your business' needs, find and display useful information, and administer the platform effectively. You'll also learn some time-saving tips, tricks, and UI shortcuts that have been built into the interface for power users to get around more quickly.

[These UI shortcuts and other pro tips will be collected online as a quick pocket-reference!]

This chapter will cover the key components of the user interface, including:

- The content and ServiceNow frames
- The application navigator
- UI settings and personalization
- UI16 interface components and configuration
- Differences between the interfaces in modern and earlier versions of ServiceNow
- Pro tips for flying around the interface like a seasoned pro

We recommend that you follow along in your own development instance as you read through this section, to gain a more intimate familiarity with the interface. See the preface of this book for more information.

Versions

Throughout this chapter, and the rest of this book, we'll be referring to various versions of ServiceNow. The versions of ServiceNow go in alphabetical order, and are named for geographic locations, beginning with **Aspen**—released in 2011. The ServiceNow versions, in order, are as follows:

- Aspen
- Berlin
- Calgary
- Dublin
- Eureka
- Fuji
- Geneva
- Helsinki
- Istanbul
- Jakarta
- Kingston
- London

This book will focus on the latest version of ServiceNow at the time of writing: **Kingston**. However, we will also reference prior versions of ServiceNow, including **Jakarta**, **Istanbul**, **Helsinki**, and **Geneva**.

Frames

ServiceNow is a cloud platform that runs inside your browser window. Within your browser, the ServiceNow interface is broken up into frames. Frames, in web parlance, are just separately divided sections of a page. This section will show you what the different frames are, what they generally contain, and the major UI elements within them.

In ServiceNow, there are two main frames: the ServiceNow frame, and the content frame. Both have different controls and display different information.

The ServiceNow frame consists of many UI elements spanning across both the top, and left side of the ServiceNow window in your browser:

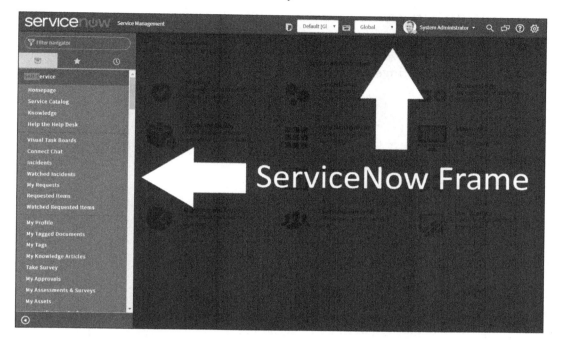

Technically, the ServiceNow frame can be further broken up into two frames: The **banner frame** along the top edge of the interface, and the **application navigator** along the left side.

Banner frame

The banner frame runs along the top of every page in ServiceNow, save for a few exceptions. There's room for company branding on the left, while on the right there contains more functional components for administrators and developers. From right to left, you'll find:

- System Settings cog
- Help and documentation button
- Conversations panel button
- Instance search button

- Profile/session dropdown
- Application picker (if enabled)
- Update Set picker (if enabled)

System settings

In your developer instance, on the far-top-right, you will see a sort of cog or sprocket. This is generally recognized as a universal settings menu icon. Clicking on that icon reveals the **System Settings** menu:

This menu is broken down into several sections:

- **General**
- **Theme**
- **Lists**
- **Forms**
- **Notifications**
- **Developer (admins only)**

The settings in this menu generally apply only to the current user who's signed in, so you can freely toggle and modify these settings without worrying about breaking anything. However, be aware that changing your time-zone only impacts your current session. To modify your time-zone permanently, you'll need to navigate to your user profile record, which can be found by clicking your username at the top-right of the page, and then clicking **Profile**.

In the **General** tab of the **System Settings** menu (as seen in the below screenshot), you'll find toggles to control accessibility options, compact the user interface, select how date/time fields are shown, select your time-zone, and even an option to display a printer-friendly version of the page you're on.

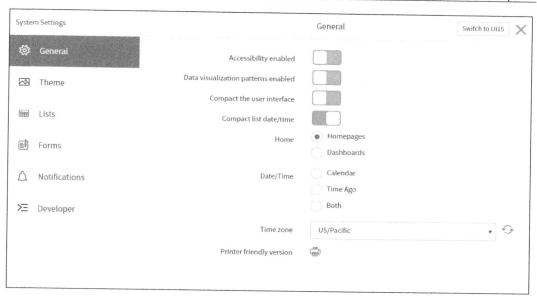

On the **Theme** tab, you'll find several pre-made ServiceNow themes with names like **System** and **Blues** (as seen in the below screenshot). One of the first things that a company often does when deploying ServiceNow, is to create a custom-branded theme. We'll go over how to do that in a later section, and you'll be able to see your custom themes here in this **System Settings** menu section.

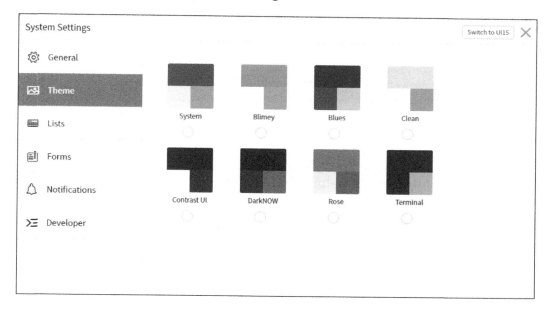

The **Lists** tab (below) contains the option to wrap longer text in list columns (which was under the **General** tab in Geneva and earlier versions of ServiceNow), as well as options to enable striped table rows (which alternates rows in a table between contrasting shades of gray, making it easier to follow with the eye from left to right) and modern cell styles. All options in the **Lists** tab except **Wrap longer text in list columns** require the List V3 plugin to be enabled before they'll show up, as they only apply to List V3.

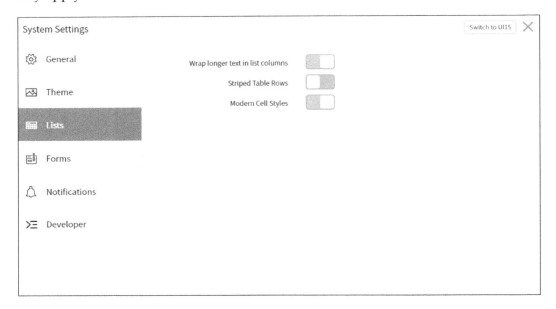

If your ServiceNow instance was set up initially on Helsinki or a later version, the **List V3** plugin will be enabled by default. However, if you've upgraded from Geneva or an earlier version, to Helsinki, you'll be on List V2 by default, and List V3 will need to be enabled. This, and any other plugins, can be enabled from **System Definition | Plugins** in the application navigator.

The **Forms** tab (below) contains settings to enable tabbed forms, as well as to control how and when related lists load.

Related lists are lists (like related tables in a spreadsheet) of related records that appear at the bottom of forms. Forms are where key data about an *individual* record are displayed, and collected. Selecting the **After Form Loads** option in the **Related list loading** section may improve load-time performance of your ServiceNow forms if there is a lot of related data to display.

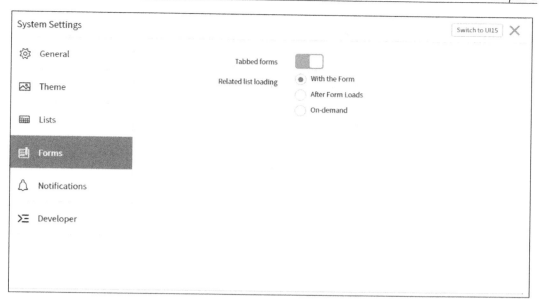

The **Notifications** tab allows you to choose whether to get notifications on your mobile device, desktop toast notifications, e-mail notifications, or audio notifications. The following image shows the Notifications settings in Istanbul and prior releases of ServiceNow:

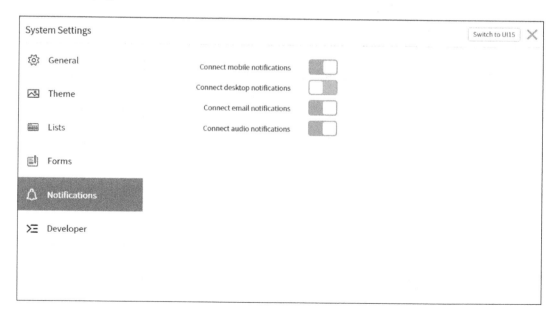

In Jakarta and later releases of ServiceNow (which you'll more likely be running), the **Notifications** menu shows the notifications that the platform may send out, organized by category. You can *unsubscribe* from them here if you choose. You will also find your **Notification Channels** listed here. Notification Channels are endpoints for notifications; such as an email address, or mobile number:

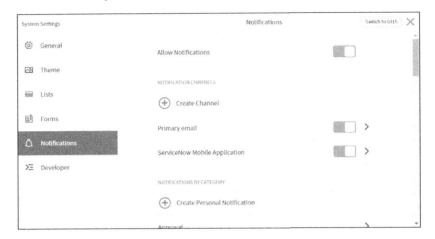

Pro Tip
In ServiceNow versions prior to Jakarta, **Notification Channels** were called **Devices**.

Finally, we have the **Developer** tab (as seen in the below screenshot). The **Developer** tab is only available to users with the *admin* role, and is where you can find settings relating to application and update set based development.

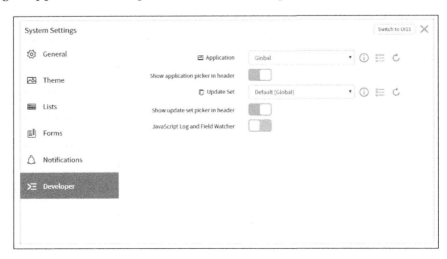

By default, your selected **Update Set** should say **Default [Global]**, which means that any configuration changes you make in the instance will not be captured in a portable update set that you can move between instances. We'll go into detail about what these things mean later on. For now, follow along with the steps below in your developer instance using your Administrator account, as we create a new update set to contain any configuration changes we'll be making in this chapter:

1. If you don't already have the **System Settings** menu open, click on the **System Settings** gear in the top-right of the ServiceNow interface.

2. If you haven't already done so, click on the **Developer** tab on the bottom-left.

3. Next, navigate to the **Local Update Sets** table:

    ○ In the main section of the **System Settings** dialog, you should see the third row down labeled **Update Sets**. To the right of that should be a drop-down with **Default [Global]** selected, followed by three buttons.

> The first button (⊕) is called a reference icon. Clicking it will take you to the currently selected update set (in this case, **Default**). The second button (≡) will take you to the list view, showing you all of the **Local Update Sets**. The third button will refresh the currently selected update set, in case you've changed update sets in another window or tab.

    ○ Click on the second button, to navigate to the **Local Update Sets** list view.

4. Click on the blue **New** button at the top-left of the page to go to the new update set form.

5. Give this update set a name. Let's enter Chapter 1 into the **Name** field.

6. Fill out the **Description** by writing in something like Learning about the ServiceNow interface!

7. Leave **State** and **Release date** to their default values.

8. Click **Submit and Make Current**.

Alternately, you could click Submit or right-click the header and click Save, then return to the record and click the Make This My Current Set related link.

Now that we've created an update set, any configuration changes we make will be captured and stored in a convenient and exportable package that we can back out or move into another instance to deploy the same changes. Now let's just confirm that we've got the right update set selected:

1. Once again, click on the **System Settings** gear at the top-right of the ServiceNow window, and open the **Developer** tab.

2. If the selected update set still shows as **Default**, click the **Refresh** (↻) button (the third icon to the right of the selected update set).

3. If the update set still shows as **Default**, just select your new Chapter 1 update set from the **Update Set** drop-down list. A notification should come up at the top of the window, as whenever you change your selected update set, the system will display an alert to confirm that you've done so.

Help

Next on the right side of the banner frame, is the **Help** icon. Clicking on this icon opens up the **Help** panel on the right side of the page:

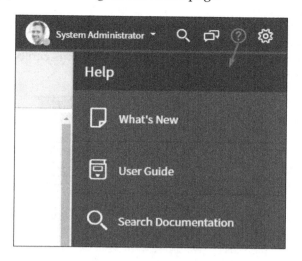

The **Help** menu is context-sensitive, and has multiple sections depending on what page you're on, such as: **What's New**, **User Guide**, and **Search Documentation**. On certain pages, help information will be displayed directly in the side-panel. On other pages, you'll see a big blue **Take Tour** button at the bottom. Clicking this button will walk you through the module, page, or whatever it is that you're viewing.

Clicking **What's New** just brings up the introduction to your instance version, with a couple of examples of the more prominent new features over the previous version.

The **User Guide** will redirect you to an internal mini-guide with some useful pocket-reference type of info. It's very slim on the details though, so you might be better off searching the developer site (`http://developer.servicenow.com`) or documentation (`http://docs.servicenow.com`) if you have any specific questions.

Speaking of the documentation site, the **Search Documentation** link in this menu will take you directly there. Clicking this link from a form or list will automatically populate a query relating to the type of record(s) you were viewing, though this often doesn't quite work and you may need to search to find what you're looking for.

Connect chat conversations

Moving further left in the banner frame, you'll find the conversations button. This opens the connect side-bar, showing an (initially blank) list of the conversations you've recently been a part of. You can enter text in the **Filter conversation** box to filter the conversation list by participant name. Unfortunately, it doesn't allow you to filter/search by message contents at this point. You can also click the plus icon to initiate a new conversation with a user of your choice. This can be a great tool for messaging users about a ticket they've submitted.

Global text search

The next link to the right in the banner frame is probably the most useful one of all—the global text search. The global text search box allows you to enter a term, ticket number, or keyword and search a configurable multitude of tables.

As an example of this functionality, let's search for a user that should be present in the demo data that came with your developer instance:

1. Click on the **Search** icon (the one that looks like a magnifying glass). It should expand to the left, displaying a search keyword input box.

2. In that input box, type in `abel tuter`. This is the name of one of the demo users that comes with your developer instance:

3. Press *Enter*, and you should see the relevant search results divided into sections.

Entering an exact ticket number for a given task (such as an incident, request, or problem ticket) will take you directly to that ticket rather than showing the search results. This is a great way to quickly navigate to a ticket you've received an e-mail about for example, or for a service desk agent to look up a ticket number provided by a customer.

The search results from the global text search are divided into *search groups*. The default groups include *Tasks, Live Feed, Policy, People & Places*, and in Jakarta: *Knowledge & Catalog*. Below each search group (or to the right, in versions prior to Jakarta), is a list of the tables that the search is run against for that group.

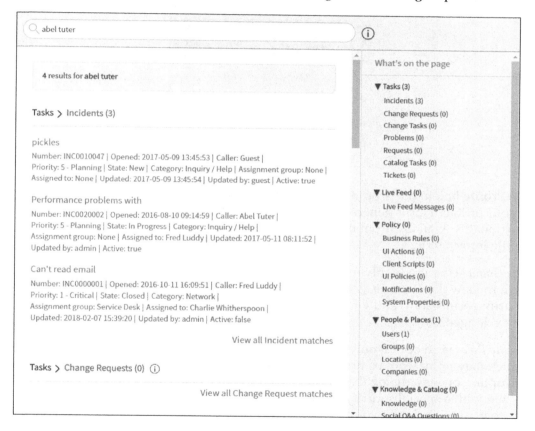

The *Policy* search group, for example, contains several script types, including *Business Rules, UI Actions, Client Scripts*, and *UI Policies*. These are different types of scripts or rules for the UI or business logic, all of which we'll learn about in future chapters.

Profile

The last item on our list of banner-frame elements, is the **Profile** link. This will show your photo/icon (if you've uploaded one), and your name. As indicated by the small down-facing arrow to the right of your name (or **System Administrator**), clicking on this will show a little drop-down menu. This menu consists of up to four main components:

- **Profile**
- **Impersonate User**
- **Elevate Roles**
- **Logout**

The **Profile** link in the drop-down will take you directly to the **Self Service** view of your profile. This is generally not what Administrators want, due to the limited functionality available from this view, but it's a quick way for users to view their profile information.

Impersonate User is a highly useful tool for administrators and developers, allowing them to view the instance as though they were another user, including that user's security permissions, and viewing the behavior of UI policies and scripts when that user is logged in.

Elevate Roles is an option only available when the *High Security* plugin is enabled (which may or may not be turned on by default in your organization). Clicking this option opens a dialog that allows you to check a box, and re-initialize your session with a special security role called `security_admin` (assuming you have this role associated with your user account). With high security settings enabled, the `security_admin` role allows you to perform certain actions, such as modifying **Access Control Lists** (**ACLs**/security rules).

Finally, the **Logout** link does just what you'd expect: it logs you out by redirecting you to the page **/logout.do** on your instance.

If you have difficulty with a session that you can't log out, you can always log out by visiting /logout.do on your instance:
http://your-instance.service-now.com/logout.do.

The application navigator

The application navigator is one of the UI components with which you will become most familiar, as you work in ServiceNow. Nearly everything you do will begin either by searching in the global text search box, or by filtering the application navigator.

The contents of the application navigator consist of modules nested underneath Application Menus. The first application menu in the application navigator is typically **Self-Service**. This application menu consists in part, of what's available to a user who doesn't have any special roles or permissions. Underneath this application menu, you'll see various modules such as **Homepage**, **Service Catalog**, **Knowledge**, and so on:

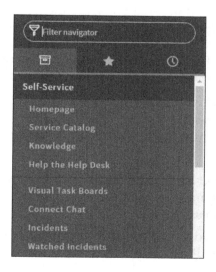

When you hear the term *application* as it relates to ServiceNow, you might think of an application on your smartphone. Applications in ServiceNow and applications on your smartphone both generally consist of packaged functionality, presented in a coherent way. However in ServiceNow, there are some differences. For example, an Application header menu might consist of modules that only have links to other areas in ServiceNow, and contain no functionality of their own. An application might not even necessarily have an application header at all.

Generally, we refer to the major ITIL processes in ServiceNow as Applications (**Incident, Change, Problem, Knowledge**, and so on) — but these can often consist of various components linked up with one another; so the functionality within an application doesn't necessarily need to be packaged in a way that it's separated out from the rest of the system.

 You'll often be given instructions to navigate to a particular module in a way similar to this: **Self-Service | My Requests**. In this example (as we'll use in this book), the left portion (**Self-Service**) is the application menu header, and the right portion (**My Requests**) is the module.

Filter text box

The filter text box in the application navigator allows you to enter a string to — you guessed it — filter the application navigator list!

It isn't strictly a search, it's just filtering the list of items in the application navigator, which means that the term you enter must appear somewhere in the name of either an application menu, or a module. So if you enter the term Incident, you'll see modules with names like **Incidents** and **Watched Incidents**, as well as every module inside the **Incident** application menu. However, if you enter Create Incident, you won't get any results. This is because the module for creating a new Incident, is called **Create New**, inside the **Incident** module, and the term Create Incident doesn't appear in that title.

In addition to filtering the application navigator, the filter text box has some hidden shortcuts that ServiceNow pros use to fly around the interface with ninja speed. Here are a few pro tips for you:

- Once you've entered a term into the filter text box in the application navigator, the first module result is automatically selected. You can navigate to it by pressing *Enter*.

- Enter a table name followed by .list and then press *Enter* to navigate directly to the default list view for that table. For example, entering sc_req_item.list [*Enter*] will direct you to the list view for the sc_req_item (Requested Item) table.

- Enter a table name followed by either .form, or .do (and then pressing *Enter*) will take you directly to the default view of that table's form (allowing you to quickly create a new record). For example, entering sc_request.form [*Enter*] will take you to the **New Record** intake form for the sc_request (Request) table.

- Enter a table name followed by `.config` to be taken to that table's configuration page. This will display all of the standard configuration options for a table, including Business Rules, Client Scripts, Security Rules, and more. You can also reach this page by going to any form or list, right-clicking the header, and going to **Configure | All**.

- Each table has a corresponding form, with certain fields displayed by default.

- Use either `.CONFIG`, `.FORM`, or `.LIST` in caps, to navigate to the list or form view in a new tab or window!

- Opening a list or form in a new tab (either using this method, by middle-clicking a link, or otherwise) breaks it out of the ServiceNow frame, showing only the content frame. More on that later in this chapter.

Try it yourself: Type `sys_user.list` into the application navigator filter text field in your developer instance, and press *Enter*. You should see the list of all the demo users in your instance!

No matter which application navigator tab you have selected when you start typing in the filter text box, it will always show you results from the **All Applications** tab and your favorites, with any of your favorites that match the filter always showing up first.

Favorites

Users can add favorites within the application navigator by clicking the star icon, visible on the right when hovering over any application menu or module in the application navigator. Adding a favorite will make it come up first when filtering the application navigator using any term that it matches. It'll also show up under your favorites list, which you can see by clicking the tab at the top of the application navigator, below the filter text box, with the same star icon you see when adding a module to your favorites.

Let's try out **Favorites** now by adding some favorites that an admin or developer is likely to want to come back to on frequent occasion.

Add the following modules to your favorites list by filtering the application navigator by the module name, hovering over the module, and clicking the star icon on the right:

- **Workflow | Workflow Editor**
- **System Definition | Script Includes**
- **System Definition | Dictionary**

- **System Definition | Business Rules**
- **System Update Sets | Local Update Sets**
- **System Logs | System Log | All**

 This one (**All**) is nested under a module (**System Log**) that doesn't point anywhere, and is just there to serve as a separator for other modules. It's not much use searching for **All**, so try searching for **System Log**!

Now that we've got a few favorites, let's rename them so they're easier to identify at a glance. While we're at it, we'll give them some new icons as well:

1. Click the **Favorites** tab in the application navigator, and you should see your newly added favorites in the list.

2. At the bottom-right of the application navigator in the ServiceNow frame, click on the **Edit Favorites** pencil icon (⬚).

3. Click on the favorite item called `Workflow - Workflow Editor`. This will select it so you can edit it in the content frame on the right:

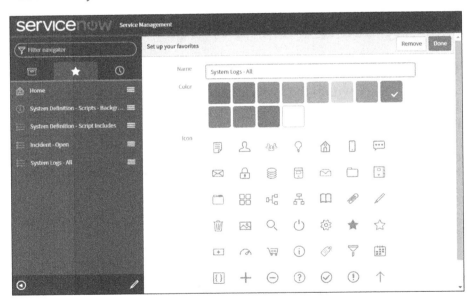

4. In the **Name** field, give it something simpler, such as `Workflow Editor`. Then choose a color and an icon. I chose white, and the icon that looks like a flowchart. I also removed my default **Home** favorite, but you may choose to keep it.

Here is what my favorites look like after I made some modifications:

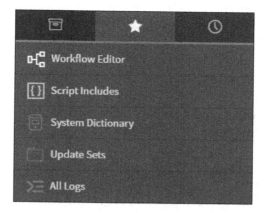

Another way to add something to your favorites is to drag it there. Certain specific elements in the ServiceNow UI can be dragged directly into your **Favorites** tab. Let's give it a try!

1. In your developer instance, head over to the **Incidents** table by using the .list trick mentioned earlier in this chapter:

    ○   Enter incident.list into the filter text box at the top of the application navigator; then press *Enter*.

2. Click on the **Edit filter** icon at the top-left of the **Incidents** list, and filter the **Incident** list using the condition builder.

3. Add the following conditions: Active is true, and Assigned to is empty. Then click on **Run**:

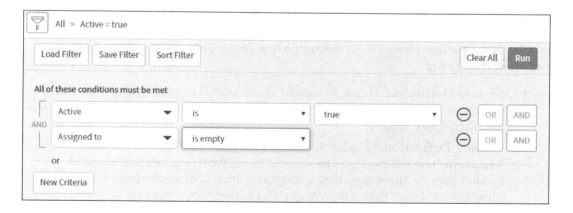

4. The list should now be filtered, after you hit **Run**. You should see just a few incidents in the list. Now, at the top-left of the **Incident** table, to the left of the **Incidents** table label, click on the **hamburger menu** (≡) (That's really what it's called). It looks like three horizontal bars atop one another.

5. In that menu, click on the **Create Favorite** button or, if you prefer, drag the last condition in the query breadcrumb at the top of the list to the application navigator to create a favorite.

6. Choose a good name, like **Unassigned Incidents**, and an appropriate icon and color. Then click **Done**. You should now have an **Unassigned Incidents** favorite listed!

Finally, if you click on the little white left-facing arrow at the bottom-left of the application navigator 🔘 , you'll notice that no matter which navigator tab you have selected, your favorites show up in a stacked list on the left. This gives you a bit more screen real-estate for the content frame.

History

Starting in the Geneva version and later, ServiceNow began storing your history in an easily accessible tab to the right of the **Favorites** tab in the application navigator. This allows you to see the pages, records, and lists you've visited during your session, and click on any of them to get back to a previous page.

Important application menus and modules

There are a few particular application menus and modules that developers and administrators should be aware of, as they're home to some of the more useful tools and parts of ServiceNow. You've already seen a few of them, and have added them to your favorites list! Here, I'll go through a few of the other more useful modules and what they're for:

- **System Definition**: Home to a great many useful modules, and contains definition information for various components of ServiceNow such as scripts and dictionary records.

- **Catalog Definitions**: Under **Service Catalog** | **Catalog Definitions**, **Maintain Items** allows you to see and modify catalog items, including related lists for their variables, categories, and other related records. Similarly, you can maintain categories, catalog shopping cart layouts, and even different service catalogs from this sub-menu.

If you aren't familiar with these terms, such as *Service Catalog* or *Catalog Items*, refer to the **ITIL** (**Information Technology Infrastructure Library**) definitions.

- **System Applications**: Using the **Studio** link in the **System Applications** menu takes you to the Application Development Studio interface, where you can build powerful scoped applications to create or enhance the functionality of your instance. This is useful, especially as some applications are installed in a special walled-off **scope** (for example, the HR application).

- **System Clone**: Using this application menu, you can create a clone target (such as adding your company's development and/or UAT instance(s) as clone targets for their production instance) and initiate a clone from one instance, over another. This is an important bit of housekeeping, since the more development work done in an instance, the further it tends to *drift* from the state of the production instance, and thus the more likely any future development that's done in it is to have issues when pushed to production. To keep instances in sync, it's usually a good idea to clone regularly.

- **Session Debug**: Under **System Diagnostics | Session Debug**, you'll find all kinds of helpful debugging options. We'll go into detail on debugging in another chapter, but suffice it to say that **Session Debug** is a very useful section. Just remember to disable debugging when you're finished, as debugging usually impacts performance for at least your session!

- **System diagnostics**: This section contains several useful diagnostic tools, including my favorite: The **Script debugger**. We'll go into more details on how this works in a later chapter, but it's a fantastic tool for debugging server-side scripts, and well-worth bookmarking!

- **System Logs**: The **System Logs** application menu contains many helpful modules, such as **System Logs | System Log | All**, which can assist in troubleshooting and debugging. Any server-side Java/JavaScript errors are generally logged to the system log.

- **System Properties**: The **System Properties** application menu contains links to properties pages for various aspects of the UI, system configuration, service catalog, and more. Properties are just system values stored in a table which can be modified to change certain behaviors. For example, the `glide.ui.ui15_switch_roles` property controls whether users can choose to manually switch between UI15 (the old version of the ServiceNow interface) and UI16 (the new interface version) using a button in the System Preferences window, based on roles.

Content frame

The content frame of the user interface is where you'll find the lists, forms, pages, and other contents. When left-clicking on a module in the application navigator, the resulting page, list, or form will load in the content frame (with a few exceptions such as the **Workflow Editor**):

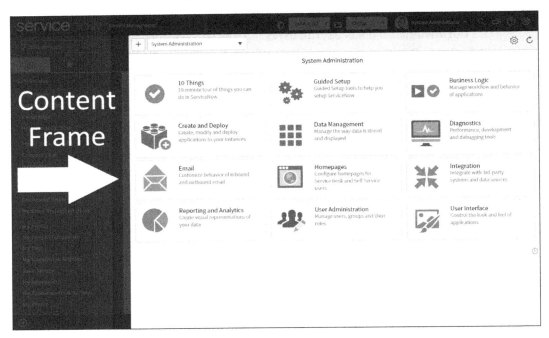

The content frame is displayed inside the ServiceNow frame (under the banner, and to the right of the application navigator). However, you can actually break the content frame out from the ServiceNow frame by opening a link in a new tab or window; for example, by middle-clicking a link in the application navigator.

Whether it's a link inside the content frame itself, or a module in the application navigator, opening the link in a new tab or window (whether from the right-click menu, by middle-clicking, or by *Ctrl*-clicking the link) will open just the content frame with the linked contents, but the banner and application navigator will not be present.

Without the content frame, the URL will look something like this:

`https://your_company.service-now.com/incident_list.do`

With the content frame, the URL will look like this:

`https://your_company.service-now.com/`**`nav_to.do?uri=`**`incident_list.do`

Adding `nav_to.do?uri=` before the rest of the URL after the forward-slash following the domain name (`service-now.com`) essentially navigates to the ServiceNow frame (located at `nav_to.do`), and passes a URL parameter (the bit after the question mark) named `uri` with a value of whatever text happens to follow the equals sign.

> URL parameters can be strung together using the ampersand (`&`), and can be accessed as name-value pairs from within client scripts. For example, have a look at this URL: `www.url.com/page?parmOne=code&parmTwo=is%20cool`. This URL contains two parameters: `parmOne` and `parmTwo`. `parmOne` is set to the string `code`, and `parmTwo` is set to the string `is cool` (because we decode the `%20` to a space).

So if you middle-click or otherwise open a link in a new tab, you'll be directed to the URL sans `nav_to.do?uri=`, but you can easily add this back into the URL. However, there's a small catch here. Only the **first** URL parameter uses the question mark. Any subsequent parameters use an ampersand.

If you find yourself opening new tabs very often, but need to pop them back into the ServiceNow frame (as I very often do!), you can create a browser **bookmarklet** to do just that using a little bit of JavaScript; or better yet, you can download a Google Chrome extension we've written, called **ServiceNow Framerizer**, from `framerizer.snprotips.com`.

UI settings and personalization

When navigating the ServiceNow UI, it's important to understand the difference between **configuration**, and **personalization**. These are defined terms within ServiceNow. As a general rule, configuration results in changes for everyone, whereas personalization results in changes just for you.

Most configuration modifies global system settings, configuration records, and properties (properties can be found in the `sys_properties` table), whereas most personalization results in modified or generated **preferences** (user preferences can be found in the `sys_user_preference` table). You *can* create **Global default** preferences by creating a preference record in the `sys_user_preference` table that isn't assigned to any particular user, but these default preferences can be overridden on a user-by-user basis, if users modify their preferences manually. It *would* be possible to create a data policy or business rule to prevent users from customizing certain preferences, but this may lead to a bad user experience. We'll discuss data policies and business rules in a later chapter.

Some examples of personalization are:

- Changing the columns that are displayed when viewing a given list, using **Personalize List Columns** from the hamburger menu at the top-left of lists:

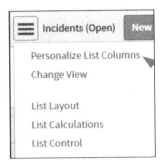

- Or by clicking the **gear** ( )menu at the top-left of the list view in Geneva and earlier.
- Adjusting your theme, list/form view preferences, or anything else from the **System Settings** gear menu at the top-right of the ServiceNow frame, in the banner.
- Adding or removing fields on a form using the **Personalize Form** ( ) button at the top-right of a form.

Some examples of **configuration** on the other hand, are:

- Changing the columns that are displayed when viewing a given list, using **List Layout** from the hamburger menu at the top-left of the list view (or by right-clicking the list header, and navigating to **Configure | List Layout** if you're using List v2). This is similar to the **Personalize List Layout** personalization option we discussed earlier, but it alters the default list layout, which impacts all users who view the list.

- Modifying the system themes from the **System UI | Themes** module in the application navigator—not to be confused with selecting a theme from the **System Settings** dialog, which constitutes personalization rather than configuration.

- Adding/removing fields or moving fields around on a form, using the **Form Designer (Configure | Form Design)**, or from **Configure | Form Layout**.

Take care not to make configuration changes when you mean to make personalization changes. Having the **admin** role can be a burden in this way. Some even avoid this by having entirely separate admin-only accounts that they must log into separately, so they won't make configuration changes by accident.

Summary

In this chapter, we learned about how content is organized on the screen, within frames—the banner frame, application navigator, and content frame. We also learned how to use the global text search functionality to find the records we're looking for, what it means to elevate roles or impersonate a user, and how to get around the application navigator, including some pro tips on getting around like a power user from the filter text box.

In the next chapter, we're going to discuss what are probably the two most important UI components: lists and forms. You'll learn how to customize and personalize your instance's lists and forms, and get hands-on experience doing just that!

2
Lists and Forms

In this chapter, we'll discover how *lists* in ServiceNow are similar to *tables* in any other relational database, and just what exactly that means for our data. We'll learn how relationships between data are created and stored in these lists, and get a brief introduction to the data types in ServiceNow. While we're at it, we'll also learn how to either personalize or configure how list data is displayed, and edited.

As an integral part of understanding data structures in ServiceNow, we'll also learn about *forms* and *form views*, the types of data that you'll see in forms and lists, and how to personalize or configure what data shows up where.

In this chapter, you'll also learn how to create a custom table as part of the foundation for your first application: a *Virtual War Room* for major incidents. This application will be used to demonstrate various pieces of functionality throughout the ServiceNow platform for the earlier chapters of this book, so it would be a good idea to follow along!

Remember: lists are where data rows and columns are displayed for multiple records. Forms are where a single record is displayed, and where work is done in ServiceNow. As you might imagine, there's a lot to learn about them both! In summary, this chapter will cover the following topics:

- The list view, and list components
- List v2 versus List v3
- Creating custom tables
- Creating update sets to track your work within tables (and elsewhere)
- Adding fields, and filtering tables

In Helsinki and later versions of ServiceNow, there are two versions of lists available: List v2, and List v3. For the most part, we'll use the example of List v3 in this book, but will attempt to call out important differences since List v2 is still used exclusively in some circumstances.

If it's not already active (such as if you've upgraded from a version prior to Helsinki), you can activate the List v3 plugin from System Definition | Plugins.

List v2 versus List v3

Before we get into a deep discussion about lists and how they work, you should be aware that there are two common versions of the list view in use presently: List v2 and List v3. You can see if the **List v3** plugin is enabled in your instance, by going to **System Definition | Plugins**, and searching for the term: list. If it is enabled, the **Status** column will show **Active** with a little green circle. Otherwise, it'll show **Inactive**.

While List v3 is the latest generation and what we're going to focus on in this book, it is important to understand List v2 as well. This is because all embedded lists, list reports, and hierarchical table lists such as the update set (sys_update_set) table list, all display in List v2 by default, since List v3 does not support those features.

A quick and easy way to tell if you're looking at a List v2 or a List v3, is to check for the personalization gear button ⚙. If you see that, then you're looking at a **List v2** list. On the other hand, if you see the **Grid** and **Split** buttons at the top of the list to the right of the search box, then you're looking at a **List v3** list.

To an admin/developer, probably the biggest difference between the two list versions is how you access configuration data (business rules, client scripts, UI actions, and so on) for the table that the list is related to.

On List v2 lists, you right-click the header row of the list, and go to **Configure**, then select the type of configuration records you'd like to see:

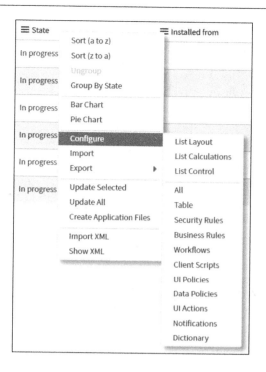

However, on List v3 lists, you click on the hamburger menu at the top-left of the page and click **Configure**:

This opens up the List v3 **Configure** modal dialog with the same options you would find in the **Configure** sub-menu in List v2 lists:

You can disable List v3 on specific lists one-by-one, by clicking the hamburger menu at the top-left of the list, then clicking on **List Control** and checking the **Disable list v3** checkbox. In this menu, you can also choose the default view mode (grid or split) for List v3.

Lists and tables

Lists in ServiceNow can be equated strongly to tables in databases. For the most part, this would be an accurate comparison. Viewing a list, is viewing a representation of a subset of records within a table on ServiceNow's database servers. The columns of that list correspond to fields within the table, and often fields which would show on the form (if configured to do so).

Each table in ServiceNow has a *label* (a friendly name), and a *name*. The label is defined in the table dictionary (something we'll discuss later in this chapter), and can contain spaces and other characters that are not allowed in the table's name. The name is often more difficult to remember, but more specific. For example, the **label** *Task* may refer to the base task table, problem tasks, catalog tasks, or a multitude of system or custom tables which contain some sort of task. However, the **name** sc_task is more specific, as a table's name is unique (but its label is not).

Creating a custom table

Let's start out by creating a custom table. This table will be the home for records created within our application of at least one type, but before we do that, we need to create an update set!

Creating an update set

In *Chapter 1*, *The Interface*, we briefly mentioned the update set selector at the top-right of the ServiceNow UI. In this chapter, we're going to create one ourselves in order to capture and track our work. We can export it and save in between clones, import it into other instances, or use the update set as a backup. Here's how:

Start by clicking on the **System Settings** gear menu at the top-right of the ServiceNow frame, in the banner. Then, click on the **Developer** tab from the left.

Just so we can keep an eye on it, let's add the update set picker to the banner section of the ServiceNow frame (if you haven't done so already) by toggling the **Show update set picker in header** option to *on*:

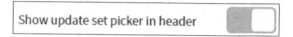

Now we'll see a little drop-down menu just to the left of our profile link and picture. This will help us keep an eye on which update set we have selected, and easily switch if we need to.

 Applications in ServiceNow can exist within their own scope, so that—unless explicitly permitted—scripts and resources in one application scope (such as the Global scope) cannot access resources within another scope. Since ServiceNow has several applications which are in a non-global **scope**, you may want to enable the **Show application picker in header** toggle as well, so you can see what application scope you're working in!

With the **Update Set** toggle switched on, click the middle icon that looks like a list ⠿ after the **Update Set** drop-down in the **System Settings** menu. This will take you to the **Update Sets** table. To create a new update set, click the **New** button and fill out some details as before. This time, set the **Name** field to Chapter 2, and click **Submit and Make Current**.

We're creating our update sets in the same order as we're developing, so as long as we also deploy/push them in the same order, we wouldn't have any issues of overlap. If we create a record in the Chapter 1 update set and then modify it in Chapter 2, that's fine. But if we then tried to migrate those update sets to another instance in the reverse order (first Chapter 2, and then Chapter 1), then the Chapter 2 update set would have us modifying a record that doesn't exist! It is important to maintain the integrity of your update sets, by understanding the order in which they were developed, and the relationship between the sets' contents. One way to do this is using update set batching, which we'll discuss in a later chapter.

After clicking **Submit and Make Current**, you should be directed back to the **Update Sets** table list. Let's demonstrate list editing by closing our previous update set (*Chapter 1, The Interface*) now that we're done with it. This will prevent us from accidentally making potentially conflicting changes to it in the future. To do so, follow these steps:

1. Ensure that the **State** column is displayed in the list view for the **Update Sets** table. If it isn't, follow these steps to add it:

    ○   Click on the personalize gear icon at the top-left of the list view. If you have Lists V3 enabled, and don't see the gear icon, click the hamburger menu preceding the filter icon at the top-right of the list, and click **Personalize List Columns**.

    ○   In the **Personalize List Columns** dialog, select the **State** field, click the right-arrow button, and then click **OK**:

This change only applies for you, since it is a personalization!

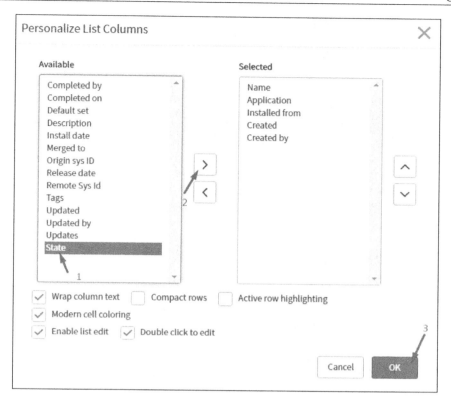

- ° The list should reload, and the **State** field should be displayed.

2. To the right of the row representing the Chapter 1 update set, double-click in the **State** column, where it says **In progress**. This should cause the field to become editable within the list view:

3. In the drop-down that appears, select **Complete**, and click the green *checkmark* button to save your update.

Not all records can be edited from the list view. Certain tables don't allow it, and ACLs (security rules) still apply. However, it is sometimes possible to bypass certain preventative measures implemented as client-side scripts and policies by editing from the list rather than the form (which is why some tables have list editing disabled). For example, if a client script exists which would remove the Complete option from the State drop-down for our Chapter 1 update set, but we viewed it through the list, we would still have been able to make this change through list editing. That script would not run on the list view.

Creating the table

Now that we've created an update set and marked it as current, we're ready to begin development. As is the case with many (though not all!) ServiceNow applications, we begin our application by creating a new table to house our data. In this case, we're creating a *Virtual War Room* application, so we'll create a table to hold *Virtual War Room* tickets.

First, in the application navigator, navigate to **System Definition | Tables**, where you'll be presented with the list view for the sys_db_object table; or you might say, the **Tables** table.

Click on the blue **New** button at the top-left of this list to get started. On the **New record** form, enter Virtual War Room for the **Label**, and press *Tab*. Once you've done that, the **Name** field should auto-populate with the value u_virtual_war_room. The u_ indicates that this is a custom, user-defined table, as opposed to a table that's built-in with ServiceNow. Scoped applications can also have custom tables which do not have names preceded by u_.

It is generally good practice to give your tables singular labels (Virtual War Room as opposed to Virtual War Rooms) as well as singular names (u_virtual_war_room, as opposed to u_virtual_war_rooms). Most built-in tables in ServiceNow adhere to this standard as well, except for the properties (sys_properties) table. ServiceNow will try to figure out the best way to pluralize the label of a record type, which is used in places like the navigation menu and the top-left of a list. However, you can custom-define the plural form when ServiceNow needs help getting it right. For example, it may pluralize *dependency* as *dependencys* rather than *dependencies*. The singular form would be used as the label on a form displaying one record.

Next, in the **Extends table** field, we have to determine whether we want our table to extend another table (and thus, inherit the existing fields, labels, and certain business logic). We'll go over what this means in more detail, in a later chapter. For now, since we are going to want access to some of the task-related goodies built in to ServiceNow, let's set our Virtual War Room table to extend the task table by entering Task into the **Extends table** field, and selecting **Task** [task] from the drop-down. If it doesn't show up there, you can click the magnifying glass and search for the table record with the name Task.

There are multiple tables with a label of Task, but only one with the **name**: task. A similar table containing catalog tasks, which was also (until a recent update) labeled **Task**, is named sc_task. More info on the **Task** table can be found in *Chapter 5, Tasks and Workflows*.

Since we want to create a new Application Menu and Module for our application, we'll leave **Create module** and **Create mobile module** checked. We'll also leave the **Add module to menu** option set to **-- Create new --**, and underneath that field, we'll leave the **New menu name** field set to the same as our table label: Virtual War Room.

You'll notice that the **Columns** tab or form section contains a list of **Table Columns**, which is currently empty. We'll leave this section alone for now, as dictionary entries for many columns are going to automatically appear for our table once we save the new table record, since we're extending another table.

Moving to the **Controls** tab/section, we've got several more options:

- **Extensible**: This indicates that other tables are able to extend this table. This might be useful if we were creating a parent table that would have child-tables that needed to share the same custom fields we created, but for our purposes we're going to leave this box **un-checked**.

- **Live feed**: This checkbox determines whether the live feed is enabled on this table. The live feed is part of the newer social IT applications, and serves as a place where users can post and share certain content. If live feed is enabled, you can have a sort of twitter-stream-like view of tickets you're interested in, and activity happening on them. Let's go ahead and **check this box**.

- **Auto-number**: This allows you to define a prefix (incidents, for example, use **INC** by default), and the system will automatically number each record in your table, beginning at the number you specify. Let's check the auto-number box, set the prefix to WAR, and leave the **Number** and **Number of digits** fields default.

Number prefixes can be virtually any number of characters, but I recommend sticking with 2-5 characters. It is also a very good idea to ensure that they're unique, as certain operations are triggered off the number field (especially on task tables). Having unique prefixes ensures that there won't be duplicate ticket numbers.

- **Create access controls**: This allows you to create a access controls, and to select (or create) a role to control access to your application. It might make sense down the line, for us to have a separate role that we can grant only to certain major-incident managing groups or users, so go ahead and leave that box checked. The **User role** field beneath it allows us to select an existing role, or create a new one. The field background color should be green, which means the value currently populated does not correspond to an existing role record, and a new role will be created for it when saved. This type of field is called a **suggest** field.

- See *Chapter 7, User Administration and Security*, for info on roles and security.

- **Application Access**: This tab/section allows us to control application-scope specific settings, but we're not concerned about that right now since we're developing in the **Global** scope, so go ahead and leave everything here as default.

> Whether the **Columns**, **Controls**, and **Application Access** sections display as tabs or stacked form sections, depends on whether you have the **Tabbed forms** toggle switched on, in the **Forms** tab of the **System Settings cog** menu. Just a reminder, this setting is a preference, meaning that it is user-specific, and won't affect other users' experience, or get captured and carried over in update sets.

Finally, right-click in the header and click **Save**. We could also click the **Submit** button, but that would redirect us back to the previous page we were on, and we're not ready for that just yet.

After saving the new table record, if you go back into the **Columns** section, you'll notice that somewhere in the ballpark of 60-70 new columns have appeared automatically! A few of these are default fields created on every table (fields like **Created**, **Updated**, **Sys ID**, and a few others), but the vast majority of the fields you'll see, came from the `Task` table:

By default, you'll see that the **Table Columns** list inside the **Columns** section of the form has several fields shown: **Column label**, **Type**, **Reference**, **Max length**, **Default value**, and **Display**. Since these are rather universal, let's go through each column and make sure we know what it means:

- **Column label**: This is the friendly name for the column (or, on the form, the field label).

- **Type**: This determines the type of field created. This dictates the default max length (which you can change), what field properties and attributes are available for this field, and what sort of values will be accepted. Changing a field type after it's been created is very difficult, and not recommended after users are actively using your application, as all data will be lost in all existing records. So, think carefully when choosing a data type!

- **Reference**: This field is only relevant to certain types of columns which reference records on other tables. We'll go into reference field types in *Chapter 4, Understanding Data and Relationships*.

- **Max length**: You can probably guess at what this field governs. It's the maximum length (in characters) that the field will accept. The default value for this is 40 for most column types, 32 for reference fields (since that's the length of a **sys ID** (a unique identifier of an individual record within the database), 4,000 for journal fields, and so on.

    - You can specify whatever length you like here, but keep in mind that the longer the field max length, the greater the overall performance impact when querying, saving, or deleting records in that table.

    - Keep in mind that if the table that the field is on extends another table, then the parent table's performance can also be impacted! For this reason, it's best not to create too many additional fields on tables that extend task, since so many others already do; long fields in particular.

- **Default value**: Also fairly self-explanatory, this is the default value for the column, to be used before the user has selected one, or if a record is saved to the database with that particular field empty.

- **Display**: Each table can have only one display value. The display value is the single column which is displayed to represent a record as a whole. On the **Incident** table for example, the display value is the **Number** column, but some companies will change it to be **Short description** instead. On the **Users** table, you might want **User ID**, or **Name** to be the display value.

You've seen the terms **field** and **column** a lot in this chapter, but it's important to be aware that these terms, in this context, are effectively interchangeable.

Adding a field

Now that we've got a table, let's go ahead and add some additional fields to our `Virtual War Room` table, within this list of table columns. To do that, we have two options.

Since **List edit insert row** (a property of this list of fields) is enabled, *option 1* is that we can actually scroll to the bottom of the list and double-click in the bottom row, where it says **Insert a new row...**, and it'll let us insert a new table column record just by specifying a few values here:

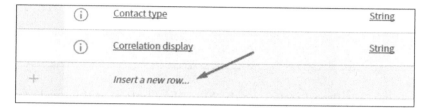

Any values we leave out will just be set to their default values, or blank if they don't have a default value. The only down-side to this, is that it doesn't allow you to see and edit all of the fields that might be relevant when creating a new table column; only those which are shown in this list formatter.

However, we've also got *option 2*: simply clicking the **New** button at the top-left of the list formatter. This will take us to the new record form for this particular table (which happens to be the `Dictionary` table, as all table and column definitions are stored there). This form has built-in logic to (for the most part) show us only fields which are relevant to what we're trying to create.

For our first custom field, let's create one to hold a reference to a particular incident ticket, since Major incidents are the sorts of tickets that we want to have result in war rooms being created for triage and remediation:

1. If you haven't already, click on the blue **New** button at the top-left of the table columns list, on the `Virtual War Room` table definition form.
2. Click on the magnifying glass on the right side of the **Type** field.
3. At the top-left of the **Field Classes** list window (next to the filter icon), click on the magnifying glass (🔍) again. Then, under the **Label** header, enter `reference` and press *Enter*. The breadcrumb text next to the filter icon will update, and you should see one field type matching your query, called **Reference**.

4. Click on **Reference** in the field classes list window, and the **Type** field will be populated. In that field, you'll see the word Reference. You'll also notice that several new fields have appeared, based on your selection.

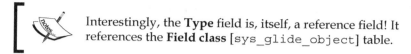 Interestingly, the **Type** field is, itself, a reference field! It references the **Field class** [sys_glide_object] table.

5. In the **Column label** field, enter Major incident. The column name should then auto-populate, and contain u_major_incident. You could change it, but this time, let's leave it as-is.

6. The **Max length** field can remain blank, as it will automatically be set to its default value for the reference field type (32 characters) after we save. However, we do want to ensure that Virtual War Rooms are not created or worked on without being associated to a Major incident; so over on the right side of the form, tick the box marked **Mandatory**.

7. In the **Reference Specification** form tab/section, there's a field called **Reference**. This is where you should enter the table in which the records you're referencing can be found. Since we're dealing with Major incidents in our Virtual War Room application, let's have this field reference the **Incident** [incident] table.

   ○ Rather than clicking the magnifying glass this time, try just typing incident into the field. You'll notice a drop-down list appears after a brief moment. You must select the one from that drop-down that is just **Incident**. It'll have the label (**Incident**) on the left, and the table name (incident) on the right, not to be confused with incident_task or anything else:

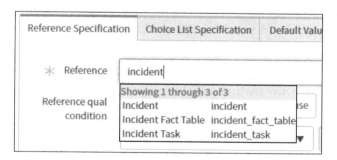

If the **Reference** field turns green, it means you didn't select a reference table from the drop-down, and ServiceNow will attempt to create a **whole new table** for you to reference. This is definitely not what we're looking for. If that happens, re-type `incident` in the **Reference** field, and make sure to select one of the options that appears below the field.

Remember when we clicked on the magnifying glass to the right of the **Type** field? The window that popped up showed us records from a specific table. This is the table specified in the **Reference** field in that particular field's dictionary.

1. Right-click on the header of the **Dictionary Entry** form, and click **Save**. This will submit the record to the database, without returning you to the previous page, so you can continue to work on the record.

Before I save a record, I usually glance up at the top-right of my screen, to make sure that I'm still in the correct update set. However, if you tend to work in multiple windows or tabs, it's easy to change your update set in one tab, but not have it reflect in the other tabs. Since which update set your work is stored in, is determined server-side, you may need to be proactive about ensuring you're still in the right set. To check if you're really in the update set that shows in your banner frame, click on the **System Settings** gear menu at the top-right, and go to the **Developer** tab. Click on the far-right refresh icon next to the **Update Set picker** drop-down, and check to make sure that the selected update set doesn't change after 1 - 5 seconds.

As you may recall, this Virtual War Room application is really meant for only `Major incidents`. Each company might have different criteria for exactly what constitutes a Major incident, but ITIL implies that generally incidents with the highest priority and the highest impact, are Major incidents.

We did make the `Major incident` field mandatory, but there's nothing currently preventing someone from creating a Virtual War Room and associating it with a low-priority incident. Luckily, ServiceNow gives us an easy way to filter the types of records that can be selected from a given **Reference** field, using a *Reference qualifier*, also known as a **reference qualifier condition** or simply **refqual**. This is a condition that is applied to the **Reference** field, so that only records which match that query can be selected from the relevant field.

In order to ensure that only incidents with the highest priority and impact are selectable, we simply add conditions using the condition builder below the **Reference** field in the **Dictionary Entry** form. The conditions should look something like this:

It's also usually a good idea to add a condition to only show active Incidents (Incidents where the **Active** field is **true**). Feel free to add that condition as well if you like, then right-click on the header of the content frame, and click **Save** again. After the frame reloads, it should look something like this:

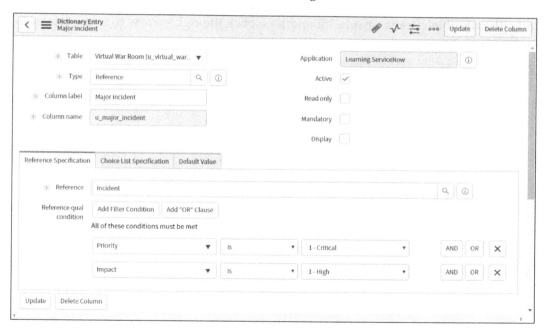

To return to the table record and column list, you can click the left-facing back arrow at the top-left of the page. In the next section, we'll head over to our application to make sure the new field shows up in the default list view for everyone, as its value is a pretty important bit of information!

List view

In the application navigator filter text box, type `Virtual War Room`, and you'll see the `Virtual War Room` application header, as well as the `Virtual War Rooms` module (automatically pluralized based on our table label). Click on that module, and you should see the `Virtual War Rooms` list view.

 You may want to click the star next to the `Virtual War Rooms` module to save it as a favorite, so it'll show up in your favorites list.

The columns displayed in the list view of a given table, such as the request item (`sc_req_item`) table, can be either personalized (modified just for you) or configured (modified for all users). You can choose to display any field within a given table in the list view, or even derived fields (fields with data from related records).

If you don't see the `Major incident` column in the `Virtual War Room` list view, click on the hamburger menu at the top-left of the content frame, and click on **List Layout**. On the next page, find the **Major Incident** field in the list marked **Available**, and either double-click it, or select it and then click the right-arrow to move it over to the **Selected** box.

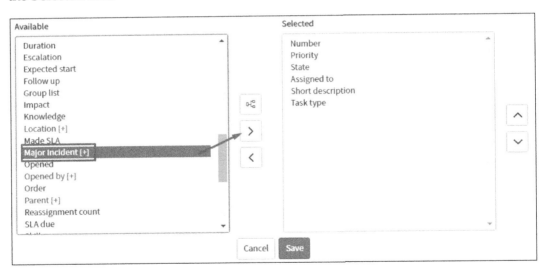

As a reminder, modify a list layout constitutes **configuration**, unless you select **Personalize List Columns**. This means that this change *is* captured in your selected update set.

Next, make sure you have that field selected and click the up-arrow on the right, until it's listed right after **Short description**.

While we're here, let's remove some superfluous columns as well. Get rid of the **Task type** and **Priority** columns by double-clicking them in the **Selected** box, so that they move back over to **Available**. Finally, click **Save**.

Congratulations, you've just created your first *custom field* on your first *custom table* in your first *custom application* in the application navigator. You're catching on quick!

If we wanted to modify the list layout just for us instead of for everyone, we could have clicked the hamburger menu at the top of the content frame, and click **Personalize List Columns**.

Users who have **personalized** the columns that show up in a list, or the order they show up in, will **not** see the changes made to a list using the above steps, even though the steps should modify the view for everyone! This is because user preferences frequently override system configuration.

In order to see the configured list view, users who have personalized their list layouts will need to click the hamburger menu, go to **Personalize List Columns**, and then click **Reset Columns** at the bottom-left of that dialog.

Condition builder

Another major component of lists is the ability to filter them using the condition builder (also sometimes called the query builder). The condition builder is one of the most powerful, and most useful tools in all of ServiceNow, and it can be found doing more than just filtering lists.

Condition builders can be included on forms as a field to store a condition value, and we've already seen how they can be used to filter the options that one can select from a **Reference** type field, while we were creating the `Major incident` field for our `Virtual War Room` application. Let's try out some examples of how the condition builder works. We'll use the incident table as an example, since it should contain a good amount of demo data in your instance, and it's got a lot of different types of fields.

To get started, navigate to **Incident | All** from the application navigator. In the list that appears, click on the filter icon (▽) at the top-left. Let's walk through several example filters, and how to build them using the condition builder.

Building a filter

For this example, let's build a query that will only show records like this:

Incidents assigned to me that are not closed or cancelled, sorted by when they were last updated (oldest first).

First, let's break this down into components:

- **Assigned to is me** (the current user, whoever it may be)
- **State is** not either **Closed** or **Cancelled**
- Sort by **Updated** (*high-to-low*)

You should be looking at two drop-down fields and one string input field, arranged in a row, like this:

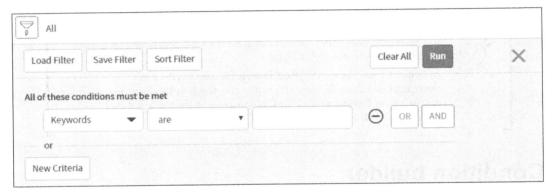

Just like in math and programming, these three fields each represent a component of a condition criteria that looks something like `<Field> <Operator> <Value>`.

Click on the first drop-down on the left of the condition builder. In this drop-down, you'll see a list of fields on the **Incident** table. The first thing we want to do is filter based on to whom the incident is assigned, so type `assigned to` into the filter box at the top of the drop-down list, and then click on **Assigned to**.

The second field is the *operator*. This determines the type of comparison we're doing. In this case, we want records where the field is equal to a certain value, so for the operator, we might want to select **is**. However, if we try to enter a value into the *value* field on the right side of the condition, we'll see that it expects us to select a user from the **Users** table (since **Assigned to** is a **Reference** field that points to that table). We could select our own user account, but we want this filter to show tickets assigned to **whichever** user views it, so that won't work. We can't make a separate custom filter for each and every user!

Luckily, for this situation, we have dynamic operators. On **Reference** fields, we can select the operator **is (dynamic)** (as opposed to just **is**), which gives us some dynamic (scripted) options for the value. The first dynamic option in this case, is **Me**. This runs a script on the server, which replaces **Me** with whatever user is viewing the list.

 These condition value fields accept JavaScript code, as long as it is preceded by `javascript:` If you were so inclined, or if you didn't have the **is (dynamic)** operator, you could use the `GlideSystem` API to get the `sys_id` of the current user for your query. You'd select **is** for the operator, and enter: `javascript:gs.getUserID();`.

So our first condition should look like this:

In order to add a second condition, we need to click the **AND** button. If we wanted to add a *one or the other* type of condition, we could use **OR**, but we want all of these conditions to match, in order for a record to show up based on this filter.

After clicking **AND**, a new query condition line will appear. For the first part of this query line, select **State** from the drop-down. For the operator, choose **is not one of**. Finally, for the value(s), hold *Ctrl*, and select both **Closed**, and **Canceled**. Your condition builder should now look pretty similar to this:

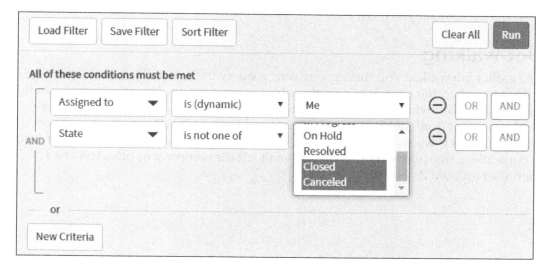

Finally, click on **Run** to filter the list of incidents. After running the filter, we then need to sort the list. There are a few ways to sort a list:

1. If the field you'd like to use to sort is displayed on the list view, you can simply click on that field header to sort by a to z (low to high). Clicking again sorts in the opposite direction. The down-sides to this method are that you can only sort on columns which display in your list view, and you can't do multi-level sorting.

2. You can also click the hamburger menu next to a column header, and choose a direction to sort.

3. Alternately, after your query is in place, you can open the condition builder and click on **Add Sort** or, in List v2, **Sort Filter**). In the section that displays, you can select one, or even multiple levels of sorting. For example, you could sort just by when the incident was updated, or you could sort by who the caller is, and sub-sort by how long ago the last update was.

For our purposes, we'll just need to sort by one field, and that field happens to be in our default list view. To sort the incident table by when each ticket was last updated, we just have to click on the **Updated** column header once. That will sort it from low to high. Dates further in the past are considered lower than more recent ones, which are lower still than dates in the future.

Note that although you cannot do multi-level sorting just by clicking on the column headers, you can do something similar by grouping records together based on certain values. For example, if you wanted to see the results of the query we just built using the condition builder, **Grouped By Priority**, but still sorted, within those groups, by the **Updated date**, you could simply right-click on the **Priority** header, and choose **Group By Priority**.

Dot-walking

The earlier lab walked you through creating a query in the condition builder using values stored on the records within the table you're viewing. This is extremely useful functionality, but what if we wanted to filter the list using a data point that is not on the incident itself, but is on one of the related records in a **Reference** field? For example, what if we wanted to show only incidents where the user in the **Caller** field is currently active (meaning that they haven't left the company or otherwise had their user account disabled).

In order to accomplish this, we'll need to make use of dot-walking. We'll explore more about dot-walking and how to do it via JavaScript later in this book, but let's have a look at how to do this in the condition builder.

In your existing **Incident** filter, click **AND** to add another condition. In the following list of fields, you'll see some fields with a little arrow inside a circle on the right:

 In List v2, in order to dot-walk, you need to first scroll to the bottom of the list of fields, and click **Show Related Fields**, then re-open the field drop-down, and select a **Reference** field from the list, that's followed by an arrow => and then a table name. When you re-open the drop-down list again, you'll see the fields from that table.

This arrow indicates a **Reference** field that can be dot-walked through. Find the **Caller** field in that list, and click the arrow to the right of it, and you'll see another list show up to the right. If this list also contains reference fields, you can continue dot-walking through them as well, up to several layers. If possible, it's recommended not to go beyond 3 layers of dot-walking, for performance reasons. For heavily utilized queries, it may even be a good idea to avoid dot-walking more than 1 or 2 layers.

Forms

As you've seen, forms are where data is displayed in ServiceNow, but you wouldn't want to display every single field in your table to all of your users! For this reason, forms have views that limit which fields are shown, and to whom.

Form views can be configured, or personalized, split into sections, and can contain and display all manner of different kinds of data. Data can be made to be displayed, made read-only, or made editable in forms based on various conditions that we'll discuss in *Chapter 6, UI and Data Policies*. In this section, we'll briefly go over how to configure and design forms, how to personalize them, and make them your own, and how to configure form sections and related lists. More details on the specific components that'll show up in forms will be covered in later chapters.

Form designer

Let's start by creating a Virtual War Room record. Follow the following steps to create a record in our application that we can use to create and modify views using the form designer:

1. In the application navigator filter text box, type Virtual War Room, and you'll see the Virtual War Room application header, as well as the Virtual War Rooms module.

2. Click on that module, and then click **New** at the top of the list, to see the Virtual War Room form and create a new record.

3. Enter Beth Anglin in the **Assigned to** field (this is a random default user included with the demo data in your development instance).

4. Click the magnifying glass next to the **Configuration item** field, and select any random configuration item from the built-in demo data.

5. Enter something for the **Short description** like test war room and something for the **Description** like this is a test ticket for the war room application.

6. Click **Submit**. This will return you to the list view.

7. Click on the Virtual War Room ticket you've just created, to go back to the form.

All of the fields you'll see on that form, are actually fields derived from the **Task** table. In fact, aside from the base system fields (**Created, Created by, Updated, Updated by**, and a few others) and our newly created Major incident field, all other fields were derived from the **Task** table.

You'll notice on this form, a number of fields and field types, including but not limited to the following:

- The **Number** field, which is a **string** type.

- The **Assigned to** field, which is a **reference** type (that points to the **Users** table).

- The **Short description** field which is a **string** type that spans two layout columns.

 The difference between the **Short description** and **Description** fields, is the **maximum length** value from the field's dictionary entry. If a **String** field has a max length of *255* characters or fewer, it will appear as a **single line** or **small** field. However, if its max length is *256* or greater, it'll be a **multi-line** field on the form.

- The **Active** field, which is a **true/false** (AKA **Boolean**) type.

- The **State** field, which is an **integer** field with a drop-down choice list.

 Though the **State** field is technically an **integer** type (meaning that the actual value in the database is an integer), the choices that can be selected are actually stored in another table, labeled choices (with the name sys_choice). This table has records that, like the table itself, have both a label, and a value. The label is what you see in the **State** field drop-down (**Open**, **Closed Complete**, **Work in Progress**, and so on) but the value is what is actually stored in the field, and in the database.

For the Virtual War Room, we're not going to need all of these fields - and anyway, this form doesn't even display our Major incident field! Let's fix that, by following the steps below:

1. Right-click on the form header, and go to **Configure | Form Design**. This will open the **Form Designer**, a handy little app within ServiceNow.

2. Since we want all Virtual War Rooms to only exist for Major incidents of the highest priority, we don't really need a **Priority** field on the war room itself. Go ahead and click the little **x** icon to the right of the **Priority** field when you hover over it.

3. Use the same method to remove the **Active** field, as well as **Parent, Short description**, and **Description**. We are going to want a short description and description on the form, but we'll get it from the Major incident.

4. Now let's add our `Major incident` field to the form. Filter the list of fields on the left to find it, and drag the `Major incident` field to the right, placing it right underneath **State**.

5. Finally, add the **Activities (filtered) (Formatter)** just under **Work notes** at the bottom. This is going to display your **journal**. More on this and activities in *Chapter 5, Tasks and Workflows*.

At this point, your **Form Design** window should be looking something like this:

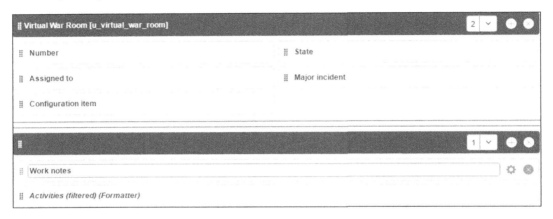

Go ahead and click the blue **Save** button at the top-right of the page, and return to the tab you were on previously. Right-click the header, and reload the form, and you should see your new, brilliantly designed form. Well done!

Form layout

In addition to the form designer, there is also **Form Layout** in the **Configure** menu when right-clicking the header (as we saw in the preceding section). This allows you to modify nearly everything that you changed through the form designer, though it isn't as user-friendly. In exchange for that lack of user-friendliness though, the trade-off is that you can easily add **derived** fields based on related records in reference type records.

Let's walk through an example, so you can see what I'm referring to:

1. Right-click in the header of the `Virtual War Room` form again, and go to **Configure | Form Layout**.

2. Scroll down to the **Major incident** field that we created. It should be highlighted in green, and have a little **[+]** next to it. This indicates that it is a **Reference** field.

3. Click on **Major incident** to highlight it, and a new icon will appear above the two arrow buttons, in-between the **Available** and **Selected** lists. Clicking this button allows you to dot-walk to access the fields on the Incident table, and add them to our Major incident table.

4. After clicking that icon, you should see a new list of options in the **Available** box on the left. From that list, double-click on **Short description**.

5. Use the arrows to the right of the **Selected** box to move the two new fields up or down so that the **Major incident. Short description** field is right before **Work notes**.

6. Click the blue **Save** button on the form layout window, and you should be returned to the form.

Now you've got the **Short description** field from the Incident table (through the **Major incident** field) displayed on your Virtual War Room form. If you want to see this value populated, just click the magnifying glass icon to the right of the **Major incident** field, and select any incident from the list that pops up. The **Short description** will populate automatically, displaying the short description from the incident you've selected!

If you have an editable **derived** (dot-walked) field on a form, and a user edits it, keep in mind that they will actually be editing the field on the record that it was dot-walked from! This can have unexpected consequences, so it's usually a good idea to make derived fields read-only.

Related lists

Related lists are powerful tools in ServiceNow, both for displaying data, and for doing work. They show up below a form, and can display any records you'd like, that are in some way associated to the record you're viewing in the form.

There are multiple ways to associate one record to another, including a custom-defined relationship that you can create using JavaScript. The simplest and most common way of relating two records though, we've already done. It's with a **Reference** field!

To understand how related lists work, you first must understand a *key* component of ServiceNow: **Keys**!

See what I did there?

In a database, it is important to be able to differentiate one record from another, with some *key* piece of information. This is a unique value that resides in a database column. This column is referred to as the *primary key* for that table. In ServiceNow, the primary key is called the *Sys ID*, stored in the database column sys_id. This is a 32-character alphanumeric value that is unique in the entire database. No two records (no matter the table) should ever share a Sys ID.

A **Reference** field is a database column that is meant to accept the primary key (**Sys ID**) from another record, often in another table. In this way, the two records are related. This is known as a one-to-many, or a parent-child relationship. In fact, there is one field on the Task table which our Virtual War Room table inherited, that's called parent, and is designed for exactly this type of relationship; though we aren't using it in this case.

 In database parlance, when your table has a column meant to accept the primary key from another record, that column is referred to as a **foreign key**.

When we created the **Major incident** reference field on the Virtual War Room table, we created a relationship between records in the **Incident** table, and records in the Virtual War Room table. We can easily see the related incident from the Virtual War Room form, by looking at the **Major incident** field; but what if we want to see any related Virtual War Rooms, from the incident form? For that, we need to use a related list.

1. To get started, navigate to the **Incident** table. Don't save your changes to the Virtual War Room ticket. Try navigating there by typing incident.list into the application navigator text filter box, and pressing *Enter*!

2. Click on any Incident record in that list to open the **Incident** form for that record.

3. Right-click on the header for that form, and go to **Configure | Related Lists**:

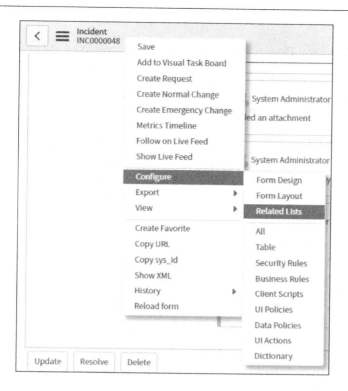

4. Scroll down in the **Available** box, until you see **Virtual War Room | Major incident**, then double-click on it, and click **Save**.

 Some of the most useful pieces of information in ServiceNow, are what something used to look like, when it was updated, and who updated it. For any records in a table that is audited (any table that's tracked in update sets), you can find the versions related list under **Configure | Related Lists** on the form.

You should now see the Virtual War Rooms related list at the bottom of the **Incident** form, and it should be empty. That means that this particular Incident doesn't have any Virtual War Rooms associated with it. Let's go ahead and fix that by clicking the blue **New** button under that related list.

You should be taken to a new record form for the `Virtual War Room` table, and the **Major incident** field should be auto-populated with the number of the incident we were just on. Be aware that although you can make the Number field unique in the incident table so that there can be no duplicates, it is not the primary key. That's the Sys ID.

In the Form Designer section of this chapter, we learned how the **State** field on the **Task** table (and tables that extend it) is actually an **Integer** field, and each of those integer values has a label, like **Open**, or **Work in Progress**, but the actual value in that field is still an integer. **Reference** fields are similar, in that-although you see the display value of the record in the **Reference** field. The actual value that it contains, is a Sys ID. Since the **Incident** table's **Number** column is set as the display value, we see the incident number in the **Major incident** reference field. If, however, we were to change the **Short description** field to be the display value instead, then we would see that instead of the number, in this and any **Reference** field which contained the Sys ID of an incident.

Just like we've done before, fill out the Virtual War Room record with any ol' information. You should notice that the **Short description** field has also auto-populated with the short description of the incident. Let's see what happens if we change the value of a field that is derived from another record. Go ahead and add the word testing to the end of the short description.

Once you've finished filling out some info and changing the short description, right-click on the header and click **Save**.

Notice that when creating an incident in this way, we've effectively bypassed the reference qualifier we created on the **Major incident** reference field! If we clear out the value in that field, the system won't let us re-populate it, but it's important to be aware that when coming at it from the child-ticket and creating a parent record in this way, we can bypass a reference qualifier. You can prevent this by removing the option to create new records from the list control of the related list, but we'll go over this in a later chapter.

When the form reloads, you'll see a *reference* icon (ⓘ) to the right of the **Major incident** field; it'll look like a lower-case letter **i** inside a circle. Click on that icon to be taken to the incident that we were on previously, and scroll to the bottom. You should now see our newly created Virtual War Room! This is because there's now a record in the Virtual War Room table that matches the default query for this related list, which you can see just to the right of the filter icon.

This is all great, and you can imagine the myriad of uses for the functionality of related lists, but we will only be using Virtual War Rooms on Major incidents, and those are pretty rare. Luckily, we can control when related lists show up easily! To see how, right-click on the list column header row in the related list, and go to **Configure | List Control**.

On the right side of the list control form, you can choose which roles are required to see the **New** or **Edit** buttons, the filter, or even links in the related list. On the left side, you can see several options for omitting the new button altogether, omitting the edit button, and other components. The option we're interested in though, is the **Omit if empty** checkbox. Tick that box, and click **Submit** to return to the Incident form.

Now, when visiting an incident that doesn't have a Virtual War Room associated with it, you won't see the related list!

Summary

In this chapter, we learned about lists—both version 2 and version 3, available in the latest versions of ServiceNow. We learned how to create custom tables, and how to manipulate forms by adding and removing fields as needed. We learned how to build qualifications for the records available in our **Virtual War Room** table, and how to sort and group by results returned in list view. And we learned how to add related lists to forms, and how to dot-walk through reference fields.

Lists and forms are fundamental to ServiceNow, so don't be afraid to come back and reference this chapter as you read on.

3
UI Customization

Now that we understand the main components of the user interface, and the basics of customizing them from a functional perspective, let's learn how to customize the look and feel of our instance and some of the major UI components.

In this chapter, we'll learn about:

- UI15 versus UI16
- Customizing the default theme
- Creating custom themes and branding your instance
- Understanding UI-impacting system properties
- Using custom CSS/SCSS properties
- Creating and branding a Service Portal

UI15 versus UI16

UI15 and UI16 are versions of the overall user interface, not too dissimilar from what we saw in earlier chapters with *List v2* and *List v3*. UI16 is the latest version, and was introduced with the Geneva release of ServiceNow.

By the time you're reading this book, it's likely that the vast majority of ServiceNow customers will be using UI16 exclusively. For this reason, UI16 is what we're going to focus on in this book. However, since UI15 is not absent, and since not *everyone* is going to be on the latest version of the UI, let's discuss some differences you'll notice between UI15 and UI16, so that you can still follow along even if you're on Fuji or earlier (as long ago as that was).

Switching between UI15 and UI16

In an instance that was setup on Geneva-or-later (meaning that it wasn't upgraded from a previous version, but was a fresh instance from Geneva or later), the **UI16** plugin is automatically active. If you want to switch between UI15 and UI16, click on **System Settings** , and you'll see a button that says **Switch to UI15** (or **Switch to UI16** if you're already in UI15):

Don't see it? Make sure that the appropriate plugin has been enabled. Go to **System Definition | Plugins** and activate the **UI16** plugin. You may want to log out and back in if you don't see the new UI:

By default, after UI16 is activated, all users should see UI16. Administrators will see the **Switch to UI15** button, but you'll need to specify some additional roles if you'd like to let other users switch freely between the two main UI versions. To do that, make sure that UI16 is activated, and navigate to the sys_properties table using .list in the Application Navigator like we learned previously. Search for a system property called glide.ui.ui15_switch_roles. It doesn't exist by default, so if you don't see it, just click **New** at the top-left of the list view, and create it. The Type value should be String. Set the value to a comma-separated list of roles for users that are allowed to switch between UI15 and UI16.

There's a little trick here. Like with many properties that expect a string containing a comma-separated list of values, you can allow all users to switch between UI15 and UI16 freely, by setting the value of this property (`glide.ui.ui15_switch_roles`) to just a comma. No text or spaces, just a simple comma. The system seems to treat this to mean simply all.

If you're already on UI16, I don't recommend switching back unless you have quite a good reason for doing so, as UI15 won't be supported, and disables some important features.

Branding your instance

If you've been following along in your own personal developer instance, what you're probably looking at when you sign into that instance, is the default ServiceNow theme. While the default theme is pretty slick, companies often appreciate a more branded and customized look for their instance.

Let's start by going to **System Properties | Basic Configuration UI16** (or **System Properties | Basic Configuration**, if you're not in UI16) to customize the instance's banner and the default theme colors. You can upload your company's logo, set banner text, and change some elements of the default color scheme. If a user has not selected a theme from the **System Settings**, this is the color scheme the user will see.

You can use predefined color names (such as white or red), RGB decimal (such as `rgb (255, 255, 255)`), or RGB hex (such as #FFFFFF) formats for CSS colors. You cannot use RGBA decimals or RGBA hex to indicate opacity for ServiceNow themes.

For more detailed editing of the UI, including table spacing and font type, navigate to **System Properties | CSS**. There are several options available for borders, buttons, backgrounds, and many more. Some of these options are also in **Basic Configuration UI16**—updating the value of an element in one form will update the value in the other as well.

Custom themes

There are already a few theme options available in the **Theme** tab of **System Settings**, but you might want to have a few other color schemes available for users to choose from. To look at the themes currently available in your instance, navigate to **System UI | Themes**. If you're in a Geneva or later instance, you'll notice quite a few themes that are not listed in **System Settings**: the additional themes are for UI15 or UI11. Here's how you can tell: Each theme has a field labeled **Device** that identifies the UI version that the theme applies to. A device value of **Browser** indicates a UI11 theme, while **Doctype** indicates a UI15 theme, and **Concourse** indicates a **UI16** theme.

I know that sounds very odd, so I'll re-state it another way:

- If the **Device** field on a given **Theme** record is set to **Browser**, then that theme only applies to UI11
- If the **Device** field is set to **Doctype**, then that theme applies to UI15
- If the **Device** field is set to **Concourse**, the theme applies to UI16

Let's get hands-on with theme building, and make ourselves a new UI16 theme. Start by navigating to **System UI | Themes**, and opening up the **Blimey** theme from the list. Once there, change the name to My Custom Theme, then right-click the form header, and select **Insert and Stay**. This will create a copy of the Blimey theme, but with the name My Custom Theme.

A UI16 theme uses CSS variables to set color values. Now that we have a new theme record, customizing this theme consists of changing the color values in the CSS field to suit the company, or personal taste. Go ahead and do that now. If you're not sure what to change, find some values that are white (#fff) and set them to a neon green color (#76EE00). This way, you can play around and experiment with different properties to see exactly what they correspond to!

After altering the colors and saving the record, refresh the whole page.

 Refreshing the whole page after a UI-impacting change is necessary, because otherwise the ServiceNow frame (the banner and application navigator) won't be reloaded. If your change impacts these UI elements, you'll need to hit your browser's *refresh* button to see the updates.

You can test the new theme by opening **System Settings**, going to the **Theme** tab on the left, and selecting **My Custom Theme**:

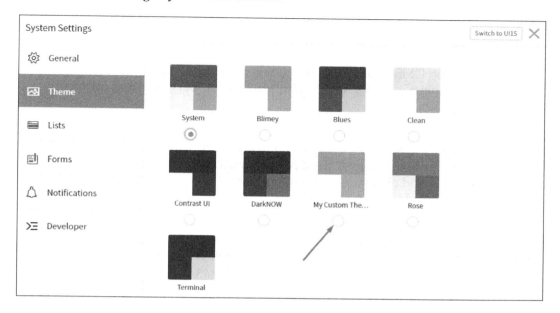

Look through all of the tabs in the application navigator, to ensure that all headings and text are still legible with the new color scheme; it can be easy to accidentally set things like background hover color ($nav-highlight-main) and text hover color ($navpage-nav-app-text-hover, $navpage-nav-mod-text-hover) to the same value, resulting in a solid color bar when hovered over, which is generally not desirable.

UI-impacting system properties

There are quite a few options for further UI customization in **System Properties | UI Properties**. You can use CSS to change the look and feel of journal fields like **Work Notes** and the **Activity Log**, alter the default number of records shown on a list, and configure button styles. It is beyond the scope of this book to go through each and every one, but you can get a good idea of what they do from their description.

Don't forget—you're in your own personal developer instance. You can't break it, so go nuts tweaking things to your heart's content, learning how things work, and generally fiddling. That's what personal developer instances are for! You can always wipe it and re-set it back to factory defaults.

Configuring service portal UI

The service portal in ServiceNow is generally used as a front page for IT, and allows users (even those without any permissive roles in ServiceNow) to submit tickets for IT (or other departments) to handle. The Service Portal is effectively a replacement for the CMS (used in Geneva and earlier), and includes many enhancements over the old Jelly-driven CMS application, but many companies will still be on a legacy CMS until they have a reason to convert/upgrade to the Service Portal for their self-service interface.

To create your own Service Portal, start by navigating to **System Definition | Plugins** to activate the **Service Portal for Enterprise Service Management** plugin (ID: `com.glide.service-portal.esm`) plugin by searching for it from the list, then right-clicking on it, and choosing **Activate/Upgrade**. Since this is your personal instance, go ahead and load demo data.

After activation, refresh the page again, and navigate to **Service Portal | Portals** in the Application Navigator. We'll use the existing default **Service Portal** as a starting point. Click on **Service Portal** to open the default built-in service portal, change the **Title** (or in earlier versions, **Name**) field to say `My Service Portal`, change the **URL suffix** field to say `my_sp`, and then right click in the header and click on **Insert and Stay** again. As before, this will create a duplicate record with the new values we've set, and redirect you to the newly created record.

There are a bunch of default values on this portal corresponding to pages in the **Service Portal | Pages** table [`sp_pages`]. Clicking on the reference icon for any of these, will take you to the page record. On these records, you'll see some CSS (if specified), and a link to open it in the Service Portal designer.

Pages in the **Service Portal** can be used in multiple portals, not just one. Catalog, header menu, and knowledge information is referenced dynamically based on the relevant fields in the portal's record. If the HR portal uses the HR catalog and the IT portal uses the IT catalog, even if both portals have `sc_home` set as the catalog homepage, the HR portal will only display HR catalog categories, and the IT portal will only display the IT catalog categories.

Now let's do some branding! Navigate to **Service Portal | Service Portal Configuration**, and open up the **Branding Editor**:

Here, you can set your portal title, company logo, homepage background color, background image, and more. In the **Theme Colors** tab on the left, you can even more granularly customize the colors of the UI elements displayed in your theme! Any changes made in the **Branding Editor** are automatically saved.

If, after making a few changes here, you navigate back to the **My Service Portal** record (from **Service Portal | Portals**), you can see that the logo and CSS variables fields will have updated to reflect the changes that you've made. You can also click the **Try It** button on the top right of the form to see the portal:

Congratulations! If you've followed the preceding steps, you now have a fully-functioning and branded **Service Portal**, completely connected to your catalog and knowledge base. No problem, right?

Creating a custom homepage

You can probably imagine that instead of the existing homepage, a company might want to have a homepage containing something different. Let's say our company wants to have three clocks with the time for the three locations where they have the most clients; **San Francisco**, **Boston**, and **London**. They also want to keep the search bar, and want a dynamic list of submitted incidents. Let's explore how we might create that for them:

1. Navigate to **Service Portal | Pages**, and create a new page by clicking **New** in the top-left.

2. Fill in the **Title** field with Home, and the **ID** field with home. The **ID** field is the URL suffix for this page. Once you're finished, right-click the header, and click Save.

3. Under the **Related Links** section of the page, click on **Open in Designer**. Inside the **Page Designer** header, you'll see a little book icon labeled **sp** next to a page icon labeled **Home**. **sp** is the URL suffix of the portal we're currently previewing this newly created page inside, and **Home** is the page currently being edited:

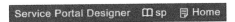

The page layout of a service portal page remains the same, no matter which portal it's being displayed in; however, different portals can have different color schemes, and display using different CSS. Click on the portal icon to change it to **my_sp**. At any point while in the **Service Portal Designer**, you can switch between **Edit** and **Preview** at the top of the designer UI, to instantly see changes you've made. Layout and widget changes made in the designer are automatically saved.

The **Service Portal Designer** provides a drag-and-drop interface for constructing page layouts and organizing widgets. First, drag a **Container** onto the form (from **Layouts**, under the **Widget** tab), then drag a **4 | 4 | 4** column layout into the container. Columns are the items beneath the **Container** option under the **Widget** tab labelled with numbers, as shown in following screenshot:

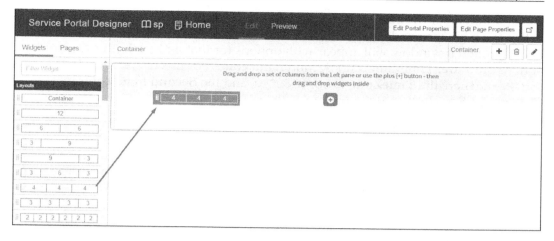

- Service Portal pages are comprised of **Widgets** inside of columns, inside of rows, and inside of **Containers**. **Widgets** are reusable, modular, customizable segments of code. Each use of a widget creates an instance record on the sp_instance table. **Widgets** often have options that are unique to each instance of the widget, and do not affect other instances of that widget. Several of ServiceNow's built-in widgets are protected and read-only, but can be cloned for customization. Creating a new record for customization instead of altering the **out-of-the-box** (OOB) widget is considered best practice, and ensures that the OOB widget can be updated in the event of future upgrades!

Type clock into the **Filter Widget** bar in the **Widgets** tab of the **Service Portal Designer**, and drag the **Cool Clock** widget into each of the columns in the container. Now you ought to have three clocks, all with either your current time, or the current time in Los Angeles (depending on your **System Settings**):

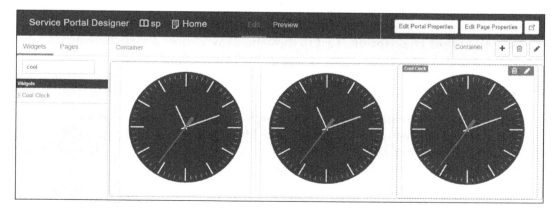

Hover your cursor over the clock on the left. A border and header should appear with a trash bin icon and a pencil icon 📝. That is the edit button. If you click on that button, a modal window will appear with options for that widget. In this case, our options are **Title**, **TimeZone**, and **Second hand color**. For this one, set the **Title** to San Francisco, the **TimeZone** to US/Pacific, and the **Second hand color** to blue. Click on the **Save** button at the bottom of the modal.

> Clicking outside of the modal window without clicking **Save** will close the window, without saving your edits! Clicking on the *pencil* icon next to the widget name in the **Widgets** tab of the **Service Portal Designer** will open that widget in the widget editor, for even more customizability.

Click the *pencil* icon again on the middle clock, and set the **Title** to Boston, the **TimeZone** to US/Eastern, and the **Second hand color** to rgb (222, 48, 146). As you can see, the color field accepts RGB values as well as color names!

Give the clock on the right a **Title** of London, a **TimeZone** of Europe/London, and a **Second hand color** of #bc3529. You may have already guessed it, but the color field also accepts hex values!

Do your clocks have different background colors? Don't worry, it's on purpose — this widget changes background colors depending on time of day for that location.

Next, we'll put in the homepage search widget. Just like in the OOB homepage, we want this widget to span most of the page, so drag in a new **Container** from the **Widgets** tab, and place it underneath the clock container. Then, drag a size **12** column into that container. Type search into the **Widgets** tab filter box to see the different search widgets available, then drag the **Homepage Search** widget into the 12 column container you just added to the page.

If you click the *pencil* icon for the **Homepage Search** widget, you'll see options for **Title** and **Short Description**. Text in those fields will show above the search bar. Go ahead and type in How can we help today? for the **Title**, and Search the Service Catalog and Knowledge Base for assistance as the **Short Description**.

There is a third option called **Typeahead Search**. This option allows you to modify the typeahead search widget embedded in the **Homepage Search** using a JSON object. In this field, enter {title: "Enter keywords to search."}. After saving, this should change the text in the search bar:

How can we help today?

Search the Service Catalog and Knowledge Base for assistance

How can we help?	Q

The last requirement for our custom homepage is a dynamic list of incidents opened by the current user (whoever happens to be viewing the page). To create that, start by dragging another container, and another size 12 column beneath the **Homepage Search** container. Search for `list` in the **Widgets** tab, and drag the **Simple List** widget into the new column.

If you click on the *pencil/edit* icon for the simple list, you'll notice that we have a lot more options available for this widget, than we did for the clock widget. Let's set it up:

- Since this is meant to be a list of incident records, set **Table** to **Incident** [`incident`].

- The default display value of the **Incident** table is the **Number** field. We can customize the primary display field for this list, but in this case, let's leave the **Display field** set to **Number**, as it's what people are used to seeing.

- To display some other useful fields in this list widget, scroll down and set the **Secondary fields** list collector field, so it contains **Short description**, **Opened**, **State**, and **Priority**.

This **Secondary fields** field is an example of how **List collector** field types work in the new service portal. It looks quite different from list collectors in the CMS or classic view (outside of the service portal or CMS).

- Finally, scroll to the bottom of the modal dialog, and click on **Save**.

- After clicking **Save**, click **Preview** at the top of the page. You should now be able to see a list of Incident tickets below your portal home page's search box. However, the list is not filtered, and you'll notice if you try to click on an Incident ticket number, that the link doesn't go anywhere. Thus, the next step is to set this up to only show records submitted by the current user (the user viewing the page). To accomplish that, rather than modify the widget by clicking the *pencil/edit* icon, we'll edit the instance of this particular widget that's displayed in this page.

Head back to the *classic view* of ServiceNow (the view with the ServiceNow frame that you see by default after logging in), and navigate to **Service Portal | Widget Instances**. Each time you use a widget in a portal page, you're effectively creating a new instance of that widget. These instances, and their unique configuration information, are stored in this table.

The **Updated** field should be the first field on the left, and if you click on the field header, it should sort the list by when each instance was last updated. Make sure it sorts so that more recent updates show up at the top of the list. If it doesn't, click on the header again. The **Simple List** widget that we just added and set up should be on the top of this list (as it was updated most recently). Click on that row to open up the instance of the simple list widget we created, then follow these steps to fill in the details:

1. Set the **Title** to **My Incidents** to change the display header of the widget on the portal page.

 Without a title, the simple list widget displays the name of the table being queried. In this case, it would display **Incident**.

2. Next, use the query builder in the **Table and Filter** form section to filter the incidents that'll be displayed in the list. We want currently active records, so set the first condition to [Active] [is] [true].

3. We also want to show only records which were opened by the current user. We'll use a dynamic filter too accomplish this. To add this dynamic filter condition, click **and** next to the first condition, and set the second condition to [Opened by] [is (dynamic)] [me].

4. In the **Fields on List**, **Appearance** form section, you can edit the maximum number of records displayed on the widget. Let's set the **Maximum entries** value to 20.

5. The **Link to this page** field allows you to determine where the user should be directed when clicking on these records. Since we're making a list of tickets, let's select **ticket** in this reference field, and the user will see the ticket that they've clicked on. Finally, right-click in the header and click **Save**.

 There is a convenient shortcut to view Widget Instances in Google Chrome. If you view the service portal page that contains the widget you're looking to edit, hover over the widget and use *Ctrl* + right click to open up the widget context menu.

Styling pages and widgets

This section assumes a basic understanding of HTML and CSS styling.

Congratulations, you've just built a functional custom homepage! It looks pretty good, but it feels a little unbalanced since the clocks are so big. Let's make them smaller.

To do this, we're going to change some of the grid size class names, and utilize the **Page Specific CSS** option for the portal. If you click on a clock widget, you'll see a thin blue line around it. If you look carefully, you'll also see not just one, but two dotted blue lined boxes drawn around it. These are the container borders. There are three containers there:

Select the **Container** surrounding the clock. Once you've selected the correct element, you'll see the word **Column** at the top-right of the page next to the three icons:

Click on the **edit** icon in the top-right of the page (not the top-right of the clock widget). You will see a field called **CSS class**, and select fields denoting size. Set the CSS class to `clock_column`, and set **Size - md** to 2. This will set the CSS class name for the widget object for later manipulation, and make the widget about half its current size. Set all other **Size** fields to **Default**, and click **Save**.

If you hover over the field headers such as **Size - md**, you'll often get field descriptions or other helpful information. In the case of this field, it tells you that it's setting the size of the widget when rendered on a desktop computer.

Repeat this procedure with the column container for each clock, and then select the row containing the clock columns by clicking outside of the clock columns to the right or left of the widgets, click the *pencil/edit* icon again from the top-right of the page, and set the **CSS class** to `clock_row`, then press **Save**.

If you preview the page after following these steps, you'll notice that while the clocks are now smaller, they are all aligned left. Rows have been styled to center content in groups of twelve columns; now that we only have six total columns' worth of content (2 for each clock), we'll need to do something to center them.

In the designer header there are a few more buttons: **Edit Portal Properties** and **Edit Page Properties**:

Clicking on either button will open a modal window containing options for the current portal and current page selected. Since we only want to change the clocks on this page, we'll be filling out the **Page Specific CSS** on the **Page Properties** modal, so go ahead and click on **Edit Page Properties**. In the **Page Specific CSS** field, enter the following:

```
.clock_row {
  text-align: center;
}

.clock_column {
  margin: auto;
  padding: 10px;
  display: inline-block;
  float: none;
}
```

This centers the content in `.clock_row`, and overrides the default `float: left` property attached to the columns. Your page properties for home should now look something like this:

The **Service Portal** supports most CSS pseudo classes and selectors, including focus, hover, and last-of-type. Unlike internal themes, Service Portal themes can use RGBA color opacity. Page-specific CSS usually overrides assigned theme and default styles, but some default styles are inaccessible. If you come across any of these, you can use the `!important` tag to override all other styles for a particular page or portal.

Now that we've created the new homepage for our portal, go back to **Service Portal | Portals**, open **My Service Portal**, and change the Homepage from **index** to **home**. Finally, click **Save**, and when the page reloads you can click on **Try It** at the top-right or bottom-left, to see your new portal page in action!

Setting up the War Room page

To prepare for the rest of our War Room application, we're going to set up a basic page that we'll customize later on. Create a new page using the same process as before, set the title to War Room and set the ID to war.

Scroll down to the **Related Links**, and select **Open in Designer**. Add in one container, and one 12 column layout into the container. Search the list of widgets for the **Form** widget, and drag it into the column. We'll leave this page like this for now, and make further customizations in a later chapter.

 The form widget will say **Record not found** in lieu of a preview or a record. This widget pulls table and sys_id information from the URL, and will not display any record if they are not included in the URL.

Styling the CMS

While this book will focus primarily on current-generation technology, we would be remiss to completely leave out the CMS. The **Service Portal** is only available for post-Geneva ServiceNow instances. For Geneva instances and the versions prior, ServiceNow uses the **Content Management System (CMS)** for users without ITIL/fulfiller roles to submit tickets through the system. CMS will continue to be supported for some time, but support may be discontinued in later versions of the Now platform. Various compatibility issues have already begun to crop up in previous releases—it is highly recommended that ServiceNow users migrate from an old Jelly-based CMS to the Service Portal as soon as possible.

The CMS and **Service Portal** are very similar, in that they are both meant to facilitate something of a *front-end* for business users to submit service requests, log Incidents, and get some basic information about their tickets. They differ though, in that the service portal is based on **Angular** (a library based on JavaScript, for building powerful web-apps), whereas the CMS is based on **Jelly** (a little-known multi-phase executable XML language, developed by Apache).

The Service Portal also provides a simple, easy-to-use interface for building your portal's front-end, based on **Bootstrap** (a paradigm of largely CSS-based design and JavaScript APIs). This simplicity and on-rails feel of the Service Portal has its down-side, though. There are some things that are much more difficult to do in **Service Portal**, than in the CMS. The CMS is almost like the wild west; a great deal of freedom and expandability, but with little in the way of standards, controls, or limitations to ensure a consistent, maintainable, or pleasant user experience.

Rather than set up a site from scratch, we'll have a quick look at the default **Employee Self-Service (ESS)** CMS as an example. Navigate to **Content Management | Sites**, and select the **Employee Self Service** site. In the **Pages** related list at the bottom of the **Site** form, open the portal page with the URL suffix main.

Layouts for the CMS are predefined **UI Macros**, and are typically written in a language called Jelly, which is a Java and XML-based scripting and processing engine for turning XML into code that can be executed. **Layouts** have drop zones, where you'll use other **UI Macros** and content blocks to display content, similar to the **Containers** and **Widgets** in the Helsinki **Service Portal**.

 UI Macros are used all over ServiceNow, including the internal lists and forms. It is considered best practice to duplicate a UI Macro and edit the duplicate, rather than edit the original record, if you'd like to make changes to one. Other developers may have used the same UI Macro elsewhere, and editing that UI Macro could have interesting consequences. Making changes to a OOB UI macro also prevents the system from upgrading that record, when you upgrade your instance to a new version!

Under the **Related Links** section of the **Portal** record, click **Edit Page**. From here, you can change the layout, and insert or edit the UI macros on the page.

To brand the CMS, let's change the header logo. Hover over the header in the layout, and you'll see the *edit* icon in the top right corner of the **UI Macro**. Click that to open the header record:

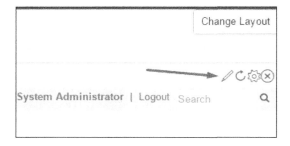

Once on the header record, you can upload a new logo, and set new background colors. Alternatively, you can use a background image for the header with your company's logo.

In addition to changing the logo, you might also want to change the colors to match the company color scheme. Navigate to **Content Management | Design | Themes** to see a list of current CMS theme records. Each theme is comprised of several style sheets that govern the styles for UI Macros and layouts in the CMS. You can click on any of the style sheets from the related list on the theme record, to modify this CSS to fit your company's branding scheme.

The **Themes** used for the CMS also include styles governing navigation list **UI Macros** and general formatting. Rather than starting a new Theme from scratch, it's a lot easier to use or duplicate the existing Style Sheets in the Default Theme, and then add a style sheet with CSS overrides to achieve the look you're going for.

Summary

In this chapter, we learned a great deal about *UI15* and *UI16*, as well as how to create custom themes using CSS UI properties. We also learned how to brand your instance for your company, which you can also use to sub-brand your dev and test instances an order to make sure they're different at a glance, to avoid making updates directly in prod by accident! We even learned about the CMS, the service portal, and how to style and customize them.

4
Understanding Data and Relationships

Data administration is about relationships. Understanding the relationships between your data, and how they tie your various tables together, is crucial to becoming a good ServiceNow administrator or developer.

There are a number of different types of data relationships, with different structures to suit different purposes. In this chapter, we're going to learn what those relationship types are, how they're structured, and how we can use them effectively within our ServiceNow instance. We'll learn not just about relationships defined by linking one record to another, but also about hierarchical relationships and inheritance.

In this chapter, we'll learn about:

- General database structures and relationships
- One-to-many relationships in ServiceNow
- Many-to-many relationships in ServiceNow
- Enforcing one-to-one relationships
- Defining custom relationships
- Database table inheritance

One-to-many relationships in ServiceNow

One-to-many relationships are one type of parent-child relationship. They consist of *one parent record*, that is linked to *many child records*. This linkage is done using database table keys.

As we briefly mentioned in a previous chapter, records have a **primary key (PK)**, and a **foreign key (FK)** column; though they aren't called that in ServiceNow. The PK in ServiceNow is the **Sys ID** [sys_id] column. Every record in ServiceNow has a Sys ID that is typically unique within the entire database (though technically a primary key only needs to be unique within a table). An example of an FK column, is any column which is meant to hold the PK of another record. These fields are reference fields in ServiceNow. The **Incident** [incident] table for example, contains an FK column with the label **Assigned to**, and an actual column name of assigned_to. This is a reference field that points to the **User** [sys_user] table, and contains the PK (Sys ID) of one of the records in that table. A reference field can only reference records in one table, specified in that field's dictionary record.

> When you look at one of these FK (reference) fields on a form, you'll see the **display value** of the record that the Sys ID it contains corresponds to. The display value is the value in whichever column has the display_value attribute set to true. For example, in the **Incident** table (and any other tables that extend the **Task** table), the display value is the **Number** column by default.

The **Assigned to** field also helps to illustrate the nature of a one-to-many relationship. As you might imagine, each incident can only be assigned to one user at a time (you can only put one Sys ID value into a reference field at one time!) However, a user may be the **assignee** of many incidents. Therefore, the relationship is one (user) to many (incidents), but not the other way around.

To get a better idea of how this relationship works, let's explore the database of an imaginary shoe-shop: Lou's Shoes.

Imagine that we have a table of customers that looks something like this:

Customers

Name (PK)	Shoe size	Preferred material
Larry Lopez	11 Men's	Leather
Sally Stewart	7 Women's	Suede
Molly Mae	8.5 Women's	Microfiber

Next, imagine that we've got a table of products, like this:

Products

Item (PK)	Color	Material
Lavender Leather Loafer	Purple	Leather
Scarlet Suede Stiletto	Red	Suede
Mahogany Microfiber Moccasin	Brown	Microfiber

 Of course, it's a bad idea to use a customer or item name as a PK like we have in the preceding two tables, because sometimes people or items have the same name! This is just for the purposes of our example. The best primary key is usually long and randomly generated, like a Sys ID!

Note that in the preceding table, we have a primary key; that's mandatory. But we don't have any foreign keys. Foreign keys are not required in a table, just primary keys are!

Finally, we've got to have a place to store orders; but orders must contain links to both an item, and to the user who ordered them. That's *two* foreign keys! That table might look something like this:

Orders

Order # (PK)	Customer (FK)	Item (FK)
018239	Larry Lopez	Lavender Leather Loafer
018240	Sally Stewart	Scarlet Suede Stiletto
018241	Molly Mae	Mahogany Microfiber Moccasin

As you can see, the **Orders** table consists of only keys-one primary (as always) and two foreign. The primary key is the order number. This is not randomly-generated, but assuming it's auto-generated and guaranteed unique, it can work for us. The other two fields/columns are both foreign keys. One links to the customers table, and one to the `items` table we defined earlier. Each record in the **Orders** table, therefore, is an order placed by a customer, for an item. For example, **Larry Lopez** placed an order for size eleven **Lavender Leather Loafers** at Lou's Shoes.

I hope he liked them.

We don't have the shoe size in the **Orders** table, but by accessing the **reference** to the **Customers** field, we can get Larry Lopez's shoe size from his profile in the **Customers** table. This is called **dot-walking**.

Of course in a real-world scenario, you could have more than one item in an order and you'd definitely want more information stored with the order (such as the price and where to ship it!) but this is just an example.

 While you can have more than one foreign key column on a table, and you can even have more than one column that should contain unique values, only one column in a given table can be the primary key.

When we added the **Major incident** field to the **Virtual War Room** table, we created a one-to-many relationship between the **Incident** and **Virtual War Room** tables, with the **Incident** being the parent, and the **Virtual War Room** being the child. We then displayed that relationship on the incident form, by showing the **related list** called **Virtual War Rooms | Major incident** (as long as it isn't empty). This is often how one-to-many relationships work, and are displayed within ServiceNow:

Many-to-many relationships in ServiceNow

Many-to-many (M2M) relationships are similar to one-to-many relationships, except that they aren't usually dependent on just a foreign key column in a child table. Instead, many-to-many relationships in ServiceNow usually rely on an entire intermediary table called an **M2M** table. This table commonly has a PK (Sys ID) of its own for each record (of course), and otherwise primarily consists (other than the default **System** fields, like **Updated** and **Created by**) of two FK columns (reference fields).

As it happens, we've already seen one example of a many-to-many table: the **Lou's Shoes Order** table we defined earlier! This table creates a many-to-many relationship between the **Customer** and **Item** tables. This structure makes sense, because any one customer might order multiple different items, and any one item might be purchased by multiple different customers.

Luckily, in ServiceNow, there is an easy and pre-defined way to create M2M tables. Follow the following steps, to see how to define a new many-to-many relationship table, and add a related list to display that relationship on both related tables (as opposed to just the parent records).

Creating a M2M table

In the following demo, we'll create a many-to-many relationship between **Problems** and **Virtual War Rooms**. This functionality would allow us to link War Rooms, to the **Problem** record that's associated with the **Major incident** and any other issues that the War Room relates to.

1. In the application navigator filter text bar, enter sys_m2m.list, and press *Enter*. This will take you to the Many to Many Definitions table. Even in your **stock developer instance**, you should see at least two or three many-to-many definitions. Note that these records are not the M2M tables themselves, they are simply the definition records for those tables. They define the many-to-many relationship; including, the names of the two tables that are linked.

> This is a great example of using the .list shortcut to navigate to a table that isn't otherwise accessible from the application navigator! It's also a great example of why it's important to remember a table's **name**, as well as its **label**.

2. At the top-left, click on **New**, to be taken to the **New record** form on the `sys_m2m` table.

3. In the **From table** field, we're going to choose our left-hand table. The left table is generally considered the primary in the M2M relationship, but this isn't important here. For our demo, select **Virtual War Room** [`u_virtual_war_room`].

4. In the **To table** field, select **Problem** [`problem`] as the right table. The other fields on the form will auto-populate.

5. You may then want to edit the pre-filled values, such as the many to many table name. I'm going to call mine `u_war_room_problem`.

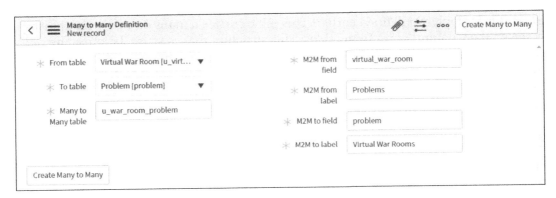

6. Finally, click on **Create Many to Many** at the top-right, or bottom-left of the form.

The result of creating this M2M table definition, is that a new table has been created with the name we specified (I used `u_war_room_prob`). This table's form will have two reference fields: One for the **Problem**, and one for the **Virtual War Rooms**. Thus, the `Problem` and **Virtual War Room** tables are now linked through this intermediary `m2m` table!

Normally when you have a reference field on one (child) table that points to a record in another (parent) table, you can add a related list on the parent table form in order to show all of a given record's child-records. However, in the case of a M2M table, the reference field isn't on the child record-it's on an intermediary record. Luckily, ServiceNow understands this M2M relationship as defined in the sys_m2m table, and makes it easy for us to display this relationship on both tables, using related lists. Here's how:

1. Head on over to the Problem table. If you want to be slick about it, enter problem.list into the application navigator filter bar, and press *Enter*.

2. Open any problem record by either clicking on the display value, or clicking on the reference icon ⓘ.

3. Note that you may need to click **Open Record** after clicking on the reference icon, if you're on List v3.

 The view that shows up when hovering over a reference icon is called the sys_popup view. By default, the **default** view is shown in the popup, but you can customize the fields that show here, by creating a new view for a given table with that name (sys_popup).

4. In the **Problem** record, right-click on the header and go to **Configure | Related Lists**:

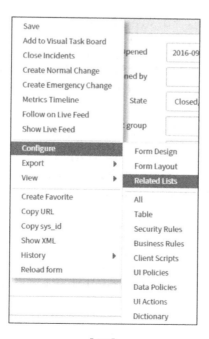

5. In the corresponding list, select the related list called simply **Virtual War Rooms**, and either double-click it, or click the right-arrow between the two list buckets:

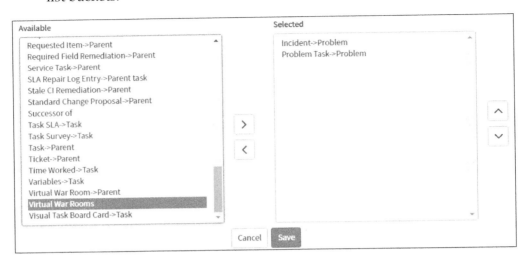

6. Click **Save**, and you should be returned to the problem form, at the bottom of which you'll see a new related list: **Virtual War Rooms**.

7. It's probably rare that we're going to be making use of this relationship since it currently requires a manual association between a **Problem** and a **Virtual War Room** record, so even though we might expect most problems to be generated from major incidents, which would also result in **Virtual War Rooms** being created, let's make sure that this related list only shows up when it has something in it. Right-click in the header of the **Virtual War Rooms** related list at the bottom of the **Problem** form, and go to **Configure | List Control**.

Check the box **Omit if empty**, then click **Save or Submit**.

Now let's repeat the preceding steps on the **Virtual War Room** table, and add the Problems related list there. Let's also similarly check the **Omit if empty** box on that related list. This way, we can see the relationship from both directions!

It's likely that most relationships between a war room and a problem will be one-to-one, but by making this M2M table and relationship, we allow for the possibility of having multiple problems generated from one major incident, and/or associated with multiple war rooms, or one problem addressed by multiple war rooms from multiple major incidents, which were only discovered later, to be related to the same problem.

Other M2M relationships

Perhaps the most well-known examples of many-to-many tables, are the `sys_user_has_role` and `sys_user_grmember` tables. These tables respectively maintain relationships between users and the roles that they have, and between users and the groups of which they are members. These M2M tables are not defined in the `sys_m2m` table, but are specially made by ServiceNow.

The `sys_m2m` table is probably the easiest way to define a many-to-many relationship, but can you think of another way to do so? That is, to create a relationship in which the left-side record can be related to an arbitrary number of right-side records, which can in turn be related to an arbitrary number of left-side records?

In terms of using a field to relate one record to one other, a reference field is pretty effective; however, that isn't the only type of field that can accept a FK value in ServiceNow. To see an example of a **List** field type, let's navigate to the `sc_catalog` table. This table stores information about the service catalogs in your instance.

On the `sc_catalog` table, open the **Service Catalog** record, and you'll see a field in the left column called **Editors**, but instead of an input field, you'll see a lock icon:

This is a `List` field type, which is a particular sort of reference field. In this case, the reference points to the `User (sys_user)` table. Clicking the lock icon opens up the field for editing. You can enter one value after another, and the field will store them in the database column as a comma-separated list of Sys IDs. You might say that this is not technically an FK column in the database, but more like a multi-FK column. It contains multiple PKs (Sys IDs).

It would be technically possible to put one of this sort of field on one table (table A) and another on another table (table B), and thus have a *pseudo-many-to-many* relationship between these two tables. In practice, this is wildly impractical, but just serves to demonstrate that there are few things that *cannot* be done in ServiceNow's database!

Enforcing one-to-one relationships

On the topic of few things being impossible in ServiceNow, let's discuss one-to-one relationships.

Strictly speaking, a one-to-one relationship doesn't truly exist in ServiceNow. In database parlance, this would require that the right-hand table records have a primary key which matches the primary key of a record in the left table. Thus, you could have a left-hand record without a right-hand one, but could never have a right-hand record without the left-hand one.

That's interesting, but ServiceNow's Sys IDs are unique, and they have to be, because of the way ServiceNow's databases are structured on the back-end. Technically, ServiceNow has a flat database structure, depending on how it's configured. In a sense, all records in the database (or all records in all tables that extend the Task table, at least) are in one monster-sized table. This means that the primary key (Sys ID) for a given record really must be globally unique.

Okay, so we can't have one-to-one relationships in the usual way you might have them in an ordinary SQL database; but remember, you can do almost anything you could need to do, in ServiceNow!

One way to create such a relationship is by propagating any changes made on one end of the relationship, to the record on the other end. Let's say for example, that we wanted to make certain that:

- Each incident could only ever possibly have one **Virtual War Room** associated with it
- Each **Virtual War Room** could only ever possibly have one incident associated with it:
    - Though this association should not be mandatory — if it exists, it should be bi-directional
- The incident associated with a war room must be the one the war room is associated with, and vice-versa

There is no out-of-the-box way to accomplish this in ServiceNow, but we can accomplish this using a business rule and just a little bit of code! Follow the following steps to see how:

First, we need to add a `virtual war room` field on the **Incident** table, which we can use to link the incident to the **Virtual War Room** table, just like the war room is currently linked to the **Incident** table by the **Major incident** field.

1. Start by navigating to the **Incident** table, using `incident.list`. Don't forget to press *Enter*!

2. Right-click on the list header, and go to **Configure | Table**. Once on the form, click on **New** at the top of the **Table Columns** embedded list, in the **Columns** tab.

 Remember that in **List v3**, there is a slightly different process to follow. You would instead click on the hamburger menu at the top-left of the list, and click on **Configure**, then on the dialog that pops up, you would click on **Table**.

3. In the **Type** field, enter `reference`, and select the autocomplete option that displays after the field. New fields will become visible based on your selection.

4. In the **Column label** field, enter **Virtual War Room**. The **Column name** field will auto-fill with the value `u_virtual_war_room`. Let's make this name a little shorter (but still clear and comprehensible), and change it to `u_war_room`.

5. Click on the **Reference Specification** tab, and type `virtual war room` and select the appropriate value from the autocomplete suggestion:

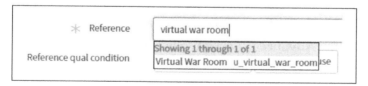

6. Finally, click **Submit**.

Now that we've got a field on the **Incident** table pointing to the **Virtual War Room** table, and one on the **Virtual War Room** table pointing to the **Incident** table, we're ready to begin enforcing this one-to-one relationship. To do that, we're going to need to create a business rule. Business rules allow us to create some basic automation functionality, or more advanced automation using scripting:

1. Return to the **Incident** table, and open an incident record. If you'd like to change the location of the `virtual war room` field in the form, you can do so with the form designer before continuing.

2. Right-click the incident form header, and go to **Configure | Business Rules**, then click on **New**.

3. On the new **Business Rule** form, the **Table** field will be automatically populated for you. Enter a name you like. I chose `Maintain 1:1 relationship with VWR`.

4. On the **When to run** column, set the filter to **Virtual war room**, **changes**. Then, check the boxes for both **Insert** and **Update**:

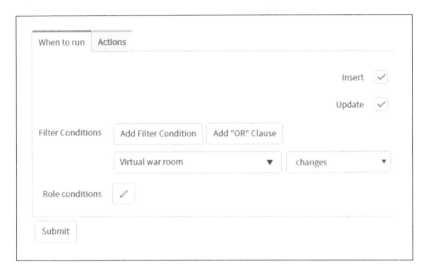

5. These two check-boxes indicate that the business rule should run whenever a record is either inserted or updated, so long as that record matches the conditions we just set at the time it's saved.

6. Next, tick the **Advanced** checkbox, click on the **Advanced** tab, and you'll see some code:

7. This is just a stub. We've got to enter our own code starting on line 3, where it says `Add your code here`. For now, delete that comment and enter the following code. It's okay if you don't understand it, because we've got a whole chapter on this kind of thing coming up:

```
(function executeRule(current, previous /*null when async*/)
{
    var grNewWarRoom;
    var grOldWarRoom;
    if (!current.u_war_room.nil()) {
        grNewWarRoom = current.u_war_room.getRefRecord();
        grNewWarRoom.setValue('u_major_incident', current.
getValue('sys_id'));
        grNewWarRoom.update();
    }
    if (!previous.u_war_room.nil()) {
        grOldWarRoom = previous.u_war_room.getRefRecord();
        grOldWarRoom.setValue('u_major_incident', '');
        grOldWarRoom.update();
    }
})(current, previous);
```

```
Script

 1 ▾   (function executeRule(current, previous /*null when async*/) {
 2
 3         var newWarRoom = current.u_war_room.getRefRecord();
 4         var oldWarRoom = previous.u_war_room.getRefRecord();
 5         newWarRoom.setValue('u_major_incident', current.getValue('sys_id'));
 6         oldWarRoom.setValue('u_major_incident', '');
 7         newWarRoom.update();
 8         oldWarRoom.update();
 9
10     })(current, previous);|
```

Just to offer a quick explanation of what's going on in this script: On lines 3 and 4, we're first getting script objects representing the actual records corresponding to the war room records in the u_war_room field on the incident table, both before the change to the record that triggered this business rule to run (oldWarRoom) and after (newWarRoom). The previous object represents the record before the change, and the current object represents the record after the change. If you used a field name other than u_war_room, you should put your chosen field name in here instead! Next, on lines 5 and 6, we're updating the u_major_incident field on the war room records we found. On the war room record that was previously (but no longer) the selected war room, we clear out the **Major incident** field since it is no longer part of this one-to-one relationship. However, on the newly associated war room, we set the major incident field to contain the sys id of the current record (the one on which this change was made). Finally, on lines 7 and 8, we call .update(), to save our changes to the database.

8. Once that business rule script is written, right-click on the header and click **Save**. This will keep us on the same record, unlike **Update**.

Note that if there are any overt errors in your script which the script editor is able to identify, it will be underlined and a red "X" icon will show up next to the line with the error.

9. Now let's create a similar-but-opposite business rule for the **Virtual War Room** table. **Without saving**, change the **Name** field to Maintain 1:1 relationship with Incident, and the **Table** to **Virtual War Room** [u_virtual_war_room].

10. At the top of the form, right-click the header, but **don't hit save** this time. Instead, click on **Insert and Stay**. This action will create a **new** record, identical to the one you were just on, except with the changes you made before clicking **Insert and Stay**. It also shows you the new record rather than the old one, like it would if you just selected **Insert**.

11. Once the form reloads, you'll be on the newly created **business rule** record that will run on the **Virtual War Room** table, so we'll need to make some changes. For starters, go to the **When to run** tab, and change the condition so **Major incident**, changes.

12. Back on the **Advanced** tab, we need to make some tweaks to our script so that it'll update the incident to the new war room when the war room's **Major incident** field is updated, rather than the other way around like we had it for the **Incident** table. Replace the script we wrote for the **Incident** table, with this new one that's tweaked just slightly for the **Virtual War Room** table:

```
(function executeRule(current, previous /*null when async*/) {
        var newWarRoom = current.u_war_room.getRefRecord();
        var oldWarRoom = previous.u_war_room.getRefRecord();
        newWarRoom.setValue('u_major_incident', current.
getValue('sys_id'));
        oldWarRoom.setValue('u_major_incident', '');
        newWarRoom.update();
        oldWarRoom.update();
    }) (current, previous);
```

```
Script
 1 ▾    (function executeRule(current, previous /*null when async*/) {
 2          var grNewWarRoom;
 3          var grOldWarRoom;
 4 ▾        if (!current.u_war_room.nil()) {
 5              grNewWarRoom = current.u_war_room.getRefRecord();
 6              grNewWarRoom.setValue('u_major_incident', current.getValue('sys_id'));
 7              grNewWarRoom.update();
 8          }
 9 ▾        if (!previous.u_war_room.nil()) {
10              grOldWarRoom = previous.u_war_room.getRefRecord();
11              grOldWarRoom.setValue('u_major_incident', '');
12              grOldWarRoom.update();
13          }
14      })(current, previous);
15
```

13. Right-click on the header, and click **Save**.

Because of these two business rules, from now on, whenever you update the **Major incident** field on a **Virtual War Room**, it'll propagate that change to the previously and newly selected Incident records. Similarly, if you update the `virtual war room` field on an incident, it'll propagate that change to the related war room(s).

It's not as elegant as a *one-to-many* relationship just using one field and a related list, and it would be seldom used, but that's one way to create a one-to-one relationship in ServiceNow!

Defining custom relationships

Adding a reference field on table A that points to table B, creates a relationship that ServiceNow can understand. This allows you to add a related list on records in table B, that displays the records from table A that are linked to it.

Creating a M2M table from the `sys_m2m` relationship definition table also creates a relationship that ServiceNow can understand. Because of this, you can add a related list on either of the two tables linked by the relationship, to show related records from the other table.

If you want to define a more complex relationship, however, ServiceNow allows you to do that as well! Let's explore an example of defining a custom relationship for tickets generated from.

service catalog requests have a sort of task-hierarchy. The **Request** [`sc_request`] record is the parent of one of more **Requested Items** [`sc_req_item`] (commonly called **RITMs**), which may be the parent of one or more **Catalog Tasks** [`sc_task`], not to be confused with the base system **Task** [`task`] table. Work is usually logged and done at the bottom of this relationship hierarchy, on the **Catalog Task** [`sc_task`] records, but the person who the request was for, is stored on the **Request** [`sc_request`] table, in a field called **Requested for** [`requested_for`].

 When I say parent, I mean parent in the parent-child relationship sense; they don't actually use the **Parent** [`parent`] field for this relationship.

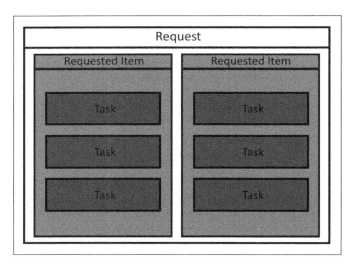

A visual representation of the Request / Request Item / Catalog Task relationship hierarchy

So if you want to be able to see `Catalog Tasks` associated with requests that were requested for a given user, in a related list on that user's record in the `sys_user` table, there would be no built-in relationship that ServiceNow can understand, that you could leverage. Instead, you would need to define a custom relationship by following these steps:

1. In the application navigator, navigate to **System Definition | Relationships**. This is a table containing defined relationships that link any two sets of records. At the top-left, click on **New**.

2. Give this relationship a name that you'll recognize. Since this will be the relationship between users, and the `Catalog Tasks` under requests that were requested for those users, let's call it **Tasks Requested for User**.

3. The **Applies to table** field is where you select the table on which the related list should be able to be **shown**. For our use case, select the **User** [sys_user] table in this field. The `parent` object in the **query with** script corresponds to records in this table.

4. The **Queries from table** field is for the table from which the items in the related list should be shown. Since our related list is going to contain catalog tasks, set this field to the **Catalog Task** [sc_task] table. The `current` object in the query with script corresponds to records in this table.

5. Once the rest of this form is filled out, we need to define the script to use for the query. We'll be covering `GlideRecord` query scripts in much more detail in a later chapter, but for now just copy the code as shown following, and then we'll go over what it's doing.

Write the following code inside the `refineQuery(current, parent { }`block:

```
var parentSid = parent.getValue('sys_id');
    current.addQuery('request.requested_for', parentSid);
```

On the first line (which, in your editor, will be either line 2 or line 3), we are creating a variable called `parentSid` (which stands for **parent Sys ID**) which will contain the value of the parent record's `sys_id` column. The parent object corresponds to the record in the `sys_user` table that the related list will be shown on, so another way of describing `parentSid`, would be to say that it contains the Sys ID of the record which is currently open, and on which the related list is displayed.

On the second line, we use a method of the `GlideRecord` class called `addQuery()`. This method is explained in great detail in a later chapter but for now, just understand that we are adding a query filter on the table that will be shown in the related list. By passing in two arguments, we're telling it that the first argument (a field name) should be equal to the second argument's value (the `sys_ID` of the parent that we acquired on the previous line). In the first argument, you might have noticed that we also used dot-walking, which we learned about in a previous chapter.

This query effectively states: Ensure that the `requested_for` field on the record in the request reference field, is equal to the `sys_id` of the record that this related list is displayed on.

Now right-click on the header, and click **Save**. The final form should look something like this:

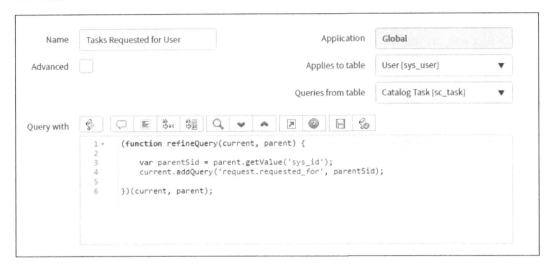

Now we need to test to make sure that our related list works as we expect. To do so, we're going to need to generate some `Catalog Tasks`. In the application navigator, go to **Self-Service | Service Catalog**, click on **Services**, and select a simple catalog item. I recommend using the **New Email Account** catalog item. Fill out the request form, and click **Order Now** on the right. Then, click **Continue Shopping** and repeat the process once more, so you'll have two separate requests, each with one requested item, and one `Catalog Task`.

Next, navigate to the `sc_task` table, using the `.list` shortcut, and find the two tasks you've just created. Write down the task numbers, and open one of them up by clicking on the task number. On the right, you should see a **Requested for** field. This field should contain your user account (**System Administrator** is the default name). Change the value of this field to some other user, such as `Abel Tuter`, and **Save** the record.

The **Requested for** field is not actually on the `sc_task` table; it's a `derived` field. This means that it actually *exists* on another table, linked via one of the reference fields on the `sc_task` table. To see that relationship, right-click on the label **Requested for**, and click on **Show - 'requested_for'**. A small dialog will appear, and you'll see **Dictionary Info** on the top line. That should show the field name, but the field name is dot-walked to: `sc_task.request_item.request.requested_for`. That means that this field is actually dot-walked two layers deep.

Now, navigate to your own user profile by clicking on your name at the top-right of your screen, and choosing **Profile**. (Note that getting to your profile using this link automatically directs you to the self service view):

On your profile page, right-click in the header, and go to **Configure | Related Lists**. On the next page, select **Tasks Requested for User** on the left, click the arrow facing right to move it to the bucket on the right side. If you wanted to make this related list appear on a view other than the self service view, you could change the **View name** field. Click **Save**.

 When you have a huge list of items in a drop-down, or **slush-bucket** field, you can usually get to the one you're looking for by selecting one value, then quickly typing the name of the value you're looking for. For example, if you're looking for a value like **Tasks Requested for User**, select any random value in the list, and type `tasks requested`, and it'll usually take you right there.

You should now see the catalog task(s) that had **System Administrator** in the **Requested for** derived field, but not the one for which you changed the **Requested for** field to `Abel Tuter`. Let's also check Abel Tuter's profile, to make sure the related list there shows that `Catalog Task`.

Navigate to the `sys_user` table using the `.list` shortcut from the application navigator filter text box again, then find and click on Abel Tuter's user profile. You will probably still be in the self service view, so your related list should still show up. If it does, you should see the task you set to be requested for `Abel Tuter`. If not, right-click at the top, and go to **View | Self Service**.

Database table inheritance

When tables share more than a few of the same fields, it is quite often beneficial to extend other tables. Indeed, there are a few tables in ServiceNow which are meant only to be extended, and never to have records created on themselves. The **Task** [`task`] table is a prime example that we already have some familiarity with. We'll go into some detail on the `task` table in particular in a later chapter, but we'll use it as an example here just to touch on the topic of inheritance.

When one table extends another table, the child table inherits any fields on the parent table. All inherited fields are on the child table, and do not need to be dot-walked to, to be accessed. This has innumerable benefits, such as being able to search for a record on a base table, and discover records in all child-tables. Again, using the `task` table as an example, you might want to see all work assigned to you. The `task` table is generally where work records are stored (incident tickets, requests, problems, changes, and so on), so you can just run one filter on the `task` table to show records where **Assigned to** [`assigned_to`] is your user account, and you'll see any records in all of the child tables where that condition is true. This is possible, because the **Assigned to** field is actually on the base/parent task table.

 You can include extended (child) table fields in base (parent) table lists by enabling a system property: `glide.ui.list.allow_extended_fields` from the `sys_properties` list.

Whenever you create a new table, it's a good idea to ask yourself: Are there other tables that do something similar? Do I need to create/use more than a couple of fields that already exist on another table? Is there some functionality linked with a base system table (such as task) that would be useful for my new table?

If so, you should carefully consider the option of extending an existing table, rather than creating one from scratch.

You can see a visual representation of all of the existing tables in your instance, and their reference-relationships to one another, by navigating to **System Definition | Tables & Columns**, selecting a table to center on (such as **Task** [task], and clicking **Schema map**. In this view, you can visit a table's dictionary, focus the view on a given table by right-clicking it, or go to the table's list:

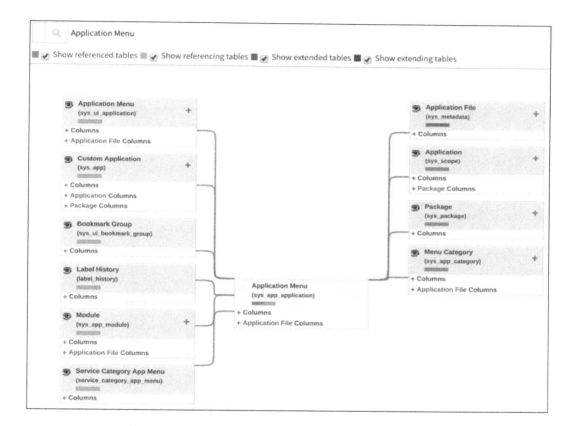

Summary

In this chapter, we learned a great deal about relationships, and database structures. We also walked through a demo of creating relationships of different sorts. This information will form a strong foundation as we go forward, and learn about the deeper structure of ServiceNow, the flat database structure of tasks, and more.

5
Tasks and Workflows

The **Task** [task] table is a special table in ServiceNow that holds records where work is done. It is a base system table, and can be extended by custom tables meant to hold task-like records. It is already the base table for various task types in ServiceNow, such as **Incident** [incident]. Like any base system table that's meant to be extended, the task table contains a number of fields that are useful for task records and the work that's done in them. For example, the need to **assign** a task is almost universal among tasks of all types, so the **Assigned to** [assigned_to] and **Assignment Group** [assignment_group] fields exists on the base task table.

 A **base table** is a table in ServiceNow that is extended by other tables, but which does not, itself, extend any other table. Recall that extending a table means inheriting its fields and some of its business logic.

The task table (or rather, tables that extend the task table) also includes task-specific functionality built-in, such as work notes and an activity log, workflow integration, SLAs, and so on!

In this chapter, we'll learn about the following:

- The **Task** [task] table and important fields on it
- Extending the task table
- How to add fields to the task table (and when not to!)
- Field dictionary overrides
- The task interceptor
- Journal fields and the activity formatter
- Approvals and workflows

- Assignment rules
- Inactivity monitors
- Visual task boards
- Major task-related pitfalls to avoid
- **SLAs** (**Service-Level Agreements**) and SLA timers

Important task fields

The task table, like any table, consists of table columns (fields) that can store data for each record. In particular, the `task` table has several fields which are supremely useful for nearly any record that could be used to track work in ServiceNow. Following are some of those fields, and a description of their purpose. These fields may or may not be shown on the form or the list of any task-extended table, but all of them exist on all tables that extend the **Task** [`task`] table (give or take some differences caused by **dictionary overrides**).

Active

Active is a Boolean field. This means that it stores a true/false value, and displays on the form as a check-box. This field is often controlled by a **business rule**. A business rule is a server-side script that runs in response to specific events on a record. In this case, an event which triggers off the **State** field is usually what determines whether the **Active** field should be set to `true` or `false`. The **Active** field is a good general indicator as to whether a given record is... well, active!

The **Active** field is also sometimes used to determine whether a user should have access to modify a ticket or not. For example, for reporting accuracy, many companies do not want Incident records modified after they've been closed. Instead, a service desk agent or user should submit a new incident record. For this reason, many companies create an **Access Control List** (**ACL**), or **Security Rule** on certain `task` tables to prevent modification by anyone except admins or managers once a task is deactivated (after it's closed).

Additional comments and work notes

The **Additional comments** and **Work notes** fields are the two **Journal** fields that are present by default on the **Task** [`task`] table (and thus, on all tables that extend the `task` table):

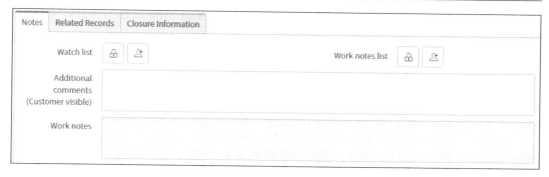

By default, the **Work notes** field can be updated only by users with the **ITIL** role, whereas the **Additional comments** field can be updated by **any** users (even those with no roles at all). This creates a separation between note types that are meant to communicate back and forth with the customer, versus notes meant to log work or serve as technical information that shouldn't necessarily be exposed to the user.

More on **Journal** fields in the next section.

Assigned to and Assignment group

The **Assigned to** [assigned_to] field is a **Reference** field type that points to the **Users** [sys_user] table. This field is generally used to designate a user to work on, or be responsible for the task. By default, this field has a **reference qualifier** set on its dictionary record that prevents any non-ITIL user from being assigned to a task (role=itil). You can override this reference qualifier on tables that extend task though, as the Project Task and Service Order tables do.

The **Assignment group** [assignment_group] field serves pretty much the same purpose as **Assigned to** [assigned_to]. The reason for having both, is that a workflow might automatically assign a certain type of task ticket to a group, but you would not want to hard-code a specific user to be responsible for such tasks (what if that user left the company?), so you'll generally assign a ticket to a group, and have a BA, manager, or the ITIL users themselves assign tickets to individual IT workers.

By default, the **Assigned to** field is also set as **Dependent on** the **Assignment group** field. The result of this, is that only users who are in the assignment group can be chosen in the **Assigned to** field.

Created, Created by, Updated, and Updated by

These fields are quite similar, but are used so frequently that we'd be remiss not to discuss them. The **Created, Created by, Updated,** and **Updated by** fields are also common to all tables in ServiceNow, for tracking purposes.

The **Created** [sys_created_on] field contains the date and time of the creation of this task record.

The **Created by** [sys_created_by] field tells you who created the record.

Updated [sys_updated_on] and **Updated by** [sys_updated_by] are the same as their corresponding **Created** fields, except that they are continually updated as the record is updated, to show when the most recent update was, and who made it. These fields can be exceptionally useful for reporting and determining who's working on what tickets, and whether any tickets are slipping through the cracks. For example, you could run a report on all open Incidents where the **Updated** field contains a date more than 30 days ago. These would represent Incidents that may have fallen through the cracks, and need someone to look into them.

Description and short description

As their names imply, **Short description** [short_description] is a field for a short description of the task (with a default character limit of 255), whereas the **Description** [description] field is for a more comprehensive explanation of the issue, often including specific instructions. As such, **Description** has a default character limit of 4,000 characters.

> The default size of a text field on a form is determined by its character limit. If a field allows the input of 256 characters or more, it is displayed as a larger, multiline input box, whereas 255 or fewer characters means it'll display as a single-line input box.

Number

The **Number** [number] field contains an identifier that is generally intended to be unique, and is the default display value for task records. As you may recall, the display value is the value that represents the record when referencing it from elsewhere in the system, such as a **Reference** field on another record. When creating a task type, you would generally select the number prefix (such as INC for Incident records).

State

The current status of a task record is indicated by the **State** [state] field (an integer field). This field may be driven by workflow, business rules, or may be manually selected by an ITIL user (usually the user in the **Assigned to** field).

Journals and the activity formatter

Journal fields technically don't store data in the table that the **Journal** field is on, but instead, create entries in the **Journal Entries** [sys_journal_field] table. These journal entries, along with other values corresponding to changes to audited fields from the **Sys Audits** [sys_audit], **History** [sys_history_line], and **Record History** [sys_history_set] tables, are displayed in the **Activity formatter**.

 Journal fields only work on audited tables. Adding such a field will modify a non-audited table's **System Dictionary** entry so that it becomes audited.

There are three types of **Journal** fields that you can add to your forms: journal_list, journal, and journal_input.

journal_list fields don't actually store data, but are used more like **formatters**. Formatters are a way of displaying data or other content (other than regular form fields) in ServiceNow forms. If you visit the dictionary record for a journal_list field (such as when you're creating it), you can navigate to the advanced view using the **Advanced view** UI action on the dictionary form. On the **Advanced view**, you'll see a **Dependent Field** form section with a **Use dependent field** check-box in it. Checking this box will reveal the **Dependent on field** field. Using this method to set the journal_list field dependent on a journal or journal_input field, will cause data entered into the selected field(s) to be shown in the journal_list field.

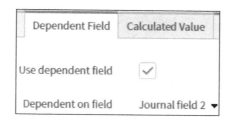

Examples of **Journal** fields include the **Work notes** and **Additional comments** fields. As you can see in the default Incident form, these fields are combined, and display the list of combined **Journal Input** fields beneath them. If you have one of these fields on your form, then all other **Journal** fields will be combined with them into one segment which you can expand to display the fields separately, or select from the select-box below the **Journal** field(s) to choose which field your input is directed into.

Just like `journal` fields, `journal_input` fields allow you to enter notes that can be displayed either in the **Activity formatter** (if that particular journal input field is tracked), or in a `journal_list` field. The difference is that if you have only `journal_input` fields on your form, the inputs will not be combined in a drop-down beneath the input boxes as with `Journal` fields:

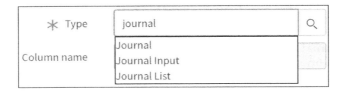

Unfortunately, the **Activity formatter** is a protected object in ServiceNow, and cannot be directly modified. However, you can customize which tables are audited, and which fields show up in the activity log when modified. To configure this, start by clicking the filter icon to the right of the **Activity formatter**, scroll to the bottom of the list, and click on **Configure available fields** as shown in the following screenshot:

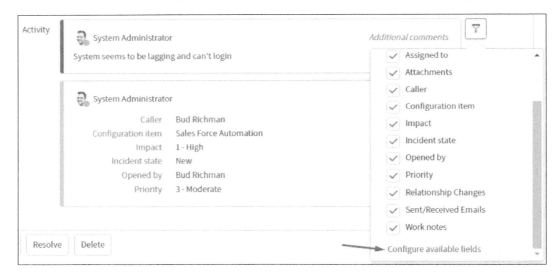

On the next page, simply double-click, or click to select a field and then click the right-arrow to move it over from the **Available** column, to the **Selected** column as shown in the following screenshot:

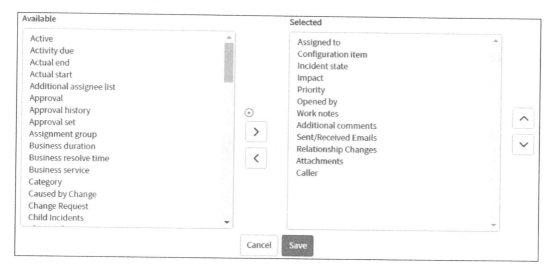

Once you make a change, you'll notice that not only future changes to the newly selected field(s) are present, but also any previous changes will show up in the activity log!

> If your table is **audited** (which you can determine from the table's record in the **System Dictionary**), changes are always being tracked in the background. This means that even if a field isn't selected to **display** in the activity log for an audited table (for example, the **Category** field on the **Incident** table), it is still tracked in the system's activity log, and any historical activity within that field will be displayed if it is configured to show in the activity log at a later time. You can also see these changes by right-clicking the form header, and going to **History > List**, or **History > Calendar**.

Extending the task table

The task table is an incredibly powerful base table, yet interestingly, no records should ever be created directly on the **Task** [task] table. Instead, task records are created on child tables; tables that extend the task table. In fact, if you attempt to create a new task directly from the task table, you'll find that you're redirected to the task **Interceptor** instead, which disambiguates which sort of task you'd like to create:

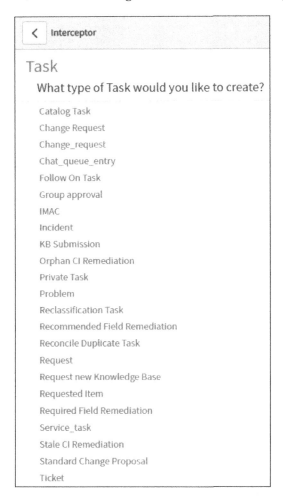

An **Interceptor** replaces a particular page (in this case, the new form page on the base **Task** [task] table) with another (in this case, a disambiguation page that links to various other task types).

To extend the **Task** table and inherit any relevant fields and business logic, start by navigating to **System Definition | Tables**. On the list of tables, click **New** from the top-left.

Since we've already created the Virtual War Rooms table (which extends the **Task** table), let's create a sub-table that also extends the **Task** table. We'll call it War Room Task, so enter that into the **Label** field of the **New** table form, then press *Tab*. The **Name** field will auto-populate with an appropriate name: u_war_room_task.

 Pressing *Tab* after entering War Room Task into the **Label** field of the new table record de-selects the **Label** field. Modifying a field and then navigating away from it (such as moving your cursor to a new field) is called a **change** event. Change events can trigger **onChange** client scripts. In this case, there is an onChange client script already running on this form, which auto-populates the table's **Name** field.

In the **Add module to menu** field, select the **Virtual War Room** application menu we created earlier, and then click the magnifying glass icon next to the **Extends table** field input box. Search for the text task, and make sure to select the correct **Task** [task] table as shown in the following screenshot:

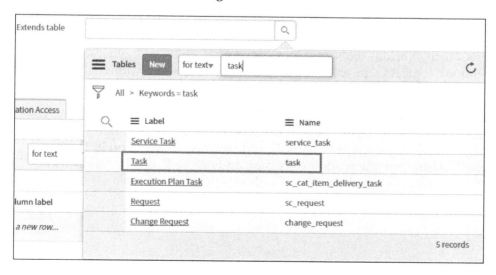

Right-click on the **New Table** form header, and click **Save**. This will display the table columns that were inherited from the system, and from the `task` table.

Next, head over to the **Controls** form section, and check the boxes for **Live feed** and **Auto-number**. This will allow users to see a live feed of the activity in the War Room Task table, and automatically generate the next war room task number for each new war room task.

Once you've checked the **Auto-number** checkbox, several new fields will show up. In the **Prefix** field, you might notice that WAR is populated there by default. This means that every war room task number will begin with WAR followed by 7 numbers. Since this is the same prefix we chose for our `Virtual War Room` records, let's choose something different. I went with WRT, but you could just as easily use four letters or even more.

Finally, replace the value from the **User role** field, with **ITIL**. This way, any ITIL user can access the war room tasks table. When you're finished, right-click the header, and click **Save** again. Congratulations, you've just created a table that extends the `task` table! This means that our new table will have fields like **Active** and **Assigned to**, as well as business logic, such as automatically deactivating after records in our table have been closed.

Tasks are not meant to sit and be stagnant; they are meant to progress through a lifecycle. That lifecycle may include assignment, approval, and manual work; or it may be *completely* automated!

Workflows

Workflows in ServiceNow are flowchart-driven automation tools with a drag-and-drop interface. Workflows can be used to automate multi-step processes using various tools, including approvals, child-task generation, notifications, logical loops and scripting, if/then control flow, timers, and they can even wait for and react to user activity.

Versions of each workflow are stored in the **Workflow Versions** [`wf_workflow_version`] table. When a task matches the criteria set up for a workflow, that workflow will execute against that task, and perform activities on it. This relationship between one workflow version and one task, is called a **context**. Contexts are stored in the **Workflow Context** [`wf_context`] table.

This setup is necessary because you might have *workflow version 1* as the published workflow version one day, and any tasks created on that day will be executed with that workflow. However, if you make changes to the workflow and re-publish it (thus creating a new version of the same workflow), you wouldn't want to start each existing task over from scratch; so the existing tasks would continue to execute with a given version of a workflow — whichever one was published when the task was created — and new tasks will execute with the now-newly-published workflow.

The graphical workflow editor (**Workflow | Workflow Editor** from the application navigator) gives you a visual representation of the contents and flow of a given workflow, in the form of a flowchart. Boxes in the workflow are referred to as (and correspond to) activities performed by the workflow. Lines drawn between the various activities correspond to the flow of the task, and are referred to as transitions:

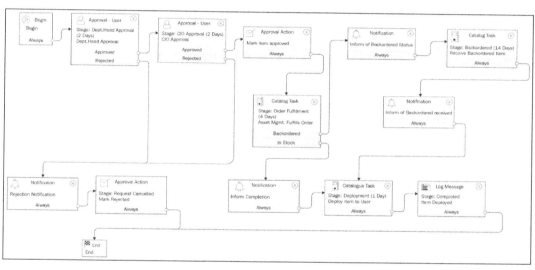

When one activity in a workflow is completed, the transition executes the next workflow activity in the flowchart. In most cases, this transition is serialized or linear; from one activity to the next. Perhaps looping back, but always executing one activity at a time:

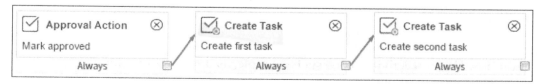

However, an activity can also have multiple lines drawn from a single exit condition, pointing to multiple activities. If this is the case, these activities will execute simultaneously:

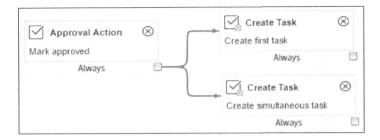

In a situation like this, it's possible to save a workflow where one of these branches doesn't have an exit condition (a transition to another activity), but it isn't recommended. Instead, ServiceNow provides a **Join** activity, which you can use to merge the divergent paths back into a single transition-flow:

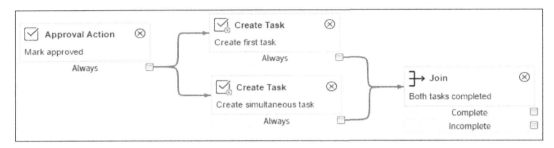

 Not too dissimilar from the **Join** activity, Workflows in ServiceNow also have a branch activity. However, using this activity is exactly the same as drawing multiple transition lines from a single exit condition on an activity!

As you may have noticed, each activity has a yellow exit condition at the bottom of the activity box. So far, the activities we've discussed have only had one exit condition called **Always**. Clicking on the small square to the right of this exit condition, and dragging a line to another activity, allows us to create a transition from the first activity, to the next. However, some activities can have multiple exit conditions. The Join activity is one such example, as it has two exit conditions: **Complete** and **Incomplete**.

If you draw a transition from two or more activities into the Join activity, the Join activity will wait for all of the activities that transition into it, to complete before transitioning to the next activity. However, in some cases, an alternative execution path might terminate on some activity that never redirects back to the **Join** activity. If this happens, then the **Join** activity's **Incomplete** exit condition will be what fires; otherwise, the **Complete** exit condition will fire. Thus, it is a good idea to draw a transition from the **Incomplete** exit condition in a **Join** activity, whenever it's possible for a preceding activity to follow a transition path that doesn't necessarily lead back to that **Join** activity; otherwise, it's possible for your workflow to become stuck!

Important workflow activities

Now that we have a basic understanding of how workflows work, let's go over some of the commonly used workflow activities, how they're used, and what they're used for. We won't go over every possible workflow activity, but to give you a good sense of how things work with workflows, we'll go over all of the most popular and useful ones.

User and group approval

Approval - Group and **Approval - User** are both workflow activities that generate approval requests, but in different ways:

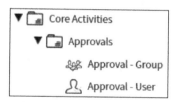

The **Approval - User** activity will create one or more approval requests for individual users. You can add both users and groups as approvers in this activity, but when adding a group, this activity will actually generate a separate approval request for each user in that group:

If you were to check the **Advanced** box, you could even use a script to generate additional users for approval, by setting a pre-defined variable (`answer`) to an array of Sys IDs corresponding to the list of users you'd like to request approval from (in addition to those specified in the **Users** and **Groups** fields.

In general, it's always best to either specify a group, or use a script to programmatically determine who the approvers should be, rather than hard-coding a list of users. Imagine if the user we've hard-coded as the approver for a certain type of request, leaves the company abruptly. Most companies have a development and approval cycle that takes days, if not weeks, to deploy a change to production, including workflow changes. However, certain things in ServiceNow are considered **data**, rather than configuration; data can generally be updated directly in production, whereas configuration (including workflows) generally cannot.

While workflows cannot usually be updated without a change request and approval, group membership and group ownership typically can; so if we can use a script to grab the owner of a certain group, then all we have to do is make sure that if one person leaves the company, any groups that they manage have someone else put in the management field instead, so that approvals continue to function.

User approvals, like group approvals, also allow you to set the conditions under which the approval request is considered **approved** (or **rejected**). You can set it to **Wait for**: anyone to approve, everyone to approve, the first response from any individual, or a condition based on a script. In a script, you could determine the total number of approvers, and then wait for more than 50% of them to approve or reject. Alternatively, you can set it so that if *anyone* rejects, then the entire approval request is rejected.

Finally, you can even set a **Due date**, so that users must reply within a specified time-frame.

The **Approval - Group** activity is highly similar to **Approval - User**, except that you can only specify groups (not individual users) to approve, and the **Wait for** conditions are more group-oriented: An approval from each group, an approval from any group, approval from everyone in all groups, and so on:

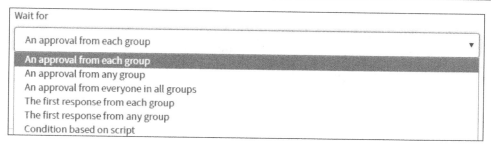

Approval coordinator

The **Approval Coordinator** workflow activity functions somewhat similar to a complex Boolean expression in programming, in that it allows you to generate an approval, the result of which is dependent upon the result of all of its preceding activities. Thus, you might have one Approval Coordinator activity that is fed by one **Approval - Group** activity, two **Approval - User** activities, and even a **Manual Approval** activity. You could then use the **Approval Coordinator** to make a determination as to the overall approval state of the record to which the workflow corresponds.

If

The **If** workflow activity does not so much perform an activity on its own, as it does control the flow of other activities in the workflow based on a condition:

A condition can be defined based on the condition builder (as seen in the preceding screenshot), or if we check the **Advanced** tick-box, we can write a script to determine if the **If** activity should return true or false. After clicking the **Advanced** tick-box, the **Script** field will be displayed. This field is auto-populated with a code-comment that provides a detailed explanation as to how to use it:

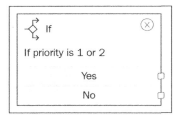

```
// This script needs to set answer to 'yes' or 'no' to indicate the state of the activity.
//
// For example,
//
// answer = ifScript();
//
// function ifScript() {
//     if (condition is true) {
//         return 'yes';
//     }
//     return 'no';
// }
```

`answer` is a pre-defined variable in the context of this advanced condition script. This variable is a string, not a Boolean; it should be set to the string `yes` or `no`.

After the script runs, whatever the answer variable is set to will determine whether the `yes` or `no` exit conditions are activated:

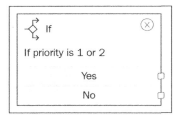

You could use this script field, for example, to look up related or child records, and divert the workflow along another path depending on whether any related records were, for example, cancelled, like so:

```
answer = 'no';
var gr = new GlideRecord('table_name');
gr.addQuery('state', '7');
gr.addQuery('parent', current.getValue('sys_id'));
gr.setLimit(1);
```

```
gr.query();
if (gr.hasNext()) {
    answer = 'yes';
}
```

 Don't worry if the preceding code doesn't make much sense to you just yet, we're going to learn all about the GlideRecord class and the Glide API later in this book.

Switch

An **If** condition activity is perfect in the event that there are only two exit states: true and false, or yes and no. If you want your workflow to follow a separate path based on a particular field's value, such as the impact of a given ticket, you might find it more advantageous or convenient to use a **Switch**. A **Switch** pivots off a field's potential values, and works especially well with drop-down fields that have a fixed number of potential values:

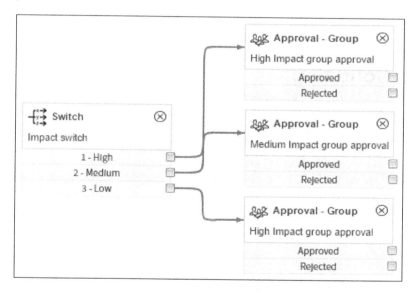

While you *can* have each exit condition transition to a different activity, it's perfectly alright to have two or more **Switch** exit conditions transition to just one activity:

When the **transitions** (the lines between the activities) intersect, it can sometimes be difficult to see where each line ends up. To see the full path one line takes, just click to select and highlight it!

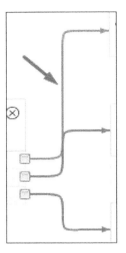

Wait for Condition

The **Wait for Condition** workflow activity allows you to specify either a simple condition (using the condition builder), or a script. Unlike a normal JavaScript function (but similar to many script fields in ServiceNow), the aim of this script is not to **return** anything, but to set a pre-defined variable (called `answer`) to either `true` or `false`. You can do just about anything you can do in any server-side script, but whatever that variable is set to after the script finishes running, will be the result:

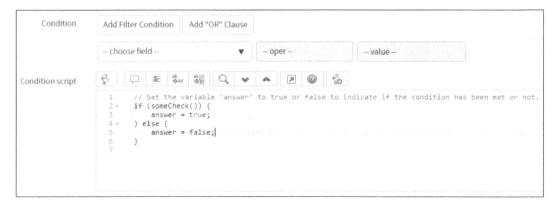

One thing to keep in mind about the **Wait for Condition** workflow activity, is that it is only (re)evaluated when the record that the workflow is associated with, is updated. Any update will trigger the re-evaluation of this condition, but updating another record will not. To help us understand this, let's imagine the following scenario:

Imagine that you've got a workflow associated to an Incident ticket, and that workflow runs a script which generates another outside record in a custom table. Next, the workflow transitions to the **Wait for Condition** activity. The **Wait for Condition** activity in this scenario, is configured to wait until that outside record is *closed*, which it determines with a script. However, the Incident workflow won't have any idea that you've updated the outside record once it is closed, so you'll need to give the incident a little *nudge* to get it to re-run the evaluation script, by updating the Incident.

One effective way of solving this problem, is to associate these two tasks together, and then use a business rule to update the parent record. For example, when generating the record in the custom `task` table, you can populate the **Parent** [parent] field with a reference to the record that the workflow is running on. You can then use a business rule on that custom table, that runs when it's closed, and updates the parent record by adding a work note. That will effectively nudge the record, and the workflow will re-evaluate the condition.

> As with most records that have both a **Condition** builder field, and a **Condition script** field, those fields in the **Wait for Condition** activity must *both* evaluate to true, if used.

Create Task and Catalog Task

These two workflow activities (**Create Task**, and **Catalog Task**) are very similar; the primary difference being that the **Catalog Task** activity specifically creates a record in the **Catalog Task** [sc_task] table, whereas the **Create Task** activity can generate a record in any task-derived table.

One important thing to remember about the **CreateTask / Catalog Task** activities, is that if the **Wait for completion** tick-box is checked, then the workflow will halt on that activity until the task is placed into a completed state:

If you want to set a pre-defined field or fields (such as fulfillment group, assigned to, short description, and/or others), set the **Task values from** field to **Fields**.

Setting the **Task values from** field to **Values** instead, allows you to set each field value to whatever you like, more granularly. In either case, you can check the **Advanced** tick-box, and use the script field to set any field value on the generated task record.

Since the script executes **after** the values are set from the static fields above it on the **Workflow Activity** form, any values set via the script take priority:

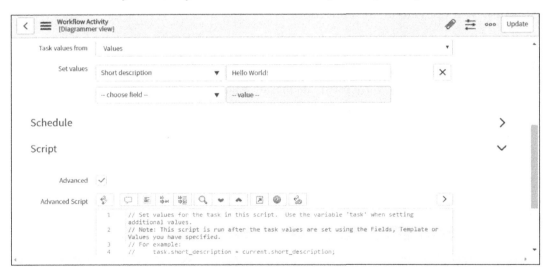

Branch and Join

As we learned at the beginning of this section, the **Branch** workflow activity behaves exactly the same as if you were to draw multiple transition lines from a single exit condition, whereas the **Join** workflow activity allows you to merge multiple transitions back into a single path, including the ability to wait for each input path to terminate or transition into the Join activity before moving forward.

Return value

Workflows, like functions, can call one another. It's possible to create re-usable workflows for commonly used processes, such as change approval, and then call them from the current workflow by simply locating one in the **Workflows** tab of the workflow editor, and dragging it into the main **Workflow** window:

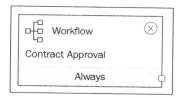

In one of these workflows, you can use the **Return value** workflow activity to return a value back to the parent workflow, just as you might when using the `return` statement inside of a function in JavaScript. In the **Workflow** subflow activity on the parent workflow, the **Map return value to** field allows you to specify the variable name to use to store the returned value. You can access this variable from the scratchpad by using `workflow.scratchpad.variableName`. In the following example, activities following the **Workflow** activity could access the returned value via the variable `workflow.scratchpad.returnedApproval`.

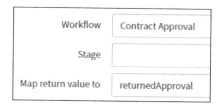

Run Script

The **Run Script** workflow activity is fairly straightforward, in that it pretty much just provides you with a script input box. This script, like all workflow scripts, has access to the workflow scratchpad, runs server-side, and can reference the record that the workflow is running against using the `current` object in the script.

The **Run Script** workflow activity is not the only way to execute a script inside a workflow. Many activity types support scripting in one form or another. All scripts that execute in the workflow context have access to several special objects including one called `workflow.scratchpad`, which can store data to be passed from one workflow activity to another.

Set Values

Much like the **Run Script** workflow activity, **Set Values** simply allows you to set one or more fields on the record against which the workflow is running, to specific values. This is often used to set the **State** field, modify the **Actual start** / **Actual end** dates, and so on:

Note that, as with most **Set Value** fields, you can dot-walk in this workflow activity to set values on related records! For example, you could set the `parent.state` field, if the record your workflow is running against is expected to have a parent, and you'd like to change the parent record's state based on something happening in the workflow. For more complex logic though, you can always use a **Run Script** workflow activity.

Pausing workflows

Starting with the **Kingston** release of ServiceNow's "Now platform", you can pause workflows in-place. This is useful for situations such as when a service that a workflow depends on goes down, in order to prevent the workflows from throwing errors. To pause a workflow, start by navigating to **Workflow | Operations | Group Pause Requests** from the application navigator, and then clicking on **New** at the top of the corresponding list.

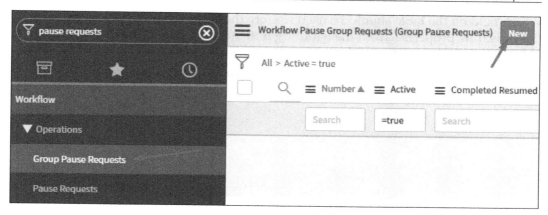

On the new record form, use the **Filter** field to narrow it down to just the workflows you want to pause like so:

This will prevent workflows of the type specified from running until they are un-paused once you're ready for them to continue.

Workflow Stages

Workflow Stages can give users a general sense of the state and progress of a given ticket, in a visual and easy to understand way.

If you've been following along, you may have noticed that each activity we've looked at, has a **Stage** field on it. This allows you to specify what stage the workflow should be at during this activity. For example, while waiting for a **Fulfillment** task to complete, you might set the **Stage** field to **Fulfilment**.

Which field on the table should be used to store the **Stage** value, can be specified in the workflow properties from the hamburger menu. Also in the hamburger menu, you can see and edit the workflow stages built into the workflow:

Demo

The simplest possible workflow in ServiceNow, would be a straight line from **Begin** to **End**:

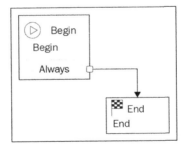

However, this workflow doesn't to very much for us. Instead, let's create a new workflow for our **Virtual War Rooms**, to drive the generation of some war room tasks. To get started, open the **Workflow Editor** from **Workflow | Workflow Editor** in the application navigator.

The **Workflow Editor** should open in a new tab or window. When it does, click on the plus icon at the top-right, under the **Workflows** tab, so we can create a new workflow for our Virtual War Room tickets:

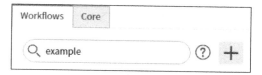

On the **New Workflow** form, set the **Name** to War Room, the **Table** to **Virtual War Room** [u_virtual_war_room], and fill out a description of your choice:

Leave the **Conditions** section blank, and click **Submit**. You'll be presented with the simplest possible workflow to start with, and it'll automatically be **checked out** by you.

Workflows exist in the **Workflow Versions** [wf_workflow_version] table. When checked out, the **Published** [published] field in this table for the specific version you're working on, is set to false. The same is true for older versions of the workflow. Each time you check a workflow out and check it back in (also known as **publishing** it), a new record in the **Workflow Versions** table is created:

If you publish a new version of the workflow while an existing published version exists, then the existing record has its **Published** field set to false, and the newly published record has its **Published** field set to true. Since we've only just created this workflow, there will only be one workflow version called War Room, and since we have not yet published it, the **Published** [published] field will be set to false:

In our imaginary company, Major Incidents are incidents with a high impact and priority. These incidents result in a `Virtual War Room` being created to validate the issue being raised, coordinate troubleshooting and resolution, and get the Incident resolved as soon as possible. Once resolved, the major incident process will hand-off to the **Problem Management** process which, per ITIL methodologies, will be tasked with identifying a root cause for the major incident, and preventing future occurrences by creating new knowledge articles, performing a change request, or otherwise taking steps to prevent this major issue in the future.

Since we're building **Virtual War Rooms** to be a *response* to major incidents, let's make it so `Virtual War Room` tickets follow this process in our workflow:

1. A validation task is created first, in which the service desk agent must ensure that the incident is indeed a major incident, and was not miscategorized. The workflow stage will be **Validation** for this task.

2. After the validation task, a diagnostic war room task is created, and assigned to the **Major Incident Response Team** group, and the workflow stage is set to **Diagnose**.

   ○ You can create this group from the **Groups** [`sys_user_group`] table by just specifying the name and leaving all other fields blank.

3. Once the diagnostic task is completed, a **Perform Fix** task will be generated. During this task, the stage will be **Fix**. Once completed, the stage will be set to **Complete** before transitioning to the **End** activity.

In order for this process to work, we'll obviously need to create some task records. It's important to understand that tasks should never be created directly in the base **Task** [`task`] table; so let's create a new table. Since we've done this once before, here are the bullet-points:

1. In the application navigator, navigate to **System Definition | Tables**, and click on the blue **New** button at the top-left.

2. On the **New record** form, enter **War Room Task** for the label, and press *Tab*. Once you've done that, the **Name** field should auto-populate.

3. In the **Extends table** field, enter **Task**, and select **Task** [`task`].

4. Leave **Create module** and **Create mobile module** checked. Set the **Add module** to menu option, to `Virtual War Room`.

5. Move to the **Controls** form tab/section. Check the **Live feed** checkbox and the **Auto-number** checkbox, then enter **WRT**.

6. Finally, right-click in the header and click **Save**.

Now that we have a table we can create `War Room Tasks` in, we can begin building our workflow. First, let's set up the stages for our workflow. Click on the hamburger menu at the top-left of the workflow editor, and click **Edit Stages**. Click **New**, and give the new stage a name of validation, and a value of validation. Click **Submit**. Repeat this process to create **Diagnose** [`diagnose`], **Fix** [`fix`], and **Complete** [`complete`] stages.

Next, click on the **Core** tab on the right side of the **Workflow Editor**, and navigating to **Tasks | Create Task**. Make sure you don't have any other activity selected in the workflow, and double-click **Create Task**. In the corresponding form, set **Name** to `Validation Task`, and set the **Stage** field to `Validation`.

Next, under the **Basics** section, set the **Task type** to **War Room Task** [`u_war_room_task`], and make sure that the **Wait for completion** tick-box is checked.

Scroll down to the **Populate task variables** form section, set the **Task values from** field to `Values`, and use the **Set values** section to set **Short description** to `Validate Major Incident Priority and Impact`:

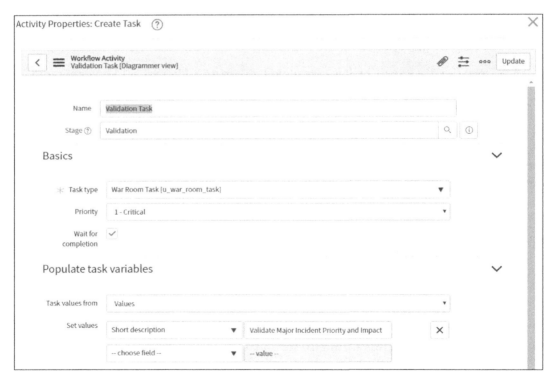

Once that's all filled out, click **Submit** and a new workflow activity will be created at the top-left. Drag it into the middle of the workflow designer, then delete the transition line connecting **Begin** and **End** by clicking on it, and pressing the *Delete* button on your keyboard. Next, drag a line from the exit condition **Always** on the **Begin** activity, to the **Create Task** activity we just created:

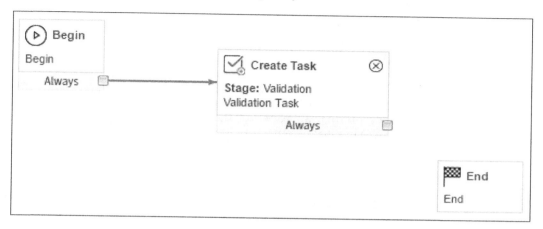

 To insert a new workflow activity in-between two others that are connected by a transition line, it is possible but not necessary to delete and re-draw the transition. Instead, you can simply drag the new activity on top of the transition line so that it turns blue, and release!

Now repeat that process to create two more **Create Task** activities:

1. **Name**: Diagnose Task
   - **Stage**: Diagnose
   - **Task type**: **War Room Task** [u_war_room_task]
   - **Wait for completion**: true
   - **Task values from**: values
   - **Set values**: Short description—diagnose the issue, and identify a possible solution

2. **Name**: Fix Task

- ° **Stage**: Fix
- ° **Task type**: **War Room Task** [u_war_room_task]
- ° **Wait for completion**: true
- ° **Task values from**: values
- ° **Set Values**: Short description—fix the issue to resolve the major incident.

 If you have a workflow activity selected while creating a new workflow activity, the new one may appear inside the selected one, as part of it. To avoid this, make sure that no other activities are selected when creating a new workflow task.

Next, create one more activity by double-clicking **Set Values** under the Utilities folder in the Core tab on the right of the Workflow Editor. Set the **Name** field to Close War Room, the **Stage** field to **Complete**, and in the **Values** section, set **State** to **Closed Complete**. Remember that this **State** field is on the Virtual War Room against which the workflow is running, not on the war room task!

Finally, complete the transition lines so that the workflow progresses from one activity to the next, in the order we defined on the previous page. It should look something like shown in the following screenshot:

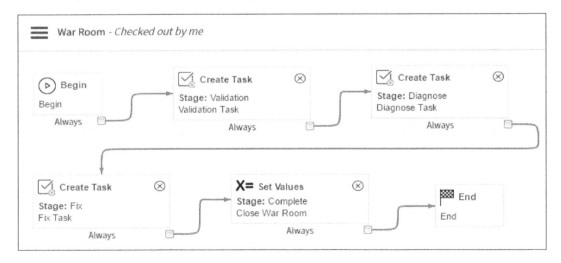

Now, simply publish your new workflow from the hamburger menu on the **Workflow Editor**, and you've got yourself a functioning workflow!

Note that, new in the Kingston release of ServiceNow's Now platform, active workflows can now be paused and resumed as needed! This is great for situations where, for example, a server or service that a workflow relies upon is down. Simply pause all contexts of that particular workflow, and resume them when the service is restored. You'll need to activate the **Workflow Pause Utility** plugin (`com.glideapp.workflow.pause`) to enable this functionality in Kingston or later versions of the Now platform.

SLAs

SLAs (Service Level Agreements) are a feature in ServiceNow that allows you to set and track a set of expectations surrounding the delivery of a given service. For example, if the user submits a given Service Request or an Incident, the SLA engine in ServiceNow can fire based on a set of conditions, and alert the assignee, their manager, or any specified user or group.

SLA Definitions can be found under **Service Level Management | SLA | SLA Definitions**:

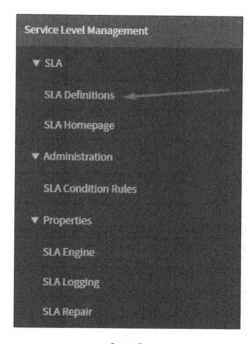

Let's start by creating an SLA for our **Virtual War Rooms**, so we can ensure that they're addressed as quickly as possible.

1. Start by navigating to the **SLA Definitions** module of the application navigator as defined above.

2. At the top of the list of **SLA Definitions**, click on **New**.

3. For the **Name** field, enter Virtual War Room Work Start.

4. Make sure that the **Type** field, if it is on your SLA Definition form, is set to **SLA**.

5. Set the **Table** field to **Virtual War Room** [u_virtual_war_room] so that the SLA will only trigger on records in our **Virtual War Rooms** table.

Pro Tip

If you have a record that operates on a particular table which is **extended** by others, it will operate on all tables that extend it as well. Be aware of this fact, when creating records like SLAs and Business Rules on tables that extend, or may be extended by, other tables.

6. The workflow that's selected by default, will be **Default SLA workflow**. This is fine for now. However, you can modify SLA workflows just like any other workflow!

7. Check the **Enable logging** toggle.

8. Set **Duration** to 3 hours, and set **Schedule** to **8-5 weekdays excluding holidays**.

9. On the **Start condition** tab, you can set **Start condition** to **State is Open**, and set **Cancel condition** to **State** is **Closed Skipped**.

10. On the **Stop condition** tab, set **Stop condition** to **State is Work in Progress**.

11. Right-click on the header, then click **Save**.

Now, if you create a new **Virtual War Room** record, the default state (Open) will trigger the SLA to fire. The SLA workflow will run, and fire off notifications or other events according to how you've configured it. By default, it just sends out a few notifications after 50%, 75%, and 100% of the duration has elapsed.

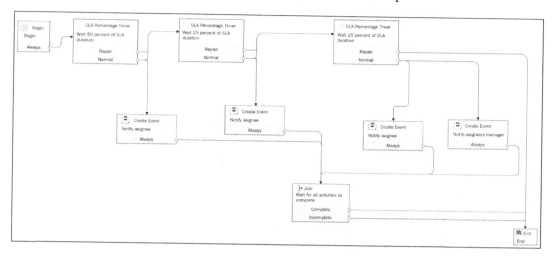

Approvals

To automate all business services would be the dream of nearly any IT Director. With ServiceNow, an astonishing degree of automation is possible, but some things must still be left to human hands. One example of a primarily human-driven process, is approval. Sure, we can set up automated approvals for a number of different circumstances. For example, orders of new hardware with a cost under a certain amount, by a manager can potentially be auto-approved. However, if an individual contributor is submitting a change request to alter a firewall rule for example, that would likely need some review.

Approvals can be requested of individual users, or of entire groups. Approvals requested of individual users, are stored within the **Approvals** [sysapproval_approver] table, whereas group approvals are stored in the **Group Approvals** [sysapproval_group] table. Approvals can be generated via approval engines, or workflows; the more common of the two being workflows. We went over these approval options in some detail in the *Workflows* section of this chapter.

Assignment

Probably the most common means of moving a task forward, is assignment. Assigning a task is the way to designate a user or group of users, as those responsible for the fulfillment of a given task.

The base **Task** [task] table (and therefore, all tables which extend it) contain two assignment fields: **Assigned to** [assigned_to], and **Assignment Group** [assignment_group]. If you've enabled Visual Task Boards, then you'll also have the **Additional assignee list** [additional_assignee_list] field.

Assignment drives a lot of default notifications, such as alerting the assignee when work notes are added by another service desk agent, or when the customer leaves comments. It's usually a very important part of the task-handling process.

Creating Task fields

One thing that's important to understand about tasks in ServiceNow, is that all task records (whether they're changes, problems, incidents, requests, request items, catalog tasks, or tasks in any other table that extends the base system **Task** [task] table) are *technically* all stored in a single database table. Although in ServiceNow, you see them as separate tables, that isn't actually the case. This is due to the *flattening* of the task table.

Each task-extending table has a field called **Task type** [sys_class_name], which defines what type of task it is (problem, change, incident, and so on.) by containing the **name** (not label) of the table that it's in (incident, problem, change_request, sc_req_item, and so on.). ServiceNow groups records with the same Task type, and treats them as though they're all in separate tables, but in the physical database on ServiceNow's servers, they're technically all in one big table. This is one of the reasons that tables that extend other tables, all share so much in the way of business logic and database fields.

This fact has far-reaching impacts on the way that the task table should be handled, some less obvious than others. For example, say you want to create a new field on the Incident form: **Assigned developer** [u_assigned_developer]. It's absolutely fine to put this field on the **Incident** table, and the **Dictionary** [sys_dictionary] will keep track of things for you; things such as where this field actually resides within the task table structure. However, what if you want to add the Assigned developer field to the **Change** table too, in case you have a change that requires a development effort? And while you're at it, perhaps you'd like to add it to the **Problem** and **Requested Item** tables.

Well, in that case, it may make more sense to add the field to the base **Task** [task] table. This way, you don't need to have multiple copies of what is essentially the exact same field in the same database table (even though you wouldn't see it as being in the same table, since ServiceNow displays each task-extending table as a separate one!). Just remember that fields are shared **down** the hierarchical chain, but not **across** it.

Here are some things to consider when it comes to the task table:

- Try not to create new fields from the **Form Designer**. Instead, navigate to the **Table record** for the table you'd like to create a field on, and create the field from the embedded related list of fields. This is because creating fields in the **Form Designer** often creates them on the base task table when you don't intend to, and doesn't give you much control over the name, type, default value, and so on.

- Think very carefully before creating new fields on either the base task table, or any table that extends it. Think both about whether that field is necessary (could an existing, possibly unused field work?), and if so, about where it should be created (on the base table, or the extended table?).

- When creating a new table where *work* might be done or tracked, carefully consider extending the task table. If you need features like workflow, an activity log and work notes, or assignment, you might be better off creating a table that extends task, rather than standing on its own. If you only need one or two fields from the **Task** table, it's probably best to start a whole new table.

- Be extremely judicious about modifying the base task table. Any time you can avoid it, it's almost always best to create a **Dictionary Override** on the extended table, rather than modifying an existing base task table field.

Summary

In this chapter, we learned about the task table, extending the task table, and workflows. We created a new task-extending table called War Room Task, and we learned how to generate and interact with records and sub-tasks. We also learned how to control and branch the flow of a workflow, as well as how to use various other workflow activity types and even SLAs with their SLA workflows.

6
UI and Data Policies

UI policies and data policies can help to prevent users from accidentally (or intentionally!) making certain changes in our database, given a set of conditions. UI policies operate client-side, while data policies run server-side. They can also be set to enforce restrictions on the client just like UI Policies, meaning that they may disable or make mandatory certain UI elements in the user's browser, or they may enforce those rules on the server.

In this chapter, we'll learn about:

- UI policies
- Catalog UI policies
- Scripting in UI policies
- "Reverse if false" functionality
- UI policy actions
- UI policy order
- Data policies
- Data policies versus ACLs
- Converting a data policy to a UI policy

UI policies

UI policies are a user-friendly way to control whether fields on a form are mandatory, read-only, or even whether they're visible. The UI policy record itself, which resides in the **UI Policy** [sys_ui_policy] table, consists of a set of conditions, a short description, a relationship to another record or set of records, and a few other odds and ends. It does not however, contain information on the **action** to be performed:

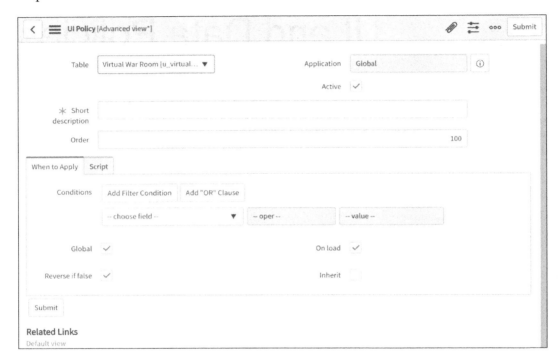

UI policy actions are stored separately, in the **UI Policy Action** [sys_ui_policy_action] table. They are related to the UI policy through a **reference** field, which—as we discussed in a previous chapter—means that they can (and by default, do) show up in a related list at the bottom of the **UI Policy** form:

These **UI Policy Actions** consist of a reference to the field to which the action applies, and drop-downs indicating whether the field should be **Visible**, **Mandatory**, or **Read only**. Each field has three options: **True**, **False**, and **Leave Alone**. As you might imagine, creating a UI policy action where the **Read only** drop-down is set to **True**, will make the field to which it applies, read only. Setting it to **False** will cause the field to *not* be read-only. The same goes for the **Mandatory** and **Visible** drop-down fields.

The **Order** field on the UI Policy table determines which UI Policy takes precedent (the last one to run effectively has the highest priority, and a blank priority field is treated as zero).

UI policy actions will only apply on the table to which the parent UI policy applies. Further, unless the **Global** tick-box is checked on the parent UI Policy (which it is, by default), all UI policy actions will only apply to the view specified on the parent UI policy's **View** field:

In order for a UI policy action to apply to a given field (or in the case of catalog UI policy actions, a given variable), it must appear on the form in question. The same is true if the field is used as part of a condition. Even if the field is not visible, it must be included on the form in order to be evaluated as part of a policy condition, or set as part of a policy action.

Catalog UI policies

Catalog UI policies are very similar to regular UI policies, except for a few key differences: catalog UI policies are stored within the **Catalog UI Policy** [catalog_ui_policy] table, as opposed to the **UI Policy** [sys_ui_policy] table. Also, rather than choosing a table on which to apply the policy actions, catalog UI policies are configured to run on either variables within a given variable set (which may be found in multiple catalog items), or variables on a specific catalog item's variables:

A catalog UI policy can only reference variables that are associated with the catalog item or variable set to which it applies. Just like UI policies, catalog UI policies can only evaluate conditions and perform actions based on variable fields which exist on the form (even if the field is hidden at all times, so long as they're included on the form in question).

As you might have guessed, catalog UI policy actions are also stored in a different table from **UI Policy Actions**: The **Catalog UI Policy Action** [catalog_ui_policy_action] table—but they otherwise behave nearly identically to other UI policies.

Reverse if false

The **Reverse if false** tick-box (which is only available on the **Advanced view** of the **UI Policy** and **Catalog UI Policy** forms), allows us to specify whether the **UI Policy Actions** (or **Catalog UI Policy Actions**) associated with our Catalog UI Policy, have their actions reversed whenever the condition associated with their parent policy does not evaluate to true.

For example, imagine we have a condition [Assigned to] [is empty] on a UI policy. When met, a UI policy action is triggered, which sets the **Assignment group** field to **Mandatory**. This way, if we don't have an assigned user, at least we can be sure we have an assigned group.

In this scenario, if we have **Reverse if false** enabled, then as soon as the assignment group field contains a value (thus making it so the condition would return false), then not only is the UI policy action which made **Assignment group** read-only no longer applicable, but instead, an action with the opposite effect is fired, actively setting the **Assignment group** field to non-mandatory. This applies even if the field is made mandatory by another means, so this is another scenario where **Order** comes into play. More on order and how to create robust policies that do not conflict, later in this chapter.

As you can imagine, **Reverse if false** can be an extremely powerful and useful tool, but it can also be the source of a great deal of confusion, if its behavior is not well understood in the context of **all** of the UI policies, client scripts, and data policies that might run on a given record or form.

It is not necessary, and not recommended, to set a field to Read-Only = False if that field is not normally read-only. Only if you need to alter some behavior, should the field's properties be set by a UI policy; otherwise, the **Leave Alone** option should be selected. **Leave Alone** does not result in any action, which means that there's nothing to reverse in the event that the condition on the UI policy is not met.

There are a few circumstances where **Reverse if false** should not be used, but the vast majority of UI and catalog UI policies will have this option enabled. It is usually only used when you have one UI policy controlling the behavior of a given field or set of fields under one condition, and an entirely separate UI policy which may conflict with the first, controlling their behavior under the exact opposite condition. In a situation like this, it's important to be careful not to modify one of the policies without modifying the other to match, or you could end up with aberrant behavior. Luckily, if this does happen, we have the ability to **debug UI policies**, which we'll learn more about in a later chapter.

If the condition on a UI policy returns false, then one of two things might happen:

- If the **Reverse if false** tick-box is selected, then the opposite of the UI policy actions are enforced. For example, if a UI policy action sets the **Short description** field to visible when the conditions are matched, then having **Reverse if false** enabled would make it so that the **Short description** field is hidden when the condition is not matched.

- If **Reverse if false** is not selected, then the UI policy simply does nothing.

  - This does not mean that the UI policy actions are undone. Say for example, that you have a UI policy which causes the **Work Notes** field to become mandatory when the **State** field is set to **Closed**, but the **Reverse if false** tick-box is unchecked. In this case, if the user set the **State** field to **Closed**, then **Work Notes** will become mandatory. However, if the user then changes their mind and sets the **State** field to another state such as **Work in progress**, then the **Work Notes** field will **remain mandatory**.

Scripting in UI policies

UI policy conditions are evaluated both on-load (if the **On load** tick-box is selected on the **Advanced view**) and whenever an update is made to any field on a form in ServiceNow. When an update is made, the condition on the UI policy is re-evaluated. If the condition returns true, then the UI policy actions run. If the conditions return false (and **Reverse if false** is enabled) then the opposite of the UI policy actions run. For example, if the UI policy turns a field **mandatory** under a certain condition, then when that condition is not met, it will typically explicitly set the field to **non-mandatory**.

Understanding that these events all happen within the browser (AKA the client) tells us that UI policies are therefore obviously evaluated client-side, which means that the client-side ServiceNow API is available. In the **Advanced view** of the UI policy form, there is a **Script** section. In this section, if the **Run scripts** tick-box is selected, two script input fields will be displayed: **Execute if true**, and **Execute if false**. Each script has a pre-defined default value, which acts as the scaffolding for the script:

```
function onCondition() {

}
```

As mentioned in the previous section, any code you write inside of that function will be executed client-side, and thus will have access to the same APIs as any client script. Using these script fields, you can define functionality to trigger when the non-scripted condition is either true or false (depending on which script field you enter it into), as well as additional logic for checking more complex conditions that you weren't able to check using the simple condition builder. One good example of when you might use this functionality, is if you need to check a value on the server in addition to certain client-side conditions in the condition builder, in order to determine whether a field should be made **Read only/Mandatory/Visible**.

We'll learn all about client scripts and the client-side APIs that we can access in a later chapter on client scripting.

UI Policy Order

The **Order** field on **UI Policies** (just like on other scripts) is very important, as it determines how UI policy actions are processed and prioritized. When two UI policies contain a UI policy action that acts upon the same field—even if they act upon different properties of that field (visible versus read-only, for example)—they can potentially conflict. Conflicting UI policy actions will be shown in the related list on the UI policy, with a red dot indicating the issue:

🔍	≡ Field name	≡ Mandatory	≡ Visible	≡ Read only
ⓘ	● assigned_to	True	Leave alone	Leave alone

If you open the UI policy action, you'll be presented with an error message indicating that the run order of the UI policy actions is unpredictable:

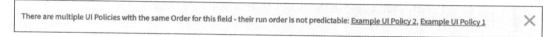

There are multiple UI Policies with the same Order for this field - their run order is not predictable: <u>Example UI Policy 2</u>, <u>Example UI Policy 1</u>   ✕

This warning will only occur when the **Order** field on the parent UI policy is set the same on both. UI policies execute in the other indicated by the **Order** field, starting with one. The higher the value, the later it executes. This also means that a higher value in the **Order** field means the policy will take priority over others with a lower order value. It won't necessarily undo any actions performed by lower-order policies, but it will overwrite them.

The default value of the **Order** field is 100. As with most numerical fields, it is generally a good idea to put some *space* in when you use a different order value for another record. For example, if we wanted to add in another UI policy that would take priority over this one, we might choose an **Order** value of 200 or so. That way, if we later decided that we wanted one or more other Policies to slot in between them in terms of the order, we could use values like 125, 150, and 175, with plenty of room in-between.

Another example of when leaving room is a good idea, is the **State** field on **Task** records. Since **State** is technically an integer field (each label, such as **New**, **Work in Progress**, **Closed Complete**, and so on, corresponds to an integer value), it's a good idea to put some space between the previous and next numbers whenever you create a new **State** option. It's always best to think ahead in situations like this, as *future you* will appreciate it.

Demo

Let's explore UI policies in a less abstract fashion: by creating one! Let's create a UI policy so that if and when the **Major Incident** field in our **Virtual War Room** records is populated, it'll be read-only. This way, a user can't create a Virtual War Room for one incident, and then switch it to another.

- To start off, navigate to the **Virtual War Room** table by typing `u_virtual_war_room.list` into the application navigator filter bar, and pressing *Enter*.

 On more recent versions of the Now Platform, you can also use the `.config` shortcut instead of `.list`, and just click on the **UI Policies** tab to get to the list of UI policies on that table.

- On the list view of the **Virtual War Room** table, click on the hamburger menu at the top-left, then click **Configure**, then **UI Policies**. On the **UI Policies** list, click **New** to create a new UI policy on the **Virtual War Rooms** table. The **Table** field will be auto-populated with our **Virtual War Room** [u_virtual_war_room].

Note that these instructions are for List V3. If you have List V2, you'll be able to access UI policies by right-clicking on the list header, and mousing over **Configure**, then clicking **UI Policies**.

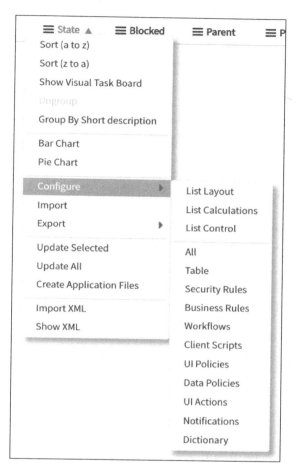

- Set the **Short description** field to something descriptive, like `Make incident field read-only when populated`.

- Add one condition to the **Conditions** field: `[Major incident] [is not empty]`. Then, right-click in the form header, and click **Save** to save the record to the database and display the **UI Policy Actions** related list.

- At the top of the **UI Policy Actions** related list, click on **New**. On the corresponding form, set the **Field name** field to `Major incident`.

- Set the **Read only** field to **True**, but leave the **Mandatory** and **Visible** fields set to **Leave alone**. Finally, click on **Submit**.

Now if you visit or create a Virtual War Room ticket with the **Major incident** field filled out, that field will be read-only; however, if you create a new Virtual War Room ticket from the list view without the **Major incident** field populated, you'll notice that the field is editable, because it doesn't yet meet the criteria specified in our **UI Policy**!

Data policies

Data policies, unlike UI policies, execute on the server. They are closely linked to UI policies in terms of behavior and functionality. They can even be used as UI policies on the client, when implemented (however, with limited functionality). Strangely, data policies reside in the `sys_data_policy2` table. That 2 is not a typo; it has been that way at least as far back as Eureka.

Data policies allow you to prevent certain changes on the server, by rejecting database updates that don't fit the criteria laid out in the data policy. You can either prevent edits by making a field read only, or you can require a field value by making a field **Mandatory**, using a data policy rule.

While data policies can be used as UI policies on the form, they lack some functionality provided by UI policies. You cannot, for example, make a field visible or hidden using data policies, because there is no server-side equivalent of a contextually hidden field. There is also no advanced view, no scripted conditions, and no UI or server-side scripting possible through a data policy (except to the extent that scripting is possible inside of any condition builder to make a determination about whether the data policy should run).

Data policies do however, have **Reverse if false** functionality. This applies to both the server-side actions, and the effective UI policy on the form, if the **Use as UI Policy on client** field is enabled.

When a data policy rejects an update, it is basically the same thing that happens when you call `current.setAbortAction(true);` in a business rule script. We'll go into more detail about business rule/server-side scripts in a later chapter.

Demo

As with UI Policies, let's explore data policies in ServiceNow by creating one! Let's create a data policy that prevents users from re-opening a Virtual War Room, once it's closed:

1. Navigate to the **Virtual War Room** table that we created in an earlier chapter, and click on the hamburger menu at the top-left. Choose **Configure**, and then click on **Data Policies**.

2. On the **Data Policies** list, click the blue **New** button at the top-left to create a new data policy record. The **Table** field will automatically be set to the **Virtual War Room** [u_virtual_war_room] table, since that was the table that was automatically added to our query on the data policies table when we navigated there from the Virtual War Room list/form.

3. On the data policy form, set the **Short description** to Prevent re-opening War Rooms, and ensure that **Use as UI Policy on client** is checked.

4. Add a condition to the **Conditions** field that contains: [State] [is one of] [Closed Complete, Closed Incomplete, Closed Skipped]. Include any other closed states in your instance, if you have any:

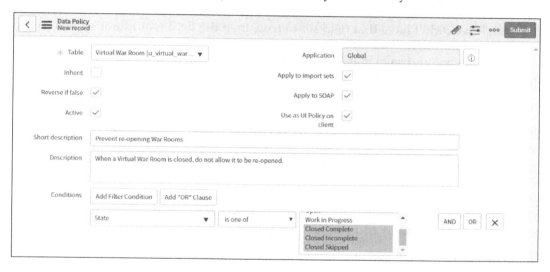

5. Right-click on the form header, and click on **Save** to save the record and reload the form without returning you to the previous page. This step, saving the record to the database and thus assigning it a Sys ID, causes the related list **Data Policy Rules** to render.

6. In the **Data Policy Rules** related list, click on the blue **New** button. The **Table** field should again be automatically populated.

7. In the **Field name** field, select **State**. Set the **Read only** field to **True**, but leave **Mandatory** as **Leave alone**. Then, click **Submit**. This will return you to the **Data Policy** record.

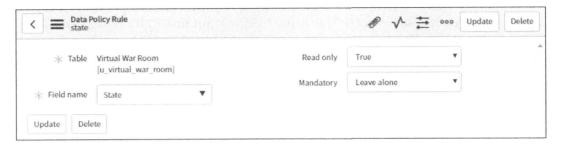

Now, if you set the **State** field on a Virtual War Room record to a **Closed** state, it will turn the field to read-only because the **Use as UI Policy on client** check-box was checked. If we didn't have that field set to true, then the field would not appear to be read-only on the client, but once a record was saved with a **Closed** state value, if you tried to re-open it and save it again, you would receive an error in the client saying **Invalid update**, and another error with a **Data Policy Exception**.

You might be thinking: *"Why not just use a UI Policy to prevent this change?"*

This is a legitimate question. The answer is that UI policies only execute on the client, and only inside of the user's browser. This means that any sufficiently clever user can bypass UI policies, but it also means that any alternative method of making a change to the database (such as via a script, a web services API, or even editing a field in the list view) can bypass this protection. For this reason, anything that's quite important to conditionally protect or require, should be done via a data policy, or some other server-side mechanism in addition to the client-side mechanism.

Data policies have a unique place and purpose within ServiceNow, just like UI policies and ACLs each have their own place.

Converting between data and UI policies

It's often possible to convert a UI policy to a data policy, and vice versa. On the UI policy form, you'll find a UI action called **Convert this to Data Policy**.

This UI action to convert a UI policy to a data policy will only show up if the following criteria are met:

1. The **Run scripts** tick-box on the **Advanced view** of the UI policy form must not be checked. This is because data policies do not support scripting, so there is no way to convert a scripted UI policy into a data policy.

2. The **Global** tick-box must be checked.

3. Any UI policy actions associated with the UI policy must not affect the visibility of a field (all Actions must have the **Visible** field set to **Leave alone**). This is because there is no way to modify the visibility of a field using a data policy.

If the preceding conditions are met, you'll see the **Convert this to Data Policy** UI Action under the **Related Links** section of the form:

Clicking this link will automatically generate a new data policy and take you to the form displaying the new record. At the bottom, you'll also see auto-generated data policy rules in the related list.

Demo

Let's navigate back to the UI policy we created earlier to ensure that the **Major incident** field on the **Virtual War Room** table becomes read-only once it's populated. You can find it by going to **System UI | UI Policies** from the application navigator.

If you don't see the **Updated** column in the list, add it by clicking on the **Personalize List** gear icon at the top-left of the list, and add it.

 If you don't see the gear icon, you may be in List v3, try clicking on the hamburger menu at the top-left of the list.

Once it's on the list view, sort the list by most recently updated, by clicking the **Updated** column header. The UI policy we created earlier in this chapter should show up near the top. Click on the name in the left column to open the UI policy.

Near the bottom, above the UI policy actions related list, there is a form section labeled **Related Links**. Under this section, you should see a link called **Convert this to Data Policy**, since our UI policy meets the conditions defined in the section above for converting to a data policy. Clicking on this link will deactivate the UI policy, and take you to a pre-made data policy, with data policy rules corresponding to the UI policy actions that were associated with the deactivated UI policy.

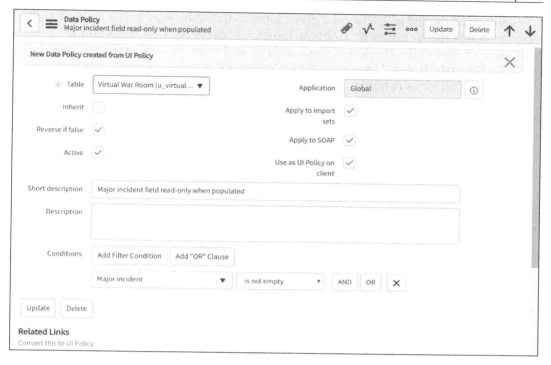

Data policies versus ACLs

Data policies are an effective means of controlling a few fields, and making a field mandatory in a data policy is probably the best way to ensure that a field has a value on the server before a record can be inserted or updated. Making a field read-only in a data policy is probably also the best way to prevent the value from changing on the server. When it comes to ensuring that a field (or a table) is fully inaccessible to users without a certain role or set of permissions however, ACLs are the way to go.

ACLs (short for **Access Control Lists** and otherwise known as **Security Rules**) are another means by which you can control access to elements within ServiceNow. They can serve much the same function as data policies, and a great deal more. One major difference between data policies and ACLs, is that ACLs are scriptable. This allows for a great degree of flexibility of functionality.

You can access the list of ACLs on a given table in the same way you'd access many other customizations: either by right-clicking the form header, or through the hamburger menu at the top-left of the list view, and then clicking on **Customize**, and then **Security Rules**. However, modifying security rules requires permissions elevation on instances running the **High Security plugin**. On such instances, you can elevate permissions by left-clicking your profile link at the top-right of the ServiceNow frame, and clicking **Elevate Roles**.

ACLs operate on a table-and-field basis, but wildcards are accepted as a replacement for either. An ACL can be a **table ACL** that grants or restricts access to an entire table, or a **field ACL** which grants or restricts access to one or all fields on a table. ACL names are broken down into two parts, separated by a **dot**: the table name, and field name:

For example, the `incident.*` ACL would grant or restrict access to all fields on the incident table, but a user must also have access to the table itself. The ACL corresponding to the whole table would have a name like, simply: `incident` (with no field name or wild-card).

Here is an example ACL that prevents modification (`Write`) on *any* field in the **Virtual War Room** table, once a war room record has been closed.

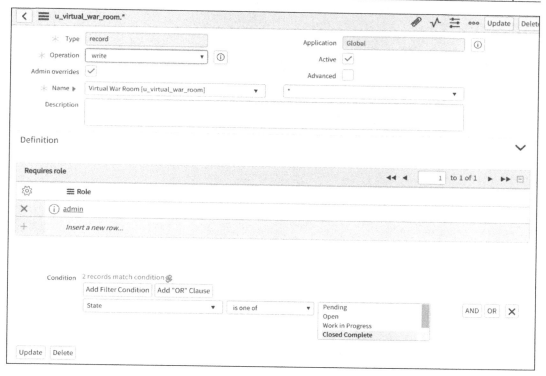

This is very similar to how a data policy would work, and it would even function similarly to a UI policy on the client. When an ACL prevents **write** access to a field, but **read** access is not prohibited, it shows on the form as a read-only field, even when not made read only by any client script or UI policy.

Best practice when it comes to security, is to always assign **roles** to **groups**; not directly to users. Once a group contains the roles you'd like to assign, add users to that group. It is much easier to manage group permissions, than to manage permissions on an individual-user basis.

Summary

In this chapter, we learned about UI policies and catalog UI policies, data policies, and how they are related. We also got to see how one can convert between data and UI policies, and how all of these tools relate to ACLs, also known as security rules.

7
User Administration and Security

User administration is one of the core duties of any ServiceNow administrator. It's important to understand what constitutes a user, how to create and manage user accounts and permissions, and even how to test changes and defects in the context of other users. In this chapter, we'll discuss those topics, and we'll learn about:

- What is a user?
- How to create a user account
- How permissions work in ServiceNow
- Creating and assigning permissions to a user
- User preferences and configuration
- ACLs / security rules
- Notifications

What is a user?

User accounts in ServiceNow are, for the most part, just another type of record in the database. User records are stored in the **Users** [sys_user] table, and define the users that can log in and access the instance. Related tables (specifically, the **Roles** [sys_user_role] table) control our users' level of access, but it's the **Users** table that defines and contains the account itself, including additional data like the user's email address, phone number, user ID (which is used to log in to ServiceNow), and even password (stored as a one-way encrypted hash):

A user is a record that corresponds to a set of permissions (roles) and groups, and of course, to a real person! User accounts can also correspond to licenses which must be purchased from ServiceNow, if they have roles. As of right now, ServiceNow does not generally charge licensing fees for users that don't require fulfiller access or any special roles. These non-roled/non-ITIL users are referred to as self-service users, and can still submit requests and do other requestor-level things that don't require special permissions or a license. It's the fulfillers - service desk agents, problem managers, and so on - that require roles, and thus, require licenses.

This applies to the Now platform's **Enterprise** edition. Licensing for the **Express** edition is typically a little different, in that you are charged for licenses for **approvers** rather than **fulfillers**. As with any licensing questions, be sure to consult your company's account representative at ServiceNow, as different companies may have different licensing schemes.

You can access the **Users** table by navigating to **System Security | Users and Groups | Users**:

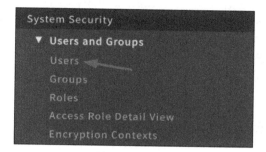

User accounts are associated with user sessions, which are instances of a user having logged in, and a context in which the user's security permissions and preferences are read from the database, and cached.

Users are members of groups, and are thereby assigned roles (through their group memberships, as we'll discuss in the following sections), and thus have permissions. Users can perform actions on objects (such as tables, records, fields, or reports) which are allowed by security rules. Users may also have notifications associated, which are triggered by events in the system, and which are sent to the user's specified **notification channels**. Effectively, a user in the Now platform is a representation and point of coalescence for all of the data, metadata, and contextual information associated with a given person.

 If you're using a slightly older version of the Now platform, notification channels may instead be unintuitively called **devices**. This update to the nomenclature was a recent, and welcome change to the platform.

Groups and roles

As we learned in a previous chapter, it's nearly always best practice to assign **roles** to **groups**, and then add **users** to those **groups**. It is virtually never a good idea to add roles directly to users. Following this best-practice guideline makes role management much, much simpler and more manageable later on.

Roles in ServiceNow correspond to specific sets of permissions. They grant access to modules within the platform, rights to perform certain actions, and more. Some roles, such as the **admin** role, grant special permissions, such as the ability to modify system records, policies, and scripts. In high security instances (instances with the **High Security Settings** plugin enabled), there is an even higher-permissions role, called `security_admin`. This role grants the ability to modify security rules (ACLs) and perform other security-related tasks.

Roles are stored in the **Role** [`sys_user_role`] table, and can be found in the application navigator, under **User Administration | Roles**. The associations between roles and users, and roles and groups, are stored in the **User Role** [`sys_user_has_role`] and **Group Role** [`sys_group_has_role`] tables respectively.

Roles are fairly simple records on their own, in that they consist primarily of a name and description. Some roles require elevation, if they have the elevated privilege tick-box checked. The `security_admin` role mentioned earlier is one such example. Elevating your privileges within an instance can be accomplished by left-clicking on your profile at the top-right of the ServiceNow interface and clicking **Elevate Roles**:

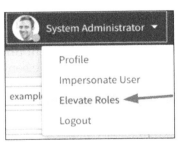

Roles can be created as they are required, and do not inherently have access to anything in ServiceNow. However, some records in ServiceNow will have the **Requires role** field, which allows you to select a role that's required to view or access that specific module, application, or object. You can also use roles to control access to UI elements, such as UI actions, or even control behavior from within scripts by using `g_user.hasRole('role_name')` on a client-side script; or `gs.hasRole('role_name')` on the server. These methods both return a Boolean `true` or `false`, allowing you to control the behavior and flow of other scripts based on whether or not the user performing the action has a given role.

Here is an example of a scripted condition field using `gs.hasRole()`:

| Condition | !current.source.isNil() && gs.hasRole('admin') |

`gs.hasRole()` is a simple API that accepts one argument: a string with the name of the role you're checking against. It returns `true` if the current user has the role, or `false` if they don't.

There is also another means of requiring a role, using the **Requires role** related list on certain record types:

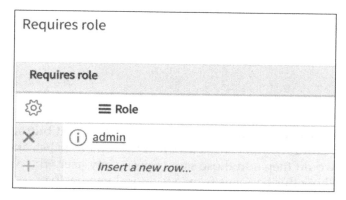

 Technically, the **Requires role** field pictured in the preceding screenshot is an embedded related list, which is just a related list that's displayed inside a form using the embedded related list formatter from the **Form Designer** (which you can access by right-clicking on the form header, and looking in the **Configure** menu).

Note that these two conditions (the **Conditions** field and the **Requires role** related list), if they both exist, are evaluated separately. If a record has a **Requires role** field, it is not necessary to use `gs.hasRole()` in a separate condition field. You may however, use any Boolean expression in that field to check some other condition. You may also ignore the **Requires role** field, and use the **Conditions** field for everything if you so choose, though this might be slightly less efficient.

Roles are linked to users through an intermediary **many-to-many** (**M2M**) table called **User Roles** [sys_user_has_role]. If the role is granted by the user's membership in a group (which, as a general rule, it ought to be), then the **Granted by** [granted_by] field is populated with a reference to the **Group** [sys_user_group] table. When a role is granted by a user's membership in a group, it means that a role has been assigned to the group, of which the user is a member. Much like the relationships between users and roles, the relationships between groups and roles are stored in a separate M2M table: **Group Roles** [sys_group_has_role].

Just like on a user record, you can grant roles to a group (and thus, to all members of that group) by modifying the **Roles** related list at the bottom of a **Groups** record:

As with any related list (any related list that has the **Omit edit button** tick-box set to false under **List Control**), you can click **Edit** at the top of the list, and add roles to a group—which would then add those same roles to any user who was a member of the group! Here's how this happens from a technical perspective:

The **Roles** related list on the **Group** form points to the sys_group_has_role table. When a new record is created in this table, this grants all members of the group the same role as the group was just granted. This is accomplished by creating a record on the sys_user_has_role table, and setting the **Granted by** field to a reference to the group to which the role was added.

> If a user is a member of two groups which grant the same role, they will appear to have that role *twice*. This is perfectly normal, and removing them from one of the groups will not remove the role granted by the other.

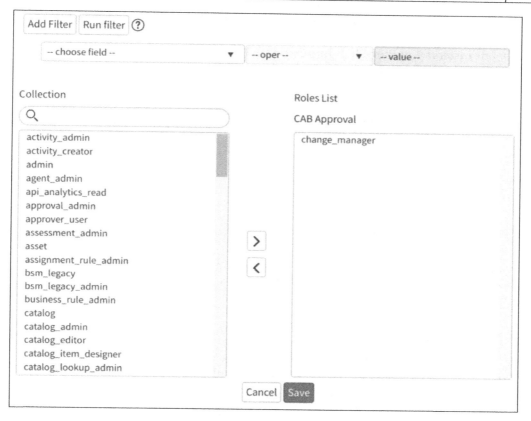

Impersonating users for testing

When testing the behavior of a form, field, ACL, or nearly any other part of ServiceNow, it can almost always be of some use to impersonate another user in order to test how things behave from a non-admin (or non-you) perspective.

Despite the name, impersonation is nothing illicit or nefarious in ServiceNow; it simply allows you to view the system from the perspective of another user. This perspective includes their user preferences, UI settings, and even their security context. A user's security context includes their roles, groups, and permissions; this way, you can see what the user would (and would not) see in the user interface, and explore the behavior of the system from their perspective. This is monumentally useful when a user claims to be having a specific issue, but you aren't able to replicate it from your user account.

Impersonating a user can be accomplished by clicking your user profile link at the top-right of the ServiceNow interface as though you were going to elevate your roles, but instead you then click **Impersonate User**. This will display a popup dialog, allowing you to select which user you'd like to impersonate, and displaying a list of the last several people you've impersonated:

Let's say we received a bug report from a user: Abel Tuter. We can use the steps to reproduce that the user provided, by impersonating them and walking through each step.

 As an admin, if you enable some form of debugging (such as security rule or UI policy debugging) and then impersonate a user, your debugging will continue, allowing you to see the results of the debugger in the context of the user that would otherwise not have access to launch a debugger. Debugging is discussed in detail, in a later chapter.

Once you're impersonating a user, you might wonder how to *stop* impersonating them. The answer is simple: Impersonate yourself! Or rather, re-open the **Impersonate User** dialog like before, but select your own user profile instead of theirs. It'll be at the top, under **Recent Impersonations**. Note that in the following screenshot, my account's display name is **System Administrator**:

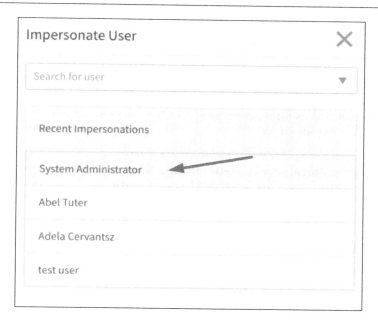

Impersonation is an extremely useful tool; not only for debugging, but for testing new development in the context of the feature's intended users!

Emails and notifications

Emails sent to and from your instance are processed by a mail server maintained by ServiceNow. This means that you don't have to manage these servers yourself and worry about connecting them to your ServiceNow database or managing communication between them. Instead, ServiceNow has pre-configured POP3 and SMTP accounts set up to send and receive emails.

These email addresses are formatted like `instance@service-now.com`. For example, if your instance name (the URL prefix you use to access your ServiceNow instance) is `my_company_name`, then the email address corresponding to that instance will be `my_company_name@service-now.com`. Sending an email to this email address will (if inbound email is enabled) result in the existing inbound email actions being evaluated.

You can configure email properties, including turning emails on or off for production or sub-prod instances, by navigating to **System Properties | Email Properties**.

> If you have a dev instance that has a name ending in dev, test, or a couple of other keywords, then emails will be automatically disabled by default. This is just something ServiceNow does automatically to try to make your life easier.

You can configure notifications by right-clicking the header of a record or list that you'd like to set notifications for, and clicking on **Configure | Notifications**.

> On List V3, you would click the hamburger menu at the top-left of a list instead of right-clicking the header.

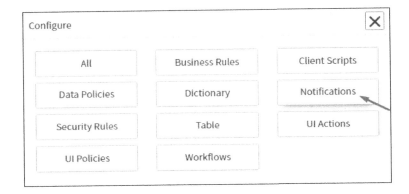

Each record in the corresponding table (the **Notifications** [sysevent_email_action] list) represents a given set of conditions, and a specific message that will be sent to users when those conditions are met. Advanced notifications also helpfully include a **Send to event creator** tick-box, which you can un-check in order to prevent a user from being overloaded by emails about changes that they themselves have made.

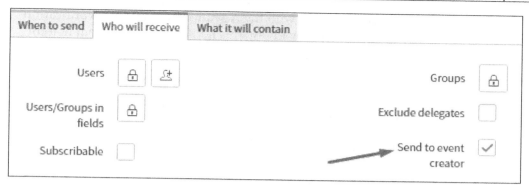

This is important, because if you have a busy IT helpdesk, they would likely make a lot of updates to helpdesk tickets, so they might end up with an inbox that's completely flooded before lunch!

Let's create a new notification in order to learn how they work!

Demo

We've built a **Virtual War Rooms** table, but we haven't assigned any notifications to it yet. How are our users going to know when these records are updated? To remedy this issue, let's create a notification on the **Virtual War Room** [u_virtual_war_room] table that alerts the assigned_to user whenever the work notes are updated by anyone other than them:

1. Let's start by going to the application navigator, and navigating to **System Notification | Email | Notifications**. At the top-left of that list, click on **New**.

2. So that we have access to all of the configuration options available on the form, let's click the **Advanced view** UI action under **Related Links** at the bottom of the form:

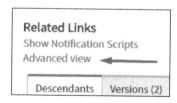

3. You should now be presented with the **Advanced view** of the **Notification** form. At the top-right, begin by giving this notification a short but helpful name. Let's use `Alert assignee on notes update`. Just below that field, set the **Table** to **Virtual War Room** [`u_virtual_war_room`]:

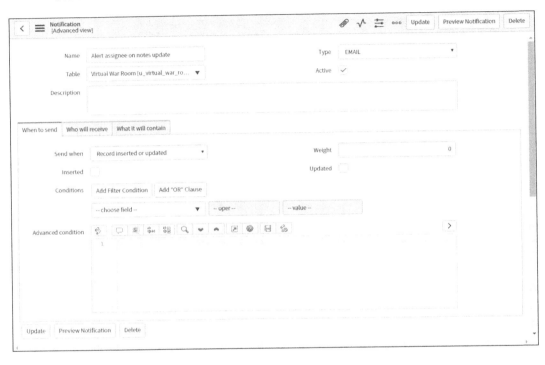

4. Next, give the notification a helpful **Description,** such as `Send an email to the person in the assigned_to field whenever the work notes are updated on the War Room record.`

5. In the **When to send** section, we want to **Send when** a **Record is inserted or updated**. However, when a record is inserted (created), we can assume that its work notes will change from undefined to whatever work notes were saved with the record initially. In fact, on insert, all fields on a given record technically change. So, of the two tick-boxes below the **Send when** and **Weight** fields, we'll check **Updated**, but not **Inserted**:

6. In the **Conditions** field, choose `[Work Notes] [Changes]`. Leave the **Advanced condition** script box empty.

   ○ As with many **Advanced condition** scripts in ServiceNow, rather than simply evaluating to `true` or `false`, a global variable called `answer` has been pre-defined as `true`. The job of the script should be to set the `answer` variable so that when the script finishes running, it should be `true` or `false` depending on whether the notification should fire or not.

   ○ Advanced notification condition scripts have access to the current variable, containing the `GlideRecord` object representing the record itself, as well as the event variable, containing information about the event that triggered the notification.

7. Next, under the **Who will receive** form section, click the lock icon 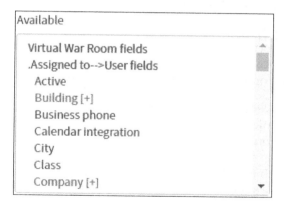 next to **Users/Groups in fields** to unlock the field, then select the **Assigned to (+)** field and either double-click it, or click the arrow to move it to the **Selected** column.

   ○ The **(+)** next to **Assigned to** indicates that this is a reference field which we can **dot-walk** through. For example, we could select **Assigned to**, then click the plus icon between the **Available** and **Selected** columns to see the available fields in the referenced table (**Users** [sys_user] in this case). This way, we can send a notification to the user in the **Manager** field, for the `assigned_to` user. This may be useful if a user is on vacation, or if an SLA is missed on a given task record for example; though we're not going to need to do that for this notification:

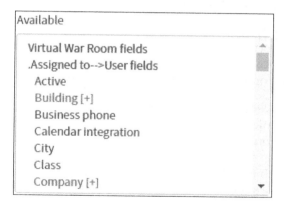

8. Un-check the **Send to event creator** tick-box so that the user doesn't get emails about their own work notes updates. Remember: if users receive too many notifications, they may begin to ignore them!

9. In the **What it will contain** section, we could select an email template; but instead, let's write our own notification for this situation, since no existing template is quite going to work for our use case. To get started, let's fill out the email's subject line. In the **Subject** field, enter `Work notes updated on Virtual War Room ${number}`.

   ○ Any field name inside of the sigil-curly brace (`${}`) block will be replaced with its value from the record. For example, since our record has an **Assigned to** field with the name `assigned_to` (like all task records), we can enter `${assigned_to}` anywhere in the notification, and when the email is sent to the user, that string will be replaced with the value of the `assigned_to` field. There are also a couple of special names we can call using this syntax, the most useful of which is probably `${URI_REF}`, which will be replaced with the **Display value** for the record, as a hyperlink to the record itself.

10. In the **Message HTML** field, enter the following:

    ```
    Virtual War Room ${URI_REF} has received new Work notes.
    Work notes: ${work_notes}
    ```

11. Right-click on the notification record header, and click **Save**. When the form reloads, click on **Preview Notification**:

    ○ If you don't have any Virtual War Room tickets with work notes created already, go ahead and create one and add a few notes to it, then return to this notification.

12. A dialog will pop up, displaying what an email for this notification would look like, when run against a specific record. In the **Event Creator** field, you'll see your user account. In the **Preview Record** field, enter a Virtual War Room ticket number for a war room that has work notes:

    ○ In the **Users** section, you'll see a list of users who will receive the notification. If a user would receive the notification, except for some condition (such as the user being the originator of the triggering event, or the user having emails turned off), the user will show up in red with a strike-through overlay. Hovering over the user's name will show you the reason they won't be included in the notification:

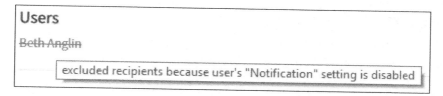

- ○ In the **Subject** section, you'll see the email subject. Where we entered `${number}`, you should now see a Virtual War Room number.
- ○ In the **Body** section, you should see the email body. It should consist of the war room ticket number with a hyperlink directly to the relevant record, followed by "**Work notes:**" and a table containing any work notes that have been saved to the record:

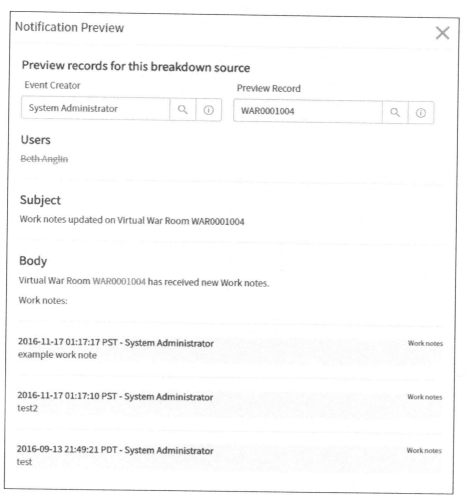

Notification devices

Notifications are sent to notification channels (formerly called **devices**) in ServiceNow. Notification channels are associated with users, and do not necessarily have to be physical devices. Due to the recent change in name from devices to channels, notification channels are stored in a table with the legacy name **Notification Device** [cmn_notif_device], and have different fields visible/mandatory based on the **Type** field:

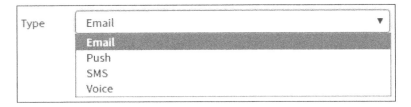

An email notification device for example, consists of a name and an email address. These devices also contain a reference field that associated them to a specific user.

Users can add and remove notification channels from the **System Settings** cog in the top-right, by clicking on the **Notifications** tab:

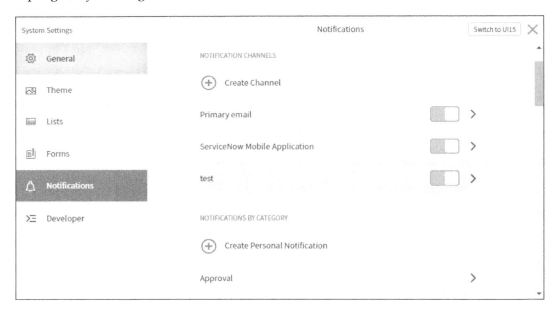

To create a new notification device record, let's navigate to the **Users** [sys_user] table, open up a user record, and click the **Notification Preferences** UI action under **Related Links**. As you'll see, this displays notification_preferences.do, a page designed to display this data in a configurable way. This lists all of the notifications that the user can receive, and whether or not they've chosen to receive them.

While we're on this page, on the left side, scroll down and click on **Virtual War Room**. This will display any notifications on the **Virtual War Room** table, including the one we just created in the preceding section:

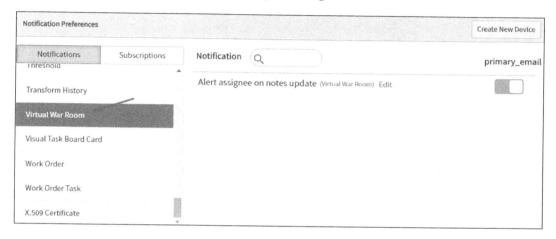

If the user wants to stop receiving this particular type of notification entirely, they can do so by simply de-selecting the toggle under primary_email on the right. primary_email corresponds to their (in this case, only) notification device. If they had multiple notification devices, they could subscribe to, or unsubscribe from specific notification types on a device-by-device basis! Notifications which have the **Subscribable** tick-box checked, will show up here.

Now, as for creating new notification devices, simply click on the **Create New Device** button at the top-right of the **Notification Preferences** page, and you'll be asked to select the device type and enter the relevant details.

User preferences

User preferences are stored in the **User Preferences** [sys_user_preference] table. Many specific user-based preferences are maintained in this table, which is structured very similarly to the **System Properties** [sys_properties] table. The main difference between a system property and a user preference, is that a user preference is associated with a specific user, whereas system properties affect all users.

One example of a user preference is the **Compact the user interface** toggle in the settings menu after clicking the cog icon in the top-right of the ServiceNow interface:

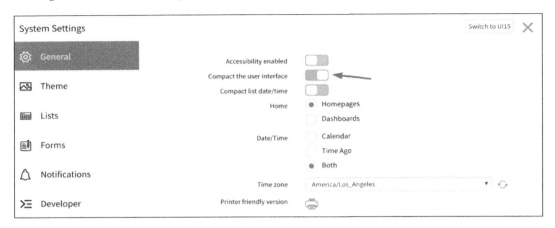

There is a user preference record corresponding to that change, called `glide.ui.compact`. Toggle this setting on, and then navigate to the `sys_user_preference` table (**User Administration | User Preferences**). If the **Updated** [`sys_updated_on`] field is not shown in the list view, add it and then use it to sort the **User Preferences** table so that more recently updated records show up on top. If you refresh the list, you should see the `glide.ui.compact` preference that you updated on the top, and set to `true`.

User Preference records consist of the following fields:

Field	Description	Example value
Name	The system property name. Usually short-hand, using dots or underscores instead of spaces.	`glide.ui.incident.stream_input`
Description	A short explanation of what this preference's value will impact.	Number of rows per page in a list
System	A Boolean (true/false) field indicating whether this represents a system-wide default.	`true`
Type	The type of data that should represent the preference itself.	`true`/`false`, string, or integer

Field	Description	Example value
User	The user account to which the preference applies. This may be blank in the case of a default preference. This is a reference field.	Abel Tuter
Value	The value or setting for the current preference.	E6afdf854f312200993533718110c7e1 (a sys_id value)

> Changing a user's preferences for them while they're logged in may not take effect until they log out and back in, since user preferences are cached with their session.

Default preferences

Boolean user preferences have a default value of `false` if they don't exist, but you can override this (or any other type of user preference value) by manually creating a new user preference record with the **System** tick-box checked, and with no username in the **User** [user] field. When those two conditions are met, the preference record becomes a **global default** for all users.

Keep in mind however, that users can override any preferences by setting a custom preference of their own (such as by toggling the **Compact user interface** switch). In fact, any users who have already configured such a preference manually will not be impacted by the addition of a new global default preference. You may however, revert all users to the global default on a one-off basis after creating that default, by deleting all instances of a given preference in the User Preferences table, that correspond to specific users, and which do not have the **System** tick-box checked.

Preferences in update sets

Another thing to note about user preferences and their defaults, is that user preferences are not tracked in update sets unless they are system-wide (that is, unless they have the **System** tick-box checked). It's important to understand this, because this can lead to unexpected behavior. If for example, you modify a preference marked as **System**, it will be saved into your update set. However, if you later un-mark it as **System** (and perhaps make further changes to it), it will still exist in your update set, but any changes made to it *after* un-checking the **System** tick-box will not be saved into your update set!

If you'd like to save a non-global user preference record to your update set, you can use the `GlideUpdateManager2` server-side API class, but unfortunately it is not an officially documented API. As such, we've written a custom tool which creates a UI action for admins to be able to force any record into an update set with the click of a button on most tables which are not already tracked in update sets. You can find this tool on our ServiceNow developer blog at the following URL: `http://updatesetinclude.snprotips.com/`

Scripting user preferences

There are situations where you may want to alter a given user preference as the result of a script running. For example, the **Make this my current update set** UI action that can be found in the **Related Links** section of the **Update Set** form changes the user preference that controls the user's currently selected update set to the `sys_id` of the currently opened update set record. Luckily, ServiceNow provides both a client, and server-side API for performing this update.

It is possible to use a client script, business rule, or any client or server-side script to modify a user preference record, by calling one of the following APIs, depending on context:

Client	`setPreference('preference_name', 'preferece_value');`
Server	`gs.getUser().setPreference('pref_name', 'pref_value');`

The client version of this script is fairly straight-forward, but the server-side script first has to get the user object on which to perform an action first, using `gs.getUser()`. the User object is similar to a GlideRecord, in that it represents an individual user's user record from the database, but it also contains associated session-specific data, such as the user's roles and permissions.

Both of the above scripts will operate within the context of the current user (whichever user triggered the action that caused the script to run), but there are ways to get the user object for other users in a script as well. More on scripting in a later chapter.

ACLs – security rules

In the previous chapter, we briefly touched on **ACLs** (otherwise known as security rules or **Access Control Lists**) and how they can be used to control whether or not a field is visible or read-only on the form. However, ACLs also have a server-side component, not entirely unlike a cross between UI policies and data policies, except that you're able to script conditions for ACLs. You can access the security rules in ServiceNow by navigating to **System Security | Access Control (ACL)** in the application navigator. This will take you to the **Access Control** [sys_security_acl] table list.

 Since we're going to be working with security rules, let's start by checking if we need to elevate our permissions. Click on the profile button at the top-right of the ServiceNow interface in the banner frame, and see if **Elevate Roles** is an option. If it is, click it, and make sure that the security_admin tick-box is selected, then click **OK**. More on High Security settings and permissions elevation shortly.

ACLs in ServiceNow specify three main components: the object being secured, the operation that it's securing the object against, and the permissions and/or conditions required to pass the security rule. The **Name** of the ACL describes and defines the type of record to which the ACL should apply: the object. The object for a field type ACL looks something like this:

The **Operation** field on the ACL record defines the operation the ACL is securing against, such as **read**, **write**, **report**, or **delete**. Another major component of ACL records, is the **Admin Overrides** toggle. If this field is set to True, then administrators will automatically have access to whatever object the ACL is securing, even if they don't have the specific role that's being checked against.

When validating permissions in a script using a function like `gs.hasRole('role_name')` in server-side scripts, or `g_user.hasRole('role_name')` in client-side scripts, having the admin role will cause these checks to always return `true` as well, if **Admin Overrides** is set to true. However, you can bypass this behavior by using the `hasRoleExactly()` API of both `g_form` in client-side scripts, and `GlideSystem` (gs) on the server.

The **Requires role** section of the form contains the roles that a user must have, to pass the role portion of the ACL. In addition to the roles, the **Conditions** field on the record, and the **Script** field (if the **Advanced** tick-box is checked) must also evaluate to `true` for the user in question to be allowed to perform the relevant action (reading, writing, deleting, and so on).

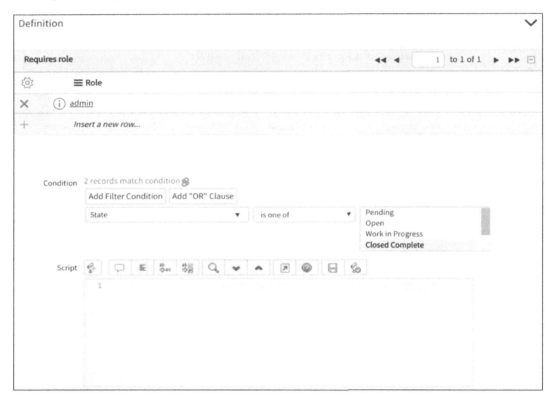

ServiceNow uses a *deny-by-default* security model, which means that any object without a permissive security rule is, by default, inaccessible.

The general access starting-point guidelines recommended by ServiceNow, include granting **Read** access to all users, for any task-related objects. Objects include tables, records, fields, and pages. They also recommend granting **Write** access to specific users or groups, based on who might need access. For example, the user in the **Assigned to** field on a given task-based record might be able to modify a given record, except perhaps for a few select fields. As for **Delete** access, ServiceNow recommends granting no one access to this functionality except in special cases. This is because deleting records can lead to some unexpected effects, including broken references. Instead, it's almost always best to deactivate a record (set its **Active** tick-box to false/un-checked). Most of this default security configuration, at least when it comes to tables such as the task and user tables, is already set up out of the box!

Table-level security rules grant or allow access to a specific table. In most cases, there is not a specific ACL granting or denying access for each field in a given table. Instead, there is usually a lower-level rule that is inherited. If you do not have access of a given operation type (read, write, delete, and so on.) to a given table, you cannot perform that action upon any record within it; even if you have the necessary field-level permissions.

Table ACLs are evaluated in a particular order - in order of specificity. First, the security evaluator checks for ACLs matching the table name (for example, `incident` or `sc_req_item`). If one is not found, then the evaluator checks for an ACL matching the parent table, if the table extends another table. If no such ACL is found (or if the table is a base table), then the evaluator finally checks for a wildcard table ACL (*).

Field-level ACLs grant or allow access on a field-by-field basis. A user must have access to both the table and the field in order to see fields on a given record. Field-level ACLs can use a wildcard (an asterisk) to control access to all fields on a given table, by using the name `table_name.*`.

To view the ACLs associated with a given table's records, first **Elevate Roles** if you have High Security Settings enabled and haven't done so already (and remember that you have to do this for every new session). Then, right-click on the header of a table of form showing the type of record you want to view ACLs for (such as the **Incident** table), and navigate to **Configure | Security Rules**. Note that this option will only show up under **Configure** if your roles are already elevated in Helsinki or later. In previous versions (Geneva and earlier) you could use this option to get to the **Security Rules** table, but you still couldn't modify anything without elevating your roles. Also remember that in List V3, you'll need to use the hamburger menu at the top-left of the list rather than right-clicking the header.

ACL process order

When a user requests access to an object (such as by loading a list or form), ACLs are evaluated to determine whether the user can see the object or not. First, the system checks whether an applicable ACL rule was found. If it was not, then the system grants access based on the default ACLs (*.*) except when the high security plugin is enabled, or when the default ACLs are set to restrictive rather than permissive. Once a relevant ACL is found, the system evaluates the access request in the following fashion:

- Does the user have one of the roles specified in the **Requires role** embedded list of the ACL?
- Does the **Conditions** specified in the ACL evaluate to `true`?
- Does the script in the **Script** field of the ACL return `true`?

If all three of these conditions return `true`, or are blank (for example, if no script is specified, we can assume that it returns `true`), then the user is granted access to the object. However, if even one of them evaluates to `false`, then the user is denied access (unless another ACL exists which overrides this one).

A user only has to pass one ACL at the table level to have access to the table, and one to have access to a given object. If there are multiple relevant ACLs, the user does not need to meet each one.

> Often, ACL results can be cached. Account permissions and security are also almost always cached in the user's session. Thus, when adjusting security rules, it's best to instruct users to log out and then log back in before testing. While testing as an admin, it is usually sufficient to un-impersonate and then re-impersonate a user's session, as that re-loads their security context just like logging out and back in.

As we learned in the previous section, when a user requests access to a given object (such as a field on a record), the first thing the system does is to evaluate whether an ACL is found for the record, but this is evaluated in a certain order as well:

1. Search for an ACL name matching `table_name.field_name`
2. If not found, search for an ACL matching `parent_table_name.field_name`
3. If not found, try `*.field_name` (`* = wildcard`) — search for ACLs on that field in any table

4. If not found, try `parent_table.*` — an ACL matching all fields on the table using a wildcard

5. Finally, if none of those worked, evaluate the wildcard `*.*` ACL which may be permissive or, if high security is enabled, restrictive

High security plugin

One of the more popular plugins to have enabled on a given instance is the **High Security Settings** plugin. You can see whether you have this plugin enabled by going to **System Definition | Plugins** in the application navigator:

One of the more important properties to understand, that is installed with the High Security Settings plugin, is `glide.sm.default_mode`, which determines whether users can access objects that only match against wildcard table ACL rules. That is, records in a table with no ACL that the user, or a given record, match; other than `*` and `*.*`.

The High Security plugin also enables the `security_admin` role, and adds two new columns to the **Properties** [`sys_properties`] table: `read_roles`, and `write_roles`, which as you might imagine, restricts read and write access respectively, to a given property. By default, properties will have a `read_roles` value of admin and the `write_roles` field will require the more elevated `security_admin` role.

It is the **High Security Settings** plugin that enables the elevated privilege options, such as elevating to the `security_admin` role. You can set the elevated privilege field to `true` in a **Role** [`sys_user_role`] record to require similar escalation in order to pass the evaluation of any ACL that requires that specific role. It would be possible to treat `security_admin` as simply a higher level of admin that is only given to specific people, but which does not require elevation, by setting the elevated privilege field to `false` on the role record.

Summary

In this chapter, we learned all about users, including what constitutes a user, how to impersonate users for testing, how users can control notifications and preferences, and how we as administrators can interact with them.

We also learned about security; specifically, ACLs, also known as security rules, which are primarily (but not solely) responsible for controlling access to tables, records, and fields in ServiceNow.

8
Introduction to Scripting

In this chapter, we're going to get a basic introduction to scripting in ServiceNow's Now platform (formerly called simply ServiceNow). As with the rest of this book, we assume a basic understanding of the JavaScript scripting language, and basic familiarity with database, programming, and ITIL terminology.

ServiceNow comes in two flavors (otherwise known as editions): **Enterprise**, and **Express**. This book is largely focused on ServiceNow Enterprise, as that is by far the more popular and more complex of the two, but most of what you've learned so far about Enterprise will translate nicely to the Express edition of ServiceNow as well.

That said, it's important to note that in this and many of the following chapters, we are going to begin focusing on scripting. Scripting is almost completely unsupported in ServiceNow Express, so if you're an Express user, these next few chapters might not be relevant to your instance.

In this chapter, we're going to learn about:

- When to employ custom or semi-custom functionality via scripting, versus using out-of-the-box functionality
- Fields and areas in the platform that support scripting, and how to script within them
- ServiceNow Integrated Development Environment (IDE) versus an external IDE
- The purposes and scopes of the different scriptable fields
- How to test client-side and server-side scripts
- Script execution order, and how it impacts behavior
- Best practices related to scripting in ServiceNow

To script, or not to script?

Once you learn how powerful scripting can be in ServiceNow, it would be easy to try and do everything with custom scripts. A wise person once said *"When all you have is a hammer, everything looks like a nail"*; however, this is quite often not the best solution for a few reasons:

- If the functionality or API are updated or deprecated, any unnecessary custom code means more maintenance costs during upgrades
- Increased custom code increases complexity, increasing the cost of development overall
- Custom code being used in lieu of out-of-the-box functionality can make it more difficult to identify the source of a given issue, making troubleshooting cumbersome
- Out-of-the-box (OOB) functionality, when it is available, is often faster and more efficient than custom code, even using extant APIs.

In the *Where scripting is supported* section of this chapter, we'll learn about the various fields and records in which scripting is supported. However, it is important to keep in mind that, as mentioned in the previous section, custom scripts do carry a small cost to offset their benefit, in terms of performance, upgradeability, and future stability.

With that said, the benefits of a custom script are very often far greater than the costs; primarily, when there is no specific functionality built into the system to accomplish what you want, without scripting. Let's look at some examples.

First, let's have a look at just a few examples where scripting is **not** necessary:

- Making a field dynamically read-only, mandatory, or hidden, based on the value of another field's value on the client (the user's browser)
- Altering the value of a field on the server upon submission
- Preventing/rejecting an update under certain conditions upon submission
- Providing an informational or error message to the user upon submission

That covers a significant percentage of the sorts of things you might need to do on a daily basis within ServiceNow, but to perform some more advanced functions, you may need to write a custom script (or indeed, leverage a script that's provided for you out of the box!) Let's look at some examples of some more advanced functionality that might require scripting:

- Setting one field based on the value of another field in the client

- Creating a new record programmatically based on a client or server-side action or event

- Setting a field value on a record that cannot be directly dot-walked to from the record that triggered the event

- Validate the contents of a field (such as ensuring that a date field is before or after a particular date) on the client

As you can see, scripting—despite not being the best way to perform certain actions—does have a myriad of uses within the platform. Generally, if it **can** be done without scripting, then it **should** be done without scripting.

Client-side versus server-side APIs

Originally, ServiceNow's name was **GlideSoft**. While that was a long time ago, there are still some indicators of the company's history, such as in the naming of ServiceNow's scripting API suite: the **Glide** API.

Scripting is an important part of ServiceNow, and many different types of records support scripting in one or more fields. Some scripts execute server side, and some execute client side. Whether a script executes on the client or on the server, determines the API that it has access to.

Server scripts, executing on the server as they do, have access to a different set of programming interfaces than client scripts, because client scripts execute within the browser. Thus, only scripts which are included in the webpage and sent from the server to the browser can be executed or called from within client scripts. Since it would be impractical and have a negative impact on performance to send over the entire scripting library from the server to the client for inclusion in each page, only a modified subset of the API is included. Luckily though, one of the things that this subset includes, is an API class for interacting with server-side scripts from the client! This API is called **GlideAjax**. More on this API later.

Additionally, it's important to be aware that the server is running **Mozilla Rhino**; an open-source implementation of JavaScript, written entirely in Java. Rhino is embedded into the ServiceNow servers, in order to provide the JavaScript API on the server. As such, this grants special access to certain Java-specific functionality (and Java-specific headaches!) for server-side scripts, that client-side scripts don't have.

Similarly, scripts which execute client side have access to a specific scope of their own. Since they're executing within the user's browser, they'll have access to JavaScript ES6 syntax (unless the user is on a very old browser), whereas ServiceNow's implementation of Mozilla Rhino only supports up to ES5 on server-side scripts (or ES3 if you're running Geneva or earlier).

While a complete description of the entire ServiceNow API is outside the scope of this book (you can find this information at `http://developer.servicenow.com/`), there are some significant differences in the APIs for client, and server-based scripts. You cannot, for example, use the `g_form` API from within a server side script. Similarly, you cannot use the `gs` (GlideSystem) API from a client-side script.

As you saw earlier, there are some short-hand references to APIs such as GlideForm. The `g_form` object is a reference to GlideForm, so you can consider the two to be interchangeable. Similarly, `g_list` is a reference to GlideList2 or GlideListV3 depending on the List version that's loaded in the page. `gs` is a reference to GlideSystem, and `g_user` is a reference to GlideUser. These APIs use **interface references** beginning with `g_`, because they have no constructor methods that would be invoked by using the `new` keyword.

While we're going to go into much more depth on the glide API in a later chapter, let's start by learning the APIs and objects that are available on the client and the server respectively. You'll notice that some objects exist on both the client and the server, but behave differently on one versus the other.

Client-side APIs

Client-side APIs are available within the browser, and load with the ServiceNow page. Let's go over some of the more commonly used client-side APIs that are available (though not an exhaustive list):

- `g_form` (a reference to the GlideForm object) allows you to access, set, and get values from form elements and fields. This object has methods to add field messages, set fields to mandatory, visible, or read-only, and so on.
- `g_user` (a reference to the GlideUser object) has methods that allow you to check if the current user (the logged-in user who loaded the page on which the script is running) has a given role, and contains properties that give you access to the user's name and ID.

- `g_list` (a reference to the GlideList2 or GlideListV3 object, depending on what list version is loaded) has methods to get, set, or change the list filter, group the list by a specified column, or set the number of records to display per page. The `g_list` API is available from UI context menus, and client-side list UI actions.

- `g_menu` (a reference to the GlideMenu object) is used in UI context menus, in the onShow script. It has methods to control the menu items that do or don't show up in a UI context menu in ServiceNow.

- GlideRecord is probably the most-used method in the glide API, because it is the means by which records in the database are generally accessed, read, and modified.

- The client-side version of GlideRecord has vital performance implications. You can read more on these implications, and how to avoid negatively impacting client performance in the *Where scripting is supported* section of this chapter.

- GlideAjax is one of the most important client-side APIs, as it allows you to execute server-side code (specifically, client-callable script includes), and receive a response back to the client. It does this asynchronously, meaning that unlike synchronous queries and scripts that execute or retrieve data from the server, it does not lock up or slow down the user's browser while it executes.

- GlideAjax is the most performance-efficient way to execute server-side queries and code from within client-side scripts. More on this in the next couple of chapters.

Server-side APIs

Just like on the client, scripts that execute on the server have a particular set of APIs that they have access to. The server-side API suite is broader than the client-side API, because making an API available on the client requires sending code from the server to the client, which can slow page load times. The server has an extremely low-latency connection to the database, which makes more robust scripting possible and much more efficient.

There are two sets of APIs: **scoped**, and **legacy**. Scoped APIs are mostly a subset of the legacy API. They are the only APIs available within scoped applications, and do have some limitations. These limitations, however, are becoming fewer and fewer with every new version of ServiceNow. Most of what you'll likely do within ServiceNow will be in the Global scope, so you won't need to worry *too much* about this difference.

Let's briefly look at some of the APIs and objects available on the server:

- **GlideAggregate**: This is an extension of the GlideRecord class, used for creating database aggregation queries such as SUM, COUNT, MIN, and MAX. For example, you can run a query with a given filter (say, all items associated with a given ticket), and get a SUM of the cost of these items in order to determine the total cost of the parent ticket.

- **GlideDateTime**: This is a class meant to help with the usage of glide_date_time fields, as well as comparing one date and time to another date and time, or formatting a date/time from a string into a date/time object that can be used for time zone conversion and date/time calculations.

- **GlideDate**: This is very similar to the GlideDateTime class, but is just for dates without times associated to them.

- **GlideRecord**: This is probably the most ubiquitous class in ServiceNow, and it is both a server-side and client-side API. It is vastly different in behavior and capability on the client, but on the server it is a powerful and efficient means of querying the database for a given record or set of records. As you can imagine, getting and setting data in the database is something you might need to do quite often in a platform like ServiceNow.

- **GlideElement**: This is a class referencing a specific field on a client-side GlideRecord object. To put it another way, you do not construct GlideElement objects in your code. Instead, each GlideRecord object contains one property (a GlideElement object) for each field on that record. This API provides methods for interacting with these fields and their values.

- **gs**: This is a reference to GlideSystem (which has no constructor method). It provides methods with all sorts of useful system functionality, including getting system properties, logging information to the system logs, and checking user permissions.

Objects that are meant to be instantiated have a constructor method. This method must be called using the new keyword. When I write var gr = new GlideRecord('table_name');, the new keyword calls the constructor method of the GlideRecord class. This constructor is often a function in the class called initialize, or it is a function itself which becomes the constructed object, which takes the argument table_name that we specified in our call. The constructor then modifies properties of the object and returns the resulting constructed object to our variable (gr, in this case).

- **GlideSession**: This is a server-side object that corresponds to the currently signed-in user's session. It provides methods to get the roles associated with a user, as well as set and retrieve data associated with their particular session. You can get an instance of the GlideSession object for the current user's session by using the `getSession()` method of the GlideSystem API like so:

    `var userSession = gs.getSession();`.

Server-side scripts that operate on a specific record (such as business rules or advanced conditions fields), also often have access to a pre-defined variable called `current`. This is an instance of the GlideRecord object which contains the record upon which the script is executing (or perhaps we should say: the record that triggered the script to run).

For example, imagine you have a business rule that executes on the **Incident** [`incident`] table, and it is triggered whenever the **State** field's value changes. If you then go to the **Incident** table, open up a record, and change the **State** field value, then the business rule will execute. When it does, in the context of the script that that business rule runs, the `current` object will correspond to the record that you just modified.

Where scripting is supported

Some records are defined as scripts, in that running a script is their primary function. An example of this type of script might be a **script includes** or **UI script**. Other records, such as **business rules**, will support scripting if you enable the **Advanced** view, but have more basic functionality even without scripting. What might be less intuitive, is that certain fields such as the condition builder, can also support scripting if the script is invoked using the `javascript:` keyword (including the trailing colon).

Later, we'll go over many of the scenarios in which scripting is supported in one fashion or another, and we'll learn what these scripts do, as well as the context in which they execute—whether on the client, or the server.

Access controls

Executes on: server

In a previous chapter, we learned about how access controls (AKA security rules / ACLs) control whether a user can access a record, or perform a certain operation upon it (read, write, delete, and so on). Access controls have a great deal of functionality without scripting, but they also have the capability to execute server-side scripts if the **Advanced** tick-box is checked:

Script

```
1   var answer;
2   if (gs.hasRole('itil') || gs.hasRole('admin')) {
3       answer = true;
4   } else {
5       answer = false;
6   }
7
8   return answer;
```

This script should evaluate to either `true` or `false`, depending on whether the ACL should allow or deny access.

Don't forget that for a user to pass an ACL challenge, all three conditions (those in the condition builder, roles list, and script field) must all evaluate to true!

Business rules

Executes on: server

Much like ACLs, business rules have a significant amount of functionality without the need for scripting. Also like ACLs, business rules support scripting when the **Advanced** tick-box is checked, in the **Script** field which will then be displayed.

Business rules execute on the server, so the usual server-side APIs are available to any scripts that might need to be run. Much like many other server-side scripts, the `current` object is also available. This object is a pre-populated GlideRecord containing the current record; that is, the record which triggered a business rules to run by being inserted, queried, or modified.

Based on the value selected in the **When** field, under the **When to run** section of the business rule form, a business rule can execute either **before** the record has been saved to the database, **after** the record has been saved, **asynchronously** (sometime after the record has been saved to the database, when the server gets around to it), or on **display** (when the record is requested from the database to be shown on a form):

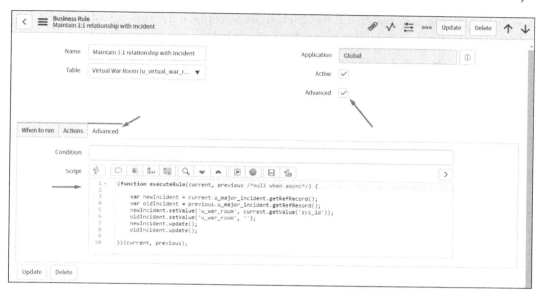

Display business rules are a special sort which execute on the server whenever a record that matches the condition in the **When to run** section is… well, displayed on a form. These business rules have access to a special object called g_scratchpad. This object can store data from the server-side script, and it can be accessed through any client-side script. In this way, you can easily present data from the server, to the client, under a given set of conditions.

Client scripts and catalog client scripts

Executes on: client

Client scripts and catalog client scripts are virtually the exact same sort of script. The differences are that client scripts execute on a form with a certain type of record, whereas catalog client scripts execute on a certain catalog item, or variable set within a catalog item.

In either case, both script types execute exclusively on the client (the user's browser). As such, they unfortunately do not have access to some very useful server-side APIs, but there are ways around that. We'll get into how to execute server-side code and APIs from a client-side script (and return the result) in a later chapter.

Client scripts can be used to show and hide options within a drop-down list, add messages to fields, show alerts to the user, or even replace the functionality of UI policy actions (though the latter is not recommended).

Depending on the value of the **Type** field, client scripts can run either **onLoad** (as soon as the form loads), **onChange** (whenever a specified field's value changes), **onCellEdit** (when a cell on a list changes value), or **onSubmit** (when the user attempts to submit the form):

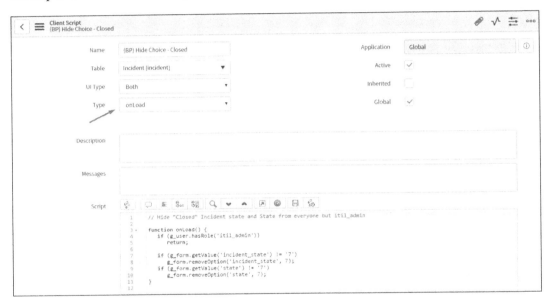

Condition builder (and the URL)

Executes on: server

Perhaps a lesser-known part of the platform that supports scripting, is the **condition builder**. You can use simple scripts to grab and return values to be used within a query, by using the keyword `javascript:` at the beginning of your query parameter:

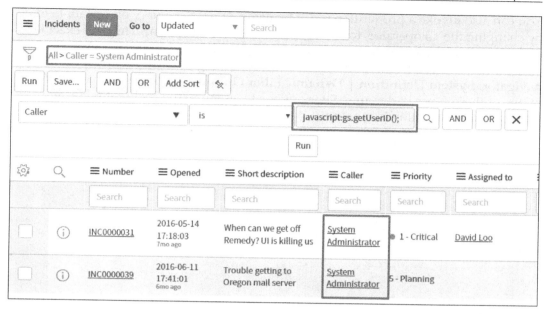

For example, if you navigate to the **Incident** list, and create a new filter that says `Caller, is, javascript:gs.getUserID();` as you can see in the previous screenshot, and click **Run**, then you'll be presented with a list of all incidents for which your user account (or the user account you're impersonating) is the **Caller**. If you then right-click the last query breadcrumb and click **Copy URL** as you can see in the following screenshot, the URL will contain the JavaScript code you used to retrieve your tickets as part of the encoded query (the part of the URL following `sysparm_query=`). If you give this link to another user, they'll see the tickets for which **they** are the caller, rather than you:

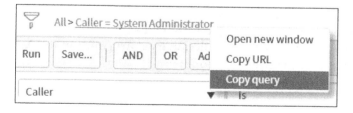

You can also invoke a pre-written script by using a `dynamic` query on certain fields by changing the `is` operator, to `is (dynamic)` (if it is an option). This will execute a server-side script and return appropriate values to be used. These dynamic filter options can be created and modified from the following module in the application navigator: **System Definition | Dynamic Filter Options**. You can see an example of one of these types of dynamic filter options by going to the **Incident** table, and filtering using the following query:

```
[Assigned to]  [is (dynamic)]  [Me]
```

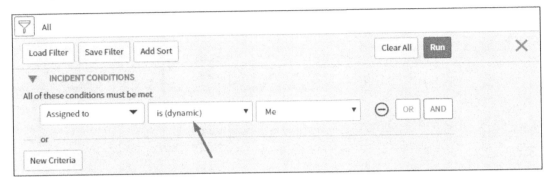

Default value

Executes on: server

Like many fields within ServiceNow, the default value field accepts JavaScript by prefacing it with the `javascript:` keyword, just like in the condition builder. Scripts within this field even have access to the `current` object, and you can dot-walk through reference fields in them.

For example, let's say you want the **Country** field in a given table to be set to the same value as the **Country** field on the **Caller's user account**. To accomplish this, you could navigate to the **Country** field's dictionary entry, and set its **Default Value** to: `javascript:current.caller_id.country`.

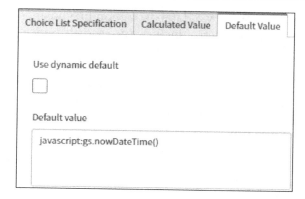

You can also use pre-defined/pre-written scripts as the default value, by checking the **Use dynamic default** checkbox. This will display a new reference field which allows you to select a dynamic default from the **Dynamic Filter Options** [sys_filter_option_dynamic] table.

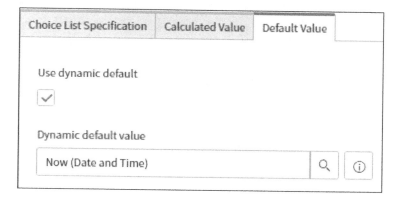

Script includes

Executes on: server

A script include is a repository for reusable code. It is available and executes on the server, and doesn't need to be included in a page or loaded with a form. Any code that executes **server-side** and in the same scope as the script include, can call it like any other API in the system.

script includes are not triggered by a database action like business rules are, or by an event like client scripts. Instead, script includes are scripts which exist on the server, and are called from other server-side scripts. You cannot directly call a script include from a client-side script, but you can make a script include accessible from a client-side script (though it still executes on the server) by making it extend the GlideAjax class. More on GlideAjax and how to use it in a future chapter. For now, suffice it to say that script includes only execute on the server, and typically only when called from another server-side script.

UI actions

Executes on: client and/or server

UI actions correspond to buttons in the banner, links under **Related Links** in the form, options in the context menu, and a few other places:

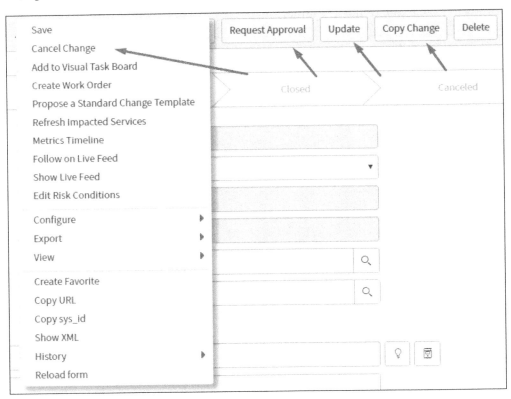

Clicking on a UI action typically results in a list or form being submitted and reloaded, so UI actions can be configured to run either client-side before the submission, or server-side after the submission (but before the reload). It is also possible to configure a UI Action to run some code on the client, and other code on the server.

As with most condition fields, the conditions for whether to display the UI action are evaluated on the server. This can have meaningful consequences. For example, consider a UI action that's configured to only be visible when the **State** field is set to **Pending**. In this case, you would have to save the form and reload it with the **State** field set to **Pending**, before the UI action's condition will be re-evaluated and the UI action will be displayed on the form.

UI policies and catalog UI policies
Executes on: client

UI policies and catalog UI policies define the behavior and visibility of fields on forms and catalog items. UI policies operate on a specific table, while catalog UI policies operate on a specific catalog item or variable set.

UI policies and catalog UI policies operate entirely client side.

UI scripts
Executes on: client

UI scripts are a lot like script includes. While script includes are libraries of code that are available to any script running **server-side**, UI scripts are libraries of code which are available to any script which runs **client-side**, on a page where the UI script is included. If the UI script has the **Global** tick-box checked, then code within it will be included on every form, list, and page on the client, except on the Service Portal. To include a UI Script on Service Portal pages, you can add it as a **JS Include**. More information on this, should you ever need to do it, can be found at: `http://attachments.sngeek.com/`.

UI scripts are a great way to avoid re-writing the same code over and over, and maintain a central repository for a given set of methods or APIs. This can save you time, and help with maintainability.

Of course, having code available on the client means that it must be sent from the server to the client, and be loaded in the user's browser. This can have performance implications during page-loads, and whenever these scripts are invoked. For this reason, it is wise to be judicious about using the **Global** tick-box on UI scripts. Instead, it would be wise to specifically load these scripts on pages and tables where you know they'll be used, and avoid loading them when they don't serve a purpose.

Workflow activities

Executes on: server

Workflow activities always execute on the server by nature and design. These scriptable activities obviously include the **Run script** workflow activity, but also include activities like **Create task**, or the **If** conditional activity. These workflow activity scripts have access to the current object, and are evaluated at the time the activity is invoked via the workflow process. If an activity is not invoked through the natural progression of the workflow, then the script(s) it contains will also not be run.

In addition to any **Script** fields, all conditions are also evaluated on the server, which means that they are not re-evaluated, and the workflow will not progress past a blocking **If** activity, until a record is saved to, or updated in the database.

Workflows also contain a special scratchpad object: an empty object which allows your activities to store and retrieve data, effectively facilitating cross-communication between the different workflow activities. For example, if I have a **Run script** activity which checks some record for some value, I might want to pass the result of that check to another workflow activity so that it can use it in its **Condition** field.

In the new **Kingston** release of ServiceNow's Now platform, the workflow wf_ context and wf_executing scratchpads support encryption! However, in order to activate that functionality, you must request the plugin (com.snc.encrypted. scratchpad) through a request in the ServiceNow HI customer service portal (hi. service-now.com).

Integrated development environment

In previous versions of ServiceNow, **Script** fields consisted of little more than string text fields with some syntax highlighting. However, in Geneva and later, the **Script** fields have become more IDE-like. These fields which are designed to accept scripts now support more advanced syntax highlighting, error checking (otherwise known as **Linting**), and even some degree of intellisense-style code auto-completion for known APIs:

For server-side scripts with access to the `current` object for example, the new **Script** field IDE will even auto-complete and predict field names (though this only works on table-specific records after the record has been saved):

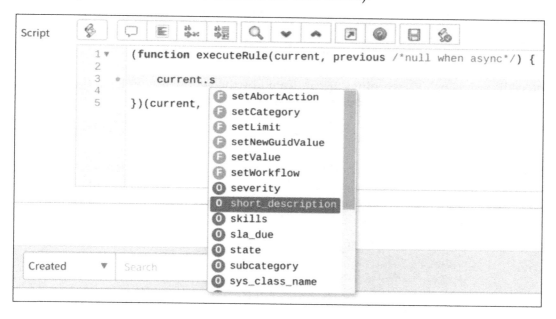

If it is not already activated on your instance, you can enable this functionality by activating the syntax editor plugin (`com.glide.syntax_editor`).

In the event of an error, the syntax editor will parse your code and attempt to detect the error for you, highlighting the appropriate line. If you attempt to submit the form, saving the code with the syntax error, a warning will be shown after the field and the update will be rejected:

```
Script
 1 ▾    (function executeRule(current, previous /*null when async*/) {
 2
 3 ●        current.setValue('short_description', 'shortDescVal");
 4 ●
 5 ●    })(current, previous);

      Could not save record because of a compile error: JavaScript parse error at line (3) column (55) problem = unterminated string literal (<refname>; line 3)
```

Warnings (in contrast with errors) will also be shown in the editor, but will not prevent the update from being saved to the database. This is a good thing, because occasionally the ServiceNow/Now script editor will (very rarely) be mistaken about some warnings.

While errors are indicated by a red dot in the editor (as on lines 3 and 5 in the preceding screenshot), warnings are indicated by the yellow dot on the left of the editor (as on line 4 in the preceding screenshot).

Script tree

Certain script records, such as business rules, have an easy way to view the glide script API tree, which gives you an expandable tree-view of the server side glide API, which you can see by clicking the **Toggle script tree** arrow at the top-right of the script editor:

```
Script
 1 ▾    (function executeRule(current, previous /*null when async*/) {      ⊞ 🗀 Fields
 2                                                                          ⊞ 🗀 GlideRecord
 3          var a = beginningOfYesterday();                                 ⊞ 🗀 GlideElement
 4                                                                          ⊞ 🗀 System
 5      })(current, previous);                                              ⊞ 🗀 System Date/Time
 6                                                                          ⊟ 🗀 System Logging
 7                                                                              ● debug
 8                                                                              ● error
 9                                                                              ● info
10                                                                              ● isDebugging
11                                                                              ● log
12                                                                              ● logError
13                                                                              ● logWarning
14                                                                              ● warn
15                                                                          ⊞ 🗀 GlideAggregate
16
17
18
19
20
21
22
```

Simply clicking on the API in the list will not auto-populate the full call, but it will populate the method call. For example, expanding the system tree, and clicking on `addInfoMessage`, it will populate `addInfoMessage(Object, String)`. You will have to write parent-object call (`gs.`).

The script tree is a great way to get a quick reference as to the exact methods available in the API you're using.

Script auto-completion

The script editor provides keyboard and action shortcuts that trigger assistive functionality for writing code and completing API calls. Here are a few examples.

While writing code, typing a period (`.`) after a valid class name or reference will open the auto-complete dialog, displaying the documented callable methods of that class:

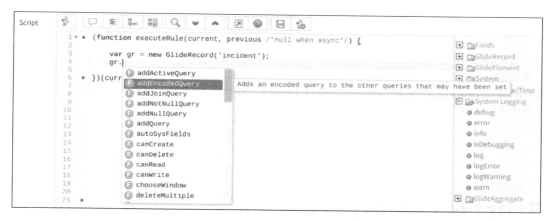

The script editor browser-based IDE can also auto-complete more than just method names. By pressing *Ctrl + Spacebar* while typing, the script editor will auto-complete:

- Class names
- Function names
- Object names
- Variable names

Just as with the other auto-completions, selecting an entry will display a short description of the class or function:

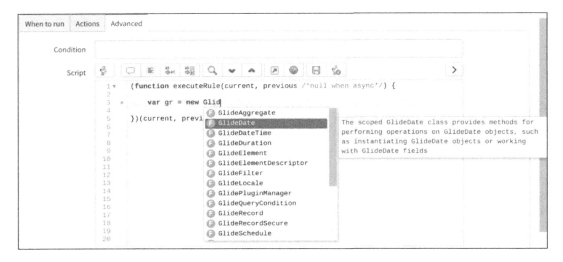

One more way to auto-complete your code (or at least get some help), is to type a documented class or function, and then type an open parenthesis: (. This will indicate what arguments the function or object constructor method expects, and what data type it expects it to be:

Script editor macros

The ServiceNow script editor/integrated IDE supports macros, which can be accessed by typing a keyword, and then pressing *Tab*. This feature is still relatively seldom-used, and we hope that ServiceNow will continue to expand it. Let's look at some of the script editor macros that are built-in, and then we'll make some enhancements to them and see how we can create a custom script editor macro ourselves! Before we get started though, remember that you can access the list and description of script editor macros any time, by typing help followed by the *Tab* key.

Documentation macro

The first editor macro is doc. Typing doc into a **Script** field and pressing *Tab* will populate some JSDoc-type headers for a function/method, including things like a section for a description of the code, what it expects as parameters, and what it returns.

JSDoc is an important JavaScript documentation standard which organizes and simplifies your code documentation so that IDEs can read and present it to anyone who may call your code in the future, as instructions on how to call it, and what to expect from it:

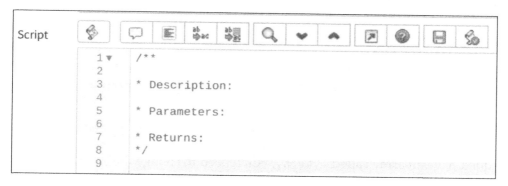

The script editor can also automatically generate a method for use within a script include, which already has the JSDoc header included. This isn't exactly standard JSDoc formatting, but it provides some basic interface information to anyone who's trying to read or reference your code, which is essential!

As you can see in the following screenshot, the macro also does not populate the method name (before the colon), input parameters (between the parentheses), and code. It's expected that you'll populate this information after the macro generates the scaffolding of the methods:

When defining a script editor macro, there's a way to define where the user's cursor ends up after the macro text is generated. We'll learn more about that shortly, when we update the method macro to be a little more helpful!

For-loop macro

A `for` loop in JavaScript is generally used to iterate over each instance of something, or to go through each child member of an object or array. For example, you might want to iterate over every member variable in an array.

You can easily generate the scaffolding of a `for` loop by typing for and pressing *Tab*. This will iterate over each element in an array called `myArray`. Of course, assuming you don't have an array called `myArray`, you'll need to change this to fit the correct name of your array variable. This is common throughout script editor macros, as they only provide a static scaffolding which you'll need to adjust to fit your purpose:

GlideRecord macros

Two macros you might just find yourself using frequently, are `vargr` and `vargror`. Both of these macros generate a GlideRecord and query.

`Vargr` adds a single query condition, but of course you're able to add more. It also generates an if block that's triggered if a record is found matching your query.

`Vargror` on the other hand, adds a condition with an `or` condition attached to it, and a `while` loop rather than an `if` block:

```
Script        🎨   💬  📧  📑  📑  🔍  ⌄  ⌃   ↗  ❓  💾  🎨
     1     //vargr:
     2     var gr = new GlideRecord("");
     3     gr.addQuery("name", "value");
     4     gr.query();
     5 ▼   if (gr.next()) {
     6
     7     }
     8
     9     //vargror:
    10     var gr = new GlideRecord('');
    11
    12     var qc = gr.addQuery('field', 'value1');
    13
    14     qc.addOrCondition('field', 'value2');
    15     gr.query();
    16
    17 ▼   while (gr.next()) {
    18
    19
    20     }|
```

Neither the `vargr`, nor `vargror` macros utilize the appropriate asynchronous client side syntax, which we'll learn about in a later chapter. As a self-study exercise, you might want to create a new syntax editor macro that generates an asynchronous client-side GlideRecord query. If you have questions about this, or almost anything else in ServiceNow, you can ask them at www.snprotips.com/help

Demo

There is already a macro for scaffolding out a for loop (Hint: It's `for`), so let's build one for a `do-while` loop.

If you're not familiar with a `do-while` loop, it's just like a `while` loop, except that the `do` comes before the `while`, so the code block executes at least once before the conditions are evaluated (whether they would evaluate to true or not). If the conditions in the `while` expression evaluate to a truthy value, then the `do` block executes **again**, until the condition evaluates to a falsey value. A `do-while` loop generally looks something like this:

```
do {
/*code that will execute at least once*/
} while(/*condition*/);
```

To create our own editor macro, let's follow the following steps:

1. In the application navigator, head over to **System Definition | Syntax Editor Macros**.

2. At the top of that list, click on the blue **New** button to create a new syntax editor macro.

3. In the **Name** field, enter the string of text that you'd like to use to trigger the macro. Since we're writing a `do-while` macro, let's use the string `dowhile` as our macro name.

4. In the **Comments** field, we'll write a description of what the macro generates. Let's enter something like `A typical do-while code block, with a blank condition at the end.`

 After we save this record, triggering the help syntax editor macro by typing `help` and then pressing *Tab* will include this help text next to the macro name.

5. In the **Text** field, enter the following code. The `$0` indicates where the user's cursor should land after the macro is triggered:

    ```
    do {
    $0
    } while(/*condition*/);
    ```

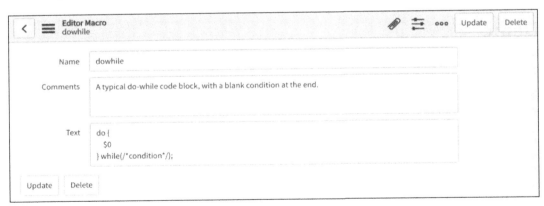

Right-click on the header, and click **Save** to submit the record to the database. From now on, you'll be able to type `dowhile` into any **Script** field, press *Tab*, and this macro will appear in the script editor!

Summary

In this chapter, we learned about when to utilize scripting in ServiceNow, as well as when not to (such as whenever it can be done using out-of-the-box functionality). We learned the differences between client-side and server-side scripts, as well as detailed examples of various types of different script records which execute client-side, server-side, or both. Finally, we learned about the built-in script editor IDE that ServiceNow provides, some of the script editor's available macros, and how to make new script editor macros!

The Server-Side Glide API

9

In 2003, CEO Fred Luddy started a company called **GlideSoft**, which specialized in IT service management applications. Three years later, the company changed its name to **ServiceNow**, but the **Glide** name stuck for the API, which is why we have APIs like GlideSystem (gs) and GlideRecord. Since then, ServiceNow has renamed its namesake platform from *the ServiceNow platform* to *the Now platform*, though the company name remains ServiceNow.

The Glide API is available on both the server and the client (though only a subset of the API is available on the client), and it consists of several classes which we'll learn about in this chapter; including:

- Server-side Glide classes:
    - GlideRecord
    - GlideAggregate
    - GlideElement
    - GlideDate and GlideDateTime
    - GlideSession
    - GlideSystem

- Client-side Glide classes:
    - GlideRecord
    - GlideAjax
    - GlideForm
    - GlideList2
    - GlideMenu
    - GlideUser

Each class in the Glide API may consist of methods (executable functions within the class), and properties (variables stored within the class, which may be set on initialization of a new instance of the class).

This chapter largely consists of details about most of the APIs you're likely to commonly use in ServiceNow development. We recommend that you read through it once, and then dog-ear this chapter so that you can come back to it for reference later on.

The structure of an API class

First, let's define a few terms. According to Mozilla's object-oriented JavaScript documentation, JavaScript is really a **classless** language. However, `class` syntax was added on top of the language, so in JavaScript, a **class** is sort of like a template for an object. A class is technically an object as well. A class definition pre-defines the methods and properties of an object generated from the class. Most experienced JavaScript developers will be familiar with a similar concept: object **prototypes**.

An **object** therefore, in this context, is simply an instance of a **class**! These classes are only slightly different from the prototype constructors you're probably familiar with, and **instances** of these classes are generated in the same way as with prototypal notation: using the `new` keyword.

```
var grIncident = new GlideRecord('incident');
```

A **method** is a function or subroutine that's declared as part of a class (and any objects that are instances of that class).

A **constructor** is a special type of function that runs when an object is declared as a new instance of a class using the `new` keyword. In ServiceNow's server-side scripts (script includes, specifically), this constructor function is usually called initialize. Any arguments passed into the class during instantiation (using the `new` keyword) will be passed into this function, which builds the object that will be returned.

Naming convention dictates that while variable names (including function names) use camelCase capitalization, class names and stand-alone constructor function names use SentenceCase capitalization.

Here's an example of what a very simple class might look like:

```
var MyClass = Class.create();
MyClass.prototype = {
    initialize: function(initArg) {
        this.localProperty = initArg;
    },
    getLocalProperty: function() {
        return this.localProperty;
    },
    type: 'MyClass'
};
```

Now let's break this down line-by-line, and see how it works.

On *line 1*, we declare our class and give it a name (`MyClass`) using a special ServiceNow API: `Class.create()`. JavaScript doesn't technically have a data type called `Class`; at least not in ES5, which is the version of JavaScript that executes on the server. Instead, this code relies on function/object prototype extensions. In order to simplify this, and provide syntax more similar to the backend Java (and more similar to what most object-oriented programming languages use), ServiceNow provides `Class.create()` as a simple way to generate a basic class-esque object.

On *line 2* and onward, we take this basic class scaffolding that we generated on line one, and extend that prototype by adding some stuff to it (everything between the curly braces: { and }).

On *line 3*, we declare the `initialize` method. This is a special method of our class, which is called automatically whenever a new object is generated (instantiated) from our class using the `new` keyword like so:

```
var myObj = new MyClass('input');
```

Any arguments passed into this instantiation process (the string `input` in the preceding case), are passed into this initialize method.

Next, on *line 4*, we set a property in the scope of the instantiated object using the keyword `this`. In this case, any time we create an instance of this class, the property called `localProperty` will be initialized with the value that was passed into the constructor function (`initArg`).

On *line 6*, we declare another method called `getLocalProperty`. This is a method that can be called from objects created from our class, and which (on *line 7*) returns the value of the property that was set on initialization.

Finally, on *line 9*, we declare the type property of our class (and instantiated objects). This is just a string that you can access to determine what class child objects were created from.

Server-side APIs

Server-side API consists of classes and methods that are available to scripts executing on the server. When a script executes on the server, it is able to do so because of an open-source implementation of JavaScript, written in the Java programming language, called **Mozilla Rhino**. This allows us to interact with Java applications such as ServiceNow by scripting in JavaScript, despite the fact that the languages are not inherently cross-compatible.

GlideRecord

The GlideRecord class is one of the most ubiquitous and useful classes in ServiceNow. Its primary function is to query a database table, and present values corresponding to each record in that table, that matches a given query. It can also be used to add, modify, or delete records. A GlideRecord object consists of properties with names corresponding to each field in the table. In the client-side Glide API, these properties usually contain strings, whereas on the server-side API, these properties contain GlideElement JavaScript Objects with their own methods and properties.

Initialize

A GlideRecord object must first be initialized by using the `new` keyword (which calls the `initialize()` constructor method) and passing in a table name as a string. This tells the new GlideRecord object what table any subsequent queries or new records are created on.

Example usage

Initialize a new GlideRecord object on the Incident table, and store it in the `gr` variable:

```
var grIncident = new GlideRecord('incident');
grIncident.addActiveQuery();
grIncident.query();
while (grIncident.next()) {
    //do something
}
```

addQuery()

The addQuery() method of the GlideRecord class can be called in three different ways, depending on whether one, two, or three arguments are supplied to it. If one argument is passed into the addQuery() method, then it'll assume that the argument is an encoded query. An encoded query is a single string that represents all of the conditions in a single query (or even multiple queries)!

There isn't any official documentation on how to construct an encoded query (though it isn't hard to figure out), but there is a very easy way to build one yourself — simply navigate to the table you want to run the query on, and use the query builder! For example, here's a query on the **Incident** table where the **Assigned to** user is active, and either the Incident is active, or the **State** is set to **New**, **In Progress**, or **On Hold**:

You can build a filter on a given table using the query builder, and then apply that same filter to your GlideRecord query by simply right-clicking the last condition in the query breadcrumbs above the list view, and clicking on **Copy query**:

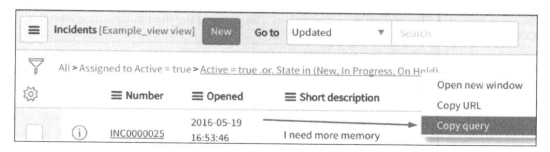

This is similar in functionality to the `addEncodedQuery()` method.

You'll see an example of this single-argument usage in the following section. On the other hand, if you pass in two arguments, then it is assumed that the first argument is the field name, and the second argument is the expected value.

Finally, if you pass in three arguments to the `addQuery()` method, you may specify not only a field and value, but an operator between them. Operators that you can use as the second argument in this case, include some rather standard operators with obvious meaning, as well as some others for more advanced functionality. You'll find a list of available operators in the following table.

Available query operators

The following table displays the query operators (which can be specified as the second argument in a GlideRecord `addQuery()` method call). These operators determine how the database query is formed on the server.

Operator	Meaning
= (equals)	The field (the first argument) must be equal to the value (the third argument).
> (greater than)	The field specified must contain a value greater than the value specified in the third argument.
< (less than)	The field must contain a value less than the value specified.
>= (greater than or equal to)	The field in the first argument must contain a value that is greater than or equal to the value specified in the third argument.
<= (less than or equal to)	The field must contain a value less than or equal to the value specified.
STARTSWITH	The field must contain a value which, as a string, starts with the value specified.
CONTAINS	The value of the field must contain the string specified in the third argument.
DOES NOT CONTAIN	The opposite of CONTAINS. The value of the field must not contain the value specified.
IN	If this is the second argument when calling the `addQuery()` method, then the third argument should contain a comma-separated list of one or more values. The value of the field specified in the first argument must then be one of the values specified in the third. Example: `gr.addQuery('state', 'IN', '1,3,5');`

Operator	Meaning
NOT IN	The reverse of IN, that is, the value of the field specified in the first argument must not also exist within the comma-separated list of values specified within the third argument.
ENDSWITH	The field value must end with the value specified in the third argument.

INSTANCEOF	This is a special operator that is meant to be used on base or parent tables, to determine if a given record's table is an instance of a given sub-table. In this case, you would specify sys_class_ name as the first argument, INSTANCEOF as the second argument, and the other table name as the third argument. For example, you might want to query the base system task table, and only see requests. The query for that would look like this:
	
	`gr.addQuery('sys_class_name', 'INSTANCEOF', 'sc_`
	`request');`
	
	This way, even if you were to extend the sc_request table, you would still see all of those records in the results of this query, since they would be in a table that was an instance of (extended from) the sc_request table.

Example usage

With a single argument, that argument is assumed to be an encoded query:

```
var gr = new GlideRecord('incident');
var encodedQuery = 'assigned_to.active=true^active=true^ORstate
IN1,2,3';
gr.addQuery(encodedQuery);
```

With two arguments, it is assumed that the first is a field name, and the second is a value to compare that field's value to for equivalency:

```
var gr = new GlideRecord('incident');
gr.addQuery('number', 'INC0012345');
```

With three arguments, the first is assumed to be a field name, the second is an operator, and the third is a value to compare the value of the first to:

```
var gr = new GlideRecord('incident');
gr.addQuery('closed_at', '>', gs.nowDateTime());
```

Or you can use the CONTAINS operator:

```
var gr = new GlideRecord('incident');
gr.addQuery('number', 'CONTAINS', '123');
```

Any of the operators listed in the table earlier in this chapter can be used in place of CONTAINS in the preceding code snippet.

addActiveQuery()

addActiveQuery() is a simple API method that accepts no arguments, but adds a query requiring that the **active** field must be **true**. It has identical functionality as if you were to write gr.addQuery('active', 'true').

addNullQuery() and addNotNullQuery()

Both addNullQuery() and addNotNullQuery() accept a single argument; a string, indicating which field should be checked.

When addNullQuery() is called on a GlideRecord object, it adds a condition to your query, stating that the field passed into the method call must be null (empty).

On the other hand, when the addNotNullQuery() method is called with a field name as an argument, a condition is added to your query stating just the opposite—that the field must contain a value—any value. It must be NotNull.

Example usage

Here, on lines two and three, we add one NullQuery and one NotNullQuery, respectively for two different fields:

```
var gr = new GlideRecord('sc_request');
gr.addNullQuery('assigned_to');
gr.addNotNullQuery('assignment_group');
gr.query();
while (gr.next()) {
    //do something
}
```

In this case, our query will return results where the assignment_group field is not blank, but the assigned_to field is blank.

canRead(), canWrite(), canCreate(), and canDelete()

These four methods can be called on a GlideRecord without any arguments, and each will return a Boolean `true`/`false` value, indicating whether the record can be read, written to, created, or deleted by the current user.

These methods take no arguments, because they apply to the entire record rather than to a given field.

Example usage

While there are use cases for calling these methods on GlideRecords inside of scripts, they are most useful inside of **Condition** fields; for example, those which determine visibility of UI actions, as you can see in the screenshot after the example code snippet:

```
current.canCreate() && gs.hasRole('itil')
```

Condition	current.canCreate()

These two conditions check whether the user can create records in that table, and whether the user has the `itil` role.

> Documenting your code—telling other developers who might read it, both what you're doing, and (most importantly) why—is critically important to being a good developer. However, condition fields must be written on a single line. There is a character limit in that field, but whenever possible, you can still comment your code using inline comments like so:
>
> ```
> current.canRead() /*User can read this record*/ &&
> gs.hasRole('admin') /*AND the user has the Admin role*/
> ```

deleteRecord() and deleteMultiple()

These two methods are for the deletion of one or more records from the database.

It should be made clear that deletion of records in ServiceNow generally is, and should be, a rare occurrence. Whenever possible, it is best to deactivate or otherwise mark a record as no longer in use, for historical and tracking purposes.

Neither `deleteRecord()` nor `deleteMultiple()` take any arguments, as both are called as methods of a specific GlideRecord object upon which they act. However, the similarities end there, as the behavior and usage of these methods are quite different.

`deleteRecord()` is used to delete a single record (in a GlideRecord) from the database. `deleteMultiple()` on the other hand, is used to delete all database records that match a given query. However, it is important to remember this: **do not** use `deleteMultiple()` on tables that contain currency fields. Instead, delete all such records one at a time, using `deleteRecord()` in this case.

Example usage

The `deleteMultiple()` method can be called either after the `query()`, or without it, but without calling `next()`:

```
var query = 'active=false^closed_atRELATIVELT@year@ago@2'; //Tickets
closed more than 2 years ago
var gr = new GlideRecord('incident');
gr.addQuery(query);
gr.deleteMultiple();
```

In this case, I'm running this on the **Incident** table, which in my instance does not have any currency fields.

Again, this method should not be called on any tables that contain currency fields due to a limitation in ServiceNow. It should also not be used in conjunction with `setLimit()`. Instead, use the following `deleteRecord()` syntax:

```
var query = 'active=false^closed_atRELATIVELT@year@ago@2'; //Tickets
closed more than 2 years ago
var gr = new GlideRecord('incident');
gr.addQuery(query);
gr.query();
while (gr.next()) {
    gr.deleteRecord();
}
```

Both of these blocks of code will delete all records matching the encoded query stored in the `query` variable. The query pulls a list of all incidents that are not active, which were closed more than two years ago, as a company might want to delete records after two years to keep the **Task** [`task`] table light.

get()

The `get()` method is an excellent shorthand for a very simple, single-condition query. It will only return one record. This method can accept either one or two arguments.

If one argument is supplied, it is expected that it'll be the `sys_id` of a record in the table specified when the GlideRecord object was instantiated.

If two arguments are specified, it is expected that the first argument will be a field name, and the second will be the value to filter by on that field. You cannot specify three arguments, which means it is not possible to use any special operators such as `CONTAINS` or `>`.

The `get()` method will only return one record, similar to using `gr.setLimit(1);`, or only calling `gr.next();` once. Even if multiple records are returned from your query (if two arguments are specified).

Calling the GlideRecord `get()` method effectively combines the steps of adding a query, calling .query(), and calling .next(), all into one step. The following example demonstrates how it works.

Example usage

With one argument, `get()` expects a `sys_id`:

```
var recordSysID = '46f09e75a9fe198100f4ffd8d366d17b';
var gr = new GlideRecord('incident');
if (gr.get(recordSysID)) {
    //do something with the record
} else {
    //do something when the record is not found
}
```

With two arguments, `get()` expects that the first argument will be the field name, and the second will be a value to compare the field value to. The following code block will return one record—the first record that matches the specified query:

```
var gr = new GlideRecord('incident');
if (gr.get('number', 'INC0000025')) {
    //do something with the record
} else {
    //do something when the record is not found
}
```

getDisplayValue()

As we learned in an earlier chapter, each table has one value that's set as the display value. This is the value that is displayed when the record is referenced in reference fields or elsewhere in the system. This field is usually, but not always, unique. The reference field can be changed by altering the dictionary record for a column in the table, but only one field can be the display value in a given table at one time. Setting a new field's **Display value** field to **true** will automatically set that field to **false** on the previous display value's dictionary entry, thus ensuring that there is only one display value at a time.

`getDisplayValue()` is quite simple, as it accepts no arguments, and returns the value of whatever field is set as the display value for the record upon which it's called.

Example usage

The following code snippet will set the value of the `displayVal` variable to `INC0010014`. INC0010014 happens to be the value of the **Number** [number] field of the incident for which the `sys_id` was passed into the `get()` API, since number is the field set as the display value in the **Incident** table:

```
var gr = new GlideRecord('incident');
gr.get('46f09e75a9fe198100f4ffd8d366d17b');
var displayVal = gr.getDisplayValue();
```

The returned value is a **primitive** (a string), so the `displayVal` variable would now contain a string containing the Incident number.

getValue() and getUniqueValue()

Both the `getValue()` and `getUniqueValue()` methods will return a value from the GlideRecord upon which they're called.

`getUniqueValue()` accepts no arguments, and simply returns the primary key (the `sys_id`) of the record.

`getValue()` on the other hand, can return the value from any table column (including `sys_id`). It accepts one argument—a field name, and will return the value therein.

Example usage

`getUniqueValue()` doesn't take any arguments, and it's a quick and easy way to retrieve the `sys_id` of a given record.

getValue() on the other hand, returns the value of a specific field or column. This can be the sys_id column, or any other column that might contain a value; simply pass the name of the field into getValue(), and it will return a primitive (string) value matching the contents of the field on the specified record:

```
var gr = new GlideRecord('incident');
gr.get('46f09e75a9fe198100f4ffd8d366d17b');
var sysIDVal = gr.getValue('sys_id');
var incNumber = gr.getValue('number');
```

hasNext()

hasNext() is a simple method that returns a Boolean value, indicating whether or not there are more records returned from a GlideRecord query, which can be accessed using .next().

If, for example, your query returns three records, you might call .next() after the query to get the first record. At this point, hasNext() will return true. Calling next() again to get the second record will leave us with one left, so once again, hasNext() will return true. However, calling next() one more time will populate the third and final record into the GlideRecord object. There being no further records to grab, if we call hasNext() once more at this point, it will return false.

Example usage

Here, we use hasNext() as the loop condition, and call next() inside the loop:

```
var query = 'active=false^closed_atRELATIVELT@year@ago@2';
var gr = new GlideRecord('incident');
gr.addQuery(query);
gr.query();
while (gr.hasNext()) {
    gr.next();
    //do something
}
```

We could simplify this loop by using .next() in the loop condition, since it returns true (when called) if it was successful in pulling a new record, and false if it wasn't. next() is documented later in this chapter. There are use-cases for using hasNext() over next(), but next() is far more common.

initialize() and insert()

If you want to create a new record in the database, you're generally going to need to call two methods: `initialize()` and `insert()`, although it is possible to generate a new record by simply using `insert()`.

Neither method takes any arguments, and their uses are functionally linked.

When you create a new GlideRecord, you're effectively generating an object that has the potential to be populated with some data. Think of this object like a blank spreadsheet. Whether you want to read data out of the spreadsheet, or save data to it, the first thing you need to do is figure out what the column headers should be. This will tell you what data goes where! This is essentially the function of the `initialize()` API.

When you create a new GlideRecord, define your filter query, and run the `.query()` method, it talks to the database and sets up the GlideRecord object so that it contains a property for each field that exists in the database, for the table you've specified. Think of these empty properties like column headers in our imaginary spreadsheet.

If we call `next()`, the system gets the next (or first) record in the database, and populates all of the GlideRecord object properties (like columns) with the values corresponding to that one record. If we use `setValue()` to modify one of these values, and then call `update()`, the system takes that modified database row and loads it into the database over the existing one, overwriting the old values.

The `initialize()` method of a GlideRecord—unlike that of a script include—does something similar to what `query()` does, in that it gets the basic structure of the database table that the `GlideRecord` corresponds to, filling in the header columns of our imaginary spreadsheet. However, rather than calling `next()` to populate the `GlideRecord` properties with an existing value from the database, we can populate it ourselves, and use `insert()` to push the values we've populated to the database. Any values we don't specify will get their default value, if one is specified.

The short version

The `initialize()` method prepares a GlideRecord to be populated by your script, while the `insert()` method pushes any values you populated it with, to the database.

Example usage

Here, we begin by declaring our GlideRecord object, initializing it on the **Incident** table, and setting a few values.

When we call the `setValue()` method on *lines 3 and 4*, we populate a GlideElement object property within the GlideRecord object, corresponding to the field specified in the first argument of the `setValue()` method call. We set the value to the value specified in the second argument of the `setValue()` call:

```
var gr = new GlideRecord('incident');
gr.initialize();
gr.setValue('short_description', 'Example record');
gr.setValue('description', 'This is a test.');
gr.insert();
```

Finally, on *line 5*, we call the `insert()` method, which pushes the GlideRecord object to the database, at which point a new record is created with the values you specified, and the default values used for any unspecified fields.

It is also possible to insert on an existing GlideRecord, thus effectively creating a duplicate. Consider the following code, which does not use the `initialize()` API:

```
var gr = new GlideRecord('incident');
gr.setLimit(1);
gr.addActiveQuery();
gr.query();
gr.next(); //Load the first active Incident from the database
gr.setValue('active', 'false'); //Set the active field to false
gr.insert(); //Insert a new record with our modification
```

First, we load the first active Incident record from the database, then we modify it by setting the `active` field to `false`. However, until we call the `update()` API, the changes only exist in our local GlideRecord variable (`gr`).

Rather than using the `update()` method of the GlideRecord API, which would have modified the existing record in the database, we used `insert()`.

next()

The `next()` method of the GlideRecord class should be called after a `query()`. Its function is to grab one row from the database table we specified when declaring our GlideRecord object, and populate that object with the values from each column/field in that record/row. This allows you to modify the record and send it back to the database using `setValue()` and `update()`, or you can read values from the record and use them elsewhere in your script by using `getValue()`.

The `next()` method takes no arguments, and returns a Boolean which is true or false depending on whether it successfully found another record or not respectively; thus, the `next()` method call can simultaneously be used as a loop condition.

Example usage

Here, we use the next() method both as an iterator to move to the next record in the database, and as a condition (since it returns true whenever it's successful) in the condition of the while loop:

```
var gr = new GlideRecord('incident');
gr.addQuery('active', 'true');
gr.query();
while (gr.next()) {
    //do something
}
```

Don't get confused between the return value of the next(), and hasNext() methods. next() will return true if it found a next record in the list matching your query filter, and will have **already** loaded it into the GlideRecord object. On the other hand, hasNext() will return true if there exists a next record in the database, but it won't load it up yet. The former tells you about the record you're currently (trying to) iterate into, and the latter looks at the **next** record to see if one exists — but does not move into it like next() does.

orderBy() and orderByDesc()

orderBy() and orderByDesc() both sort the results of your query before they're returned, so that when you iterate through the results using the next() method, you get the results in the appropriate order.

The orderBy() and orderByDesc() methods both accept one argument: The name of a field in the database table specified when instantiating the GlideRecord object you're calling this method on. This is the field that will either be sorted low-to-high/ a-to-z/past-to-present if you used the orderBy() method, or the opposite if you called orderByDesc().

Example usage

orderBy() and orderByDesc() are both called in exactly the same way. Simply specify the field you'd like to sort the results by after your query is run:

```
var gr = new GlideRecord('incident');
gr.addQuery('active', 'true');
gr.orderBy('priority');
gr.query();
while (gr.next()) {
    //do something
}
```

These APIs should be called prior to calling the `query()` method, as the database will sort the query results before returning them to your script.

query()

The `query()` method of the GlideRecord class is one that (unless you use `get()` to retrieve a single record) is used any time you want to use a GlideRecord to retrieve data from the database.

When you call the `query()` method, you're submitting the query to the database. The result is retrieving some data which you can think of like a spreadsheet/list of results. You can iterate through the rows of those results using the `next()` method.

Example usage

Except when using `get()`, or in a situation such as a business rule where a GlideRecord is already defined for you, calling the `query()` method is usually a necessary step before you can do anything to any records that already exist in the database:

```
var gr = new GlideRecord('incident');
gr.addActiveQuery();
gr.orderBy('priority');
gr.query();
while (gr.next()) {
    //do something
}
```

setAbortAction()

This method is one that's most commonly used inside of business rules to abort whatever database action was being performed that triggered the business rule to fire. Calling this method on the `current` object in a business rule means that no changes will be committed to the database.

There are other ways to prevent a database action (data policies and ACLs, for example), but this allows you some finer-grain control over how and when it happens. For example, you might write a script in a business rule which checks several conditions—even conditions based on external records or system properties—and determines whether to abort the database action based on that.

The `setAbortAction()` method accepts one argument: a Boolean. Whatever Boolean value this method was last called with when the script finishes running, will determine whether the database action is actually aborted or not.

In other words, calling `setAbortAction(true)` in one part of your script, and then later calling `setAbortAction(false)`, will result in the database action not being cancelled.

Example usage

This example assumes it's running inside of a before business rule, which means that the current object is pre-populated with a GlideRecord corresponding to whichever record was inserted or updated, triggering the business rule to run:

```
if (current.getValue('active') === 'false') {
    current.setAbortAction(true);
}
if (gs.hasRole('admin')) {
    current.setAbortAction(false);
}
```

You may also default to aborting the action, and then conditionally allow it. In the following example, the operation will only be aborted if the record is not active:

```
current.setAbortAction(true);
if (current.getValue('active') === 'true') {
    current.setAbortAction(false);
}
```

setLimit()

The `setLimit()` method of the GlideRecord class takes one argument: a number corresponding to the maximum number of records that should be returned from the database. This can be used to limit potential performance implications of a large query, or by combining it with `orderBy()` or `orderByDesc()`, and can further extend the usefulness of this method.

Example usage

Let's look at an example where you want to have a script pull up to 10 incidents from the database in order to assign them to a particular user, whose `sys_id` is stored in the `assignee` variable. But you don't just want to assign 10 random incidents from the queue; you would probably want to make sure that you got the highest priority ones first, so we order by the **Priority** field:

```
var gr = new GlideRecord('incident');
gr.addQuery('assignment_group', assignmentGroup);
gr.orderBy('priority');
gr.setLimit(10);
```

```
gr.query();
while (gr.next()) {
    gr.setValue('assigned_to', assignee);
    gr.update();
}
```

setValue()

Except for setting journal fields, `setValue()` is used to update any field value in a GlideRecord object. After updating a field value, you must submit the new data to the database using a method such as `insert()`, `update()`, or `updateMultiple()`.

`setValue()` accepts two arguments: A field name, and a new value for that field. It does not return a value.

You'll often see code (including out-of-the-box code!) that does not use `setValue()`, but instead sets the field directly like so: `current.short_description = 'Example short description';`. This is **not a best practice**. It will technically work (usually), but because of JavaScript's **type coercion** and **pass-by-reference** features, this can cause issues that are extremely difficult to troubleshoot and pin down.

The same rule applies to the `getValue()` method: It should be used nearly any time you need to retrieve a value from a GlideReord field. There are some exceptions to this rule, but you should get into the habit of using `getValue()` and `setValue()` as standard practice.

 You can learn more about the importance of using `getValue()` and `setValue()`, as well as the exceptions to this rule, by checking out the article at `pbr.sngeek.com`.

Example usage

Here, we use `get()` with two arguments to retrieve a RITM (from the `sc_req_item` table) by number, and then we use `setValue()` and `gs.getUserID()` to set the `assigned_to` field to the current user. Finally, we use the `update()` method to commit the change to the database:

```
var ritmGR = new GlideRecord('sc_req_item');
ritmGR.get('number', 'RITM0010455');
ritmGR.setValue('assigned_to', gs.getUserID());
ritmGR.update();
```

setWorkflow()

The `setWorkflow()` method accepts one argument: a Boolean `true`/`false` value. This argument will determine whether any business rules should be triggered by any database actions performed by your GlideRecord script. For example, if you make a change and call the `update()` method, calling `setWorkflow()` and passing in `false` will prevent any business rules that would normally be triggered by that update from running. It also prevents other script engines (such as the workflow engine) and audit scripts from running.

This is exceptionally useful for when you need to make a mass update to a lot of records but you don't want to trigger any additional actions. For example, perhaps an error caused all incidents generated over the past week to be created without a **Description** field value, but you want it to default to the same value as the **Short description** when no other value is specified. Once you've corrected the **Default value** field on that column's dictionary record, you might then want to find all records where the **Description** field is empty but the **Short description** field is not, and set the former to the latter.

To avoid running business rules and sending notifications as a result of that change, you can use the `setWorkflow(false)` API.

This method returns no value.

Example usage

The following script would result in a database record being updated, but no business rules would be triggered by this update:

```
var grRitm = new GlideRecord('sc_req_item');
grRitm.get('number', 'RITM0010455');
grRitm.setValue('assigned_to', gs.getUserID());
grRitm.setWorkflow(false);
grRitm.update();
```

update() and updateMultiple()

Both `update()` and `updateMultiple()` will result in a database update. The main difference is that `update()` operates on one record at a time, whereas `updateMultiple()` updates any and all records returned from your GlideRecord query, without using `next()` to iterate through each one. `update()` returns the Sys ID of the updated record.

`update()` accepts one optional argument: the reason for the update. This reason will be logged in the audit history for the updated record.

`updateMultiple()` on the other hand, accepts no arguments, and returns no value. It should not be used in conjunction with `setLimit()`.

> While it's possible to modify a field's value by using `gr.ield_name = 'new_value';`, this is generally not best except with journal fields. This is especially critical while using `updateMultiple()`. You should never directly set a value like that before using `updateMultiple()`. You must use `setValue()` instead, or the update could ignore the query filter, updating every record in the table. That would be bad. Each field in the database table becomes an element of the GlideRecord object (`gr` in the previous snippet). This element is not just a string or number, but a specific Object type, called a GlideElement. More on that API later in this chapter.

Example usage

Here, we use `update()` to modify a single record:

```
var ritmGR = new GlideRecord('sc_req_item');
ritmGR.get('number', 'RITM0010455');
ritmGR.setValue('assigned_to', gs.getUserID());
ritmGR.update();
```

In the following example, we will demonstrate the `updateMultiple()` method by assigning one user (stored in the `assignee` variable) to all unassigned Incident tickets:

```
var gr = new GlideRecord('incident');
gr.addNullQuery('assigned_to'); //checks for blank assignee field
gr.query();
gr.setValue('assigned_to', assignee);
gr.updateMultiple();
```

Note that we don't use the `next()` method here at all, because we're using the `updateMultiple()` method. We are also sure to use `setValue()`, rather than directly setting the value as a property.

GlideElement

The GlideElement class is not generally instantiated on its own, but it is used for elements in a GlideRecord object, and provides methods for interacting with them. An element generally refers to a data column in the record, such as the number field on a task record, or the `sys_updated_on` field of a record. You can access a GlideElement from a server-side GlideRecord object (for example, by using `gr.number`), or by using the `getElement` method of a GlideRecord object.

Best practice dictates that you **always** use the getter and setter functions: `getValue()`, and `setValue()` if you want to get or set the value of the field. Directly accessing the server-side `GlideElement` property, however, will give you a reference to the GlideElement object.

Let's say for example, that we have a table with a column called `short_description`. When we query this table, we get a GlideRecord object populated with various properties. Each field in the table becomes a property in the GlideRecord object, but those properties are not just strings and numbers and other basic/primitive data types. Instead, each property corresponding to a field in the record is an object that is an instance of the GlideElement class.

That means that the field/property, `gr.short_description`, corresponds to a **GlideElement** object, with all of the methods you'll see next, and more. We're going to cover the most useful methods that developers are likely to use on a relatively frequent basis, here.

The fact that a GlideRecord's properties are objects rather than primitives isn't without implications. Perhaps you've heard JavaScript referred to as a **loosely typed** language. This isn't just a colloquial term; it means that the data types in JavaScript are fluid. In many other languages, when you declare a variable and initialize it, you intrinsically link it to a given data type: string, integer, float, Boolean, and so on. However, in JavaScript, you can declare a `var`, set it to a **string** value, and then later modify its value so it contains a **number**, or any other type—including both **primitive** and **object** types.

This is useful in some situations; for example, you can set the value of the `short_description` field with a line of code such as `gr.short_description = 'New short description."`;. However, as we've mentioned a few times in this chapter, this can actually be a bad thing, since you're overwriting the GlideElement object that used to be in the parent GlideElement object's `short_description` property. Using the GlideRecord's `setValue()` method, however, correctly sets the value within the GlideElement object.

By the same token, due to JavaScript's **pass-by-reference** feature, you should not set a variable using the following syntax:

```
var userReference = gr.assigned_to;
```

The above line of code will **not** set the userReference variable to the **value** of the assigned_to field. Instead, it will set the variable to a **reference** to the **object** that exists at the location gr.assigned_to.

Imagine that we have a GlideRecord object in the variable gr, with a query that should give us two incidents: First INC0000001, and then INC0000002. What do you think would be logged on the last line?

```
var incNumber; //declare above loop to prevent repeat declaration
while (gr.next()) { //Iterate over the two returned Incidents
    //If the number is INC0000001
    if(gr.getValue('number') === 'INC0000001') {
        //set the variable to the "number" property of gr.
        incNumber = gr.number;
    }
}
gs.log(incNumber);
```

You would not be silly to think that this script would print out the Incident number INC0000001, since we only set the variable's value if the Incident number is INC0000001. However, since we are setting the incNumber variable to a reference to the gr.number object rather than a primitive value like a string, it is merely a pointer to the object located at gr.number. When the while loop is finished running, the gr.number variable contains an object with the value INC0000002, so even though we set the variable when gr.number had a value of INC0000001, when the last line runs, the same object contains a different value, so the reference to the object contained in the variable should also contain a different value: INC0000002.

changes(), changesFrom() and changesTo()

The changes(), changesFrom(), and changesTo() methods of the GlideElement class are generally called from within business rules that run before or after a given database update is made. These methods return a Boolean value indicating whether a field has changed at all, whether it's changed from a specified value, or whether it's changed to a specified value, respectively.

The changes() method does not accept any arguments. It doesn't need to, because it's being called from the GlideElement corresponding to the field, so it already knows which field is being checked.

changesFrom() and changesTo() however, both take one argument—a value to compare the old or new value of the field to, respectively.

All three methods return a Boolean true/false indicating whether the expression is accurate, as you can see in the following example usage.

Example usage

Here, imagine we have a record where the active field is set to false because the ticket has been closed for some time. Normally, there would be an ACL or data policy in place to prevent users from reopening such tickets if we didn't want them to, but imagine that in this case, we have no such thing. Instead, just for this demonstration, we're using a business rule to make that determination, because a business rule can be scripted and use more complex logic:

```
if (current.active.changesFrom(false) && !gs.hasRole('admin')) {
    gs.addErrorMessage('Non-admins cannot re-open closed tickets after
they've been deactivated.');
    current.setAbortAction(true);
}
```

As you can see in the preceding example, this script checks two conditions: The active field changes from false, and the user does not have the admin role. If this condition evaluates to true, then we abort the operation and display a message to the user about why we've done that; otherwise, we allow it to go through by simply doing nothing.

In other words, we're allowing admins to reactivate records, but nobody else.

In the condition for the if block, we could also use changes() and compare the new value to true explicitly, or we could use changesTo() instead of changesFrom(), as you can see in the following condition:

```
current.active.changesTo(true) && !gs.hasRole('admin')
```

getDisplayValue()

Both the GlideRecord and GlideElement classes contain a getDisplayValue() method. While the method of the GlideRecord object (gr.getDisplayValue()) gets the display value for the record based on the field that's marked as the display value in the field dictionary, the getDisplayValue() method of the GlideElement class (gr.field_name.getDisplayValue()) gives you the value that is displayed for the field's value.

You might think a field's value and display value are the same, but certain field types can have a disparity between the actual value, and the display value. For example, drop-down fields can have a label as well as a value. It's the value that gets stored in the actual database. The **State** field on **Task** tables are another example, as the value is an integer, but the display value is something else like **Draft** or **Pending**. Similarly, reference fields have both display values (which is generally the record's display value from the table being referenced), and actual values (the sys_id of the referenced record). If you call getValue() and pass in a reference field, you'll get the record's sys_id, but if you use getDisplayValue() on the GlideElement for that field, you'll get the display value—often the number field for task records.

Example usage

Here, we get the ticket number of the parent task from a specified Incident record, and save it into the parentTask variable:

```
var gr = new GlideRecord('incident');
gr.get('46f09e75a9fe198100f4ffd8d366d17b');
var parentTaskNumber = gr.parent.getDisplayValue();
```

You could alternatively **dot-walk** to the referenced record to get the number field's value by using gr.parent.number, but the example above is actually more efficient because it does not require the server to perform a query to look up the referenced record to grab that field's value.

getED()

The getED() method of the GlideElement class is the only way to get a GlideElementDescriptor object, which provides information about specific fields, rather than the data inside those fields.

The GlideElementDescriptor class provides methods that facilitate unique functionality, such as getEncryptionType() and getAttachmentEncryptionType() to get the type of encryption used in the field that the element was acquired for by using getED() if Edge Encryption is enabled on the field. You can also use isEdgeEncrypted() to check whether Edge Encryption is enabled for the field.

You can also use getLabel() or getName() to get the element's field label or field name respectively, and getLength() to get the element's character limit.

Example usage

The following script gets the `short_description` field's element descriptor, and then logs some info about it:

```
var gr = new GlideRecord('incident');
gr.get('46f09e75a9fe198100f4ffd8d366d17b');
var element = gr.short_description.getED();
var description = 'The ' + element.getLabel() + ' field has the name:
' + element.getName() + '. ';
if (element.isEdgeEncrypted()) {
    description += 'It is ' + element.getEncryptionType() + '
encrypted.';
}
gs.info(description);
```

This code will return `The Short description field has the name: short_description`. —if it's encrypted, it'll also add a sentence stating the encryption type.

getReferenceTable() and getRefRecord()

These two methods of the GlideElement class exist to retrieve information about reference fields and the data that they reference.

Neither method accepts an argument (they don't need to, as they're called from the GlideElement containing the reference information).

The `getReferenceTable()` method returns the name of the table being referenced by the given reference element. The `getRefRecord()` method on the other hand, returns a GlideRecord object that's pre-populated with the record, the `sys_id` for which is the value of the field. In other words, the record referenced in that reference field is returned.

Example usage

Here, we print out some data about the parent field on a given Incident record:

```
var gr = new GlideRecord('incident');
gr.get('46f09e75a9fe198100f4ffd8d366d17b');
var tableName = gr.parent.getReferenceTable();
var parentGR = gr.parent.getRefRecord();
gs.info('The Parent field references the ' + tableName +
' table, and currently contains the ' + parentGR.getDisplayValue()
+ ' record.');
```

nil()

This nil() method determines if a field is null or empty. It's usually the same result as a Boolean expression comparing the results of calling getValue() and passing in the field name, with a blank string.

nil() returns a Boolean value—true if the field is null or empty, and false if it contains a value.

Example usage

The following snippet checks if a specified Incident isn't assigned to anyone. If it's not assigned, the script logs a message to the system logs:

```
var gr = new GlideRecord('incident');
gr.get('46f09e75a9fe198100f4ffd8d366d17b');
if (gr.assigned_to.nil()) {
    gs.info('Please assign ' + gr.getValue('number') + ' to a user.');
}
```

toString()

The toString() method of the GlideElement class returns the field's value as a string. In most cases, this is essentially the same as the result of calling getValue() on the GlideRecord object and passing in the field's name as an argument.

If a field has a **value** and a **display value**, such as in the case of a reference field, this will return the **value**.

Example usage

Here, we log a message with the sys_id of the caller for the Incident:

```
var gr = new GlideRecord('incident');
gr.get('46f09e75a9fe198100f4ffd8d366d17b');
var callerSysID = gr.caller_id.toString();
gs.info('The caller's sys_id is ' + callerSysID);
```

GlideDateTime

The GlideDateTime class is for working with date/time fields and date/times in general.

Constructing a new GlideDateTime object using the new keyword with no arguments initializes it to the current date and time in GMT. You can also initialize while passing in an argument: either another GlideDateTime object or a date-formatting string (in the UTC timezone) in the format: yyyy-MM-dd HH:mm:ss.

> An easy way to convert the value in a date/time field to a GlideDateTime object, is by using the getGlideObject() method of the GlideElement class. Example:
>
> ```
> var gdtStart = current.start_time.getGlideObject()
> ```

Adding or removing time

There are multiple methods for adding or removing time from a GlideDateTime object once it's initialized. Here are a few of the more useful ones.

The add() method accepts one of two types of arguments: either a GlideTime object (an object containing a specific duration or amount of time), or a number of milliseconds.

You can add a specific number of days (local time or UTC) using addDaysLocalTime() or addDaysUTC() respectively. Neither method returns a value.

The same is true for adding time week-by-week (addWeeksLocalTime() and addWeeksUTC()), month-by-month (addMonthsLocalTime() and addMonthsUTC()), and even year-by-year (addYearsLocalTime() and addYearsUTC()).

The following snippet demonstrates several ways to add time to a GlideDateTime object.

Example usage

The following code declares a GlideDateTime object, initializes it with the current date and time, then adds 3 months and 2 days by first adding 24 hours in milliseconds, 1 day in days, and then 3 months. Finally, it sets a date/time field on the current record to the value in the date/time object:

```
var gdt = new GlideDateTime(gs.nowDateTime()); //current date/time
gdt.add(24*60*60*1000); //Add 24 hours
gdt.addDaysLocalTime(1); //Add another day
gdt.addMonthsLocalTime(3); //Add 3 months
current.setValue('start_time', gdt.getValue());
```

getDayOfMonth() and getDayOfWeek()

One often has the need to figure out the day of the month or week, either right now, or for a date/time in a given field. For example, certain events should only occur on weekends, or on the first day of the month. These methods both have UTC and local time versions (`getDayOfMonthUTC()` or `getDayOfWeekLocalTime()`, for example).

These methods can be called on a GlideDateTime object that's already been initialized with a value. They take no arguments, but return a number value representing the day of the week (1-7) or the day of the month.

> Note that while `getDayOfWeekUTC()` and `getDayOfWeekLocalTime()` return a number, the returned value doesn't adhere to the standard Sunday-through-Saturday week. Monday is the first day of the week to a GlideDateTime object, and it returns the value 1. Sunday will return 7.

Example usage

The following snippet returns 7, since the day specified falls on a Sunday:

```
var gdt = new GlideDateTime("2017-12-03 12:00:00");
gs.info(gdt.getDayOfWeekLocalTime());
```

GlideSession

The GlideSession class has no constructor, but it is returned from the `getSession()` method of the GlideSystem API (`gs.getSession();`). This API allows you to get and set data related to the current session.

getClientData() and putClientData()

The `getClientData()` and `putClientData()` methods allow you to set data in the user's session from a server-side script using `putClientData()`, and then retrieve that data using `getClientData()` from a client-side script.

This functionality can be extremely useful for passing data back-and-forth between the server and client, without performance-costly synchronous queries or time-consuming Ajax calls. Usually a display business rule and using `g_scratchpad` would make more sense, but there are plenty of use-cases for these APIs as well.

Example usage

In a business rule on the **Incident** table, we can place some data in the user's client session like so:

```
var userSession = gs.getSession();
session.putClientData('ticket_number', current.getValue('number'));
```

And then in a client script, you can access this data like so:

```
var ticketNumber = g_user.getClientData('ticket_number');
```

GlideSystem

The GlideSystem server-side API is not constructed using the new keyword, but is available to all server-side scripts via the variable gs. This API allows us to get various kinds of useful information about the system, the user's session, the current date/time, or other bits of useful info. It also allows you to interact with the user, by displaying informational or error messages.

addErrorMessage() and addInfoMessage()

The addErrorMessage() method will display a red error message at the top of the user's browser window on the next page they load after the server-side script that calls this method runs. This same functionality can also be achieved from a client-script, using the g_form API (g_form.addErrorMessage()).

This is an error message.	✕

addInfoMessage() has the same effect, but instead displays a blue informational message as opposed to a red error message.

Example usage

The following script could run inside of a business rule or other server-side script, and show a message indicating whether the operation was allowed or not:

```
if (current.active.changesFrom(false)) {
    if (gs.hasRole('admin')) {
        gs.addInfoMessage('This record has been re-activated');
    } else {
        current.setAbortAction(true);
```

```
            gs.addErrorMessage('This record can only be re-opened by an
    Administrator.');
        }
    }
```

debug()

The debug() method allows you to write a debug message to the system log. This method uses the standard Java MessageFormat placeholder replacement pattern. This means that in addition to the first argument—the debug message—you can specify up to five additional arguments, which will then be used to replace variables inside the message indicated by {1}, {2}, and so on.

Example usage

The following code will write a string like the following to the debug log:

The current incident, INC0001234, with a Short Description "Example Incident", is in a state of Resolved.

```
gs.debug(
    'The current incident, {0}, with a Short Description "{1}", is in
a state of {2}.',
    current.getValue('number'),
    current.getValue('short_description'),
    current.state.getDisplayValue()
);
```

eventQueue()

The eventQueue() method of the GlideSystem (gs) API accepts several arguments: first, a string containing the event to trigger. Events can be created in the event registry from **System Policy | Events | Registry**. The name of one of these events is what should be specified in the first argument.

The second argument is the context in which the event should run. Most events run against a particular record, so this argument should be a GlideRecord object containing the record against which this event should run.

The third and fourth arguments are event parameters. Event parameters are available to the triggered script or action. For example, the first or second parameter in an event which triggers an email notification to be sent might contain a recipient's email or user sys_id.

This method does not return a value.

Example usage

The following `eventQueue()` method call will trigger an event called `incident.commented` from the event registry. The event will be triggered in the context of the record in the `current` variable, and the event's `parameter1` will be the current user's `sys_id`.

This event can trigger other actions, such as notifications or business rules, using the other arguments provided to the method call:

```
gs.eventQueue('incident.commented', current, gs.getUserID(),
gs.getUserName());
```

getProperty()

System properties (stored in the `sys_properties` table) can be accessed in order to determine the behavior, or expected behavior, of all manner of functionality in ServiceNow. You can even create your own custom properties to control how custom functionality should behave.

The `getProperty()` method of the GlideSystem (`gs`) API accepts one mandatory argument, and one optional one: respectively, the property name, and a default value to return if the property is not found. It returns the value contained within the property or, as you might expect, the value of the second argument if the property is not found. If no second argument is specified and the property is not found, it returns null.

Example usage

Here, we determine whether to display a message based on the value returned from a `true`/`false` property:

```
if (gs.getProperty('custom_app.module.show_message') === 'true') {
    gs.addInfoMessage('some message');
}
```

In the preceding snippet, we strictly compare the property value with the string `true`, because the `getProperty()` method returns a string value.

getUser()

The `getUser()` method of the GlideSystem API accepts no arguments, but returns a reference to the GlideUser object corresponding to the currently logged in user.

Example usage

Here, we get the currently logged in user's GlideUser object, and from that, print out the user's sys_id:

```
var currentUser = gs.getUser();
gs.info(currentUser.getID());
```

getUserID()

The getUserID() method of the GlideSystem class accepts no arguments, and simply returns the currently logged in user's sys_id.

Example usage

```
var gr = new GlideRecord('sys_user');
gr.get(gs.getUserID());
gs.info('The current user's company is ' +    gr.getValue('company'));
```

hasRole()

The hasRole() method is for checking if the currently logged in user has a specific role. It accepts one argument (the name of the role to check that the user has, and returns a Boolean value indicating whether the user has the specified role or not).

Example usage

Here, we see a snippet from a business rule that prevents a database action if the user does not have the admin role:

```
if (!gs.hasRole('admin')) {
    current.setAbortAction(true);
    gs.addErrorMessage('Only Admins can perform this action.');
}
```

GlideUser

The GlideUser API class in ServiceNow provides methods that allow you to get information about the current user, their roles and permissions, and their preferences; all without needing to rely on much slower GlideRecord queries.

The GlideUser class has no constructor method, and instead it is generally declared by calling the GlideSystem method: gs.getUser(), which returns the GlideUser object.

getPreference() and savePreference()

The getPreference() method of the GlideUser class allows you to retrieve the value of one of the user's user preferences. User preferences are stored within the sys_user_preference table, and consist of things like how many records to display per page in a given list, or what update set is currently selected.

This method accepts one argument: a string containing the name of the preference to retrieve.

The getPreference() method returns a string containing the value of the preference requested, or null if no such preference is defined.

savePreference() on the other hand, accepts two arguments: the name of the preference, and the new value to set it to. savePreference() does not return a value.

Example usage

Here, we check a user preference to see whether they have annotations turned on. If they do, we show an additional message on the screen:

```
var currentUser = gs.getUser();
if (currentUser.getPreference('glide.ui.show_annotations') === 'true')
{
    gs.addInfoessage('This form is for [purpose]. You can do
[instructions].');
}
```

Next, we have a business rule that we can imagine runs on the sys_user table, and checks a custom field, u_show_annotations. When this field is toggled off, this business rule sets the user's preference the same way:

```
var currentUser = gs.getUser();
if (current.u_show_annotations.changesTo('false')) {
    currentUser.savePreference('glide.ui.show_annotations', 'false');
}
```

hasRole()

This method, like others that share its name, simply returns true or false to indicate whether the user has the specified role. It accepts one argument: the name of the role to check, and it returns one value: a Boolean indicating whether or not the user has that role.

Example usage

Here's a simple example, where we log true or false, depending on whether the user has the admin role:

```
var currentUser = gs.getUser();
gs.info(currentUser.hasRole('admin'));
```

isMemberOf()

`isMemberOf()` is nearly identical in functionality to `hasRole()`, in that it accepts one argument, and returns a Boolean indicating whether the user has membership in that argument. However, rather than checking if the user has a specified role, `isMemberOf()` checks if the user is a member of a specific group.

This is great for situations where you want to make sure that only certain group members can perform certain actions, but (for some reason) you don't have a role associated specifically with that. For an example of this, see the following code snippet.

Note that unless the role is configured as an elevated privilege, the `hasRole()` method will always return `true` if you check if an admin has a given role. However, this is not true for `isMemberOf()`. The admin role does not override group membership lookups. To avoid this behavior when checking for a role, use `gs.hasRoleExactly()`.

Example usage

Here we have a business rule that checks whether the user is a member of the assignment group of the ticket, and rejects updates if they are not.

```
var currentUser = gs.getUser();
if (!currentUser.isMemberOf(current.assignment_group.
getDisplayValue())) {
    current.setAbortAction(true);
}
```

Remember that business rules are not the best way to reject updates from users; we're just using this as a simple example. A better way to enforce this functionality would be through ACLs or possible UI/data policies.

Also, if we were writing this for use in a real-world scenario, we would probably want to add a message indicating the reason the update was rejected to avoid a bad user experience.

Summary

In this chapter, we learned about a number of powerful server-side ServiceNow APIs, including GlideUser, GlideSystem, GlideSession, and more. We also learned about some exclusively client-related APIs, such as GlideAjax and the `g_form` API. We've learned not only how certain APIs work, but why they work the way they do, and when to use them to maximize productivity and create a positive user experience!

This chapter can serve as a reference for some of the ServiceNow APIs we'll be using in the coming chapters, so feel free to bookmark it, and flip back now and then for reference.

10
The Client-Side Glide API

Similarly to the previous chapter, this chapter will focus on the Glide API. Unlike the previous chapter though, this chapter will go over some of the more common client-side Glide API classes, including the following:

- GlideRecord
- GlideAjax
- GlideForm
- GlideUser

Each class in the Glide API may consist of methods (executable functions within the class object), and properties (variables stored within the class, which may be set on initialization of a new instance of the class).

Remember that while the Glide API extends the functionality of client-side scripts, this is done by simply adding certain JavaScript files into the browser's scope. Client-side scripts **do not execute on the server** (perhaps obviously), and thus **do not execute within Mozilla Rhino (the server-side implementation of JavaScript)**. This means that you do not have access to certain *Java-ish* functionality, but also that you do have access to the browser's scope, certain UI elements and client-side functionality such as **DOM (Document Object Model)** manipulation and whatever syntax version of JavaScript is supported by the browser. For example, at the time of publication, all modern browsers support up to ES6 JavaScript syntax standards, whereas server-side scripts in ServiceNow Geneva and later, only support up to ES5 syntax. It should be noted though, that DOM manipulation is very rarely a good idea.

This chapter largely consists of API documentation with explanations and use examples. We recommend that you read through it once, and then dog-ear this chapter so that you can come back to it for reference later on.

Client-side APIs

The client-side Glide API is partly a subset of the server-side API, but it also provides APIs for dealing with forms and lists. These APIs allow for the control and manipulation of the behavior of elements of the ServiceNow interface, and interaction with the database, user, and session information.

Many client-side APIs don't provide constructor methods, or require instantiation. For example, rather than declaring a new instance of the GlideUser class, we simply have access to the g_user object.

One of the most important things to understand about client-side code is that it can have serious impact on the user experience, in terms of performance. Querying a record from the database, for example, requires constructing a query, sending it across to the server, waiting for the response, and then waiting for all of the data associated with the response to that query (and all of the records contained therein) to be sent back to the client from the server.

Since JavaScript executes within a single thread, while all of this happens, the user's browser session is effectively locked up, which can make for a very negative user experience. Luckily though, nearly any time you need to do something that would result in potentially locking up or slowing down the user's browser session for any noticeable period of time, client-side APIs provide the option to specify a callback function.

In JavaScript, functions are first-class objects, similar to strings, arrays, and other capital-O Objects. Functions can be stored inside of variables, passed into functions as arguments, and returned from functions. This way, you can pass a function in as an argument to be called once the code in the called function finishes executing! This is called a **callback function**.

A callback function is a function that's passed into another function as an argument, and then executed at some point within the body of the function to which it was passed; often with some specific argument, that is the result of execution.

If you want to test out any of the APIs you see here, you can navigate to a page on which the API should be present (for example, navigate to a record form to test out the g_form API), and then press *Ctrl + Shift + J*. You should notice that in addition to your browser's **Console** window/pane opening up, a client-side JavaScript executor shows up. Any code that you write or paste in this window can be executed in the same context as any client script, UI script, or UI policy script:

GlideAjax

The GlideAjax class allows a client-side script to make an AJAX (Asynchronous JavaScript And XML) call to the server, execute a server-side script include, and even return a value. GlideAjax might be one of the least well understood client-side APIs in ServiceNow, in part because it has both a client-side, and a server-side component.

First, let's discuss the server-side component. A GlideAjax call from a client-side script will ultimately execute a script include (which as we learned in a previous chapter, is a server-side script), so let's create a script include for our GlideAjax script to talk to.

For our example, we're going to create a simple script include that'll return the value of a system property we specify, so we'll create a script include called **GetPropertyAjax**. Once we enter this name and then tab out of the **Name** field, the default scaffolding of the script include is populated into the **Script** field.

To make this script include accessible from client-side scripts through GlideAjax though, we need to check the **Client callable** tick-box. This will alter the contents of the **Script** field, so that our script include extends the `AbstractAjaxProcessor` class. It also removes the initialize method, since we won't be initializing this class from the server.

Next, we'll define a method of our GlideAjax script include that'll do the work of retrieving the value of the system properties and returning it to the client.

```
var GetPropertyAjax = Class.create();
GetPropertyAjax.prototype = Object.extendsObject(AbstractAjaxProcess
or, {
    getProp: function() {
        var propName = this.getParameter('sysparm_prop_name');
        return(gs.getProperty(propName));
    },
    type: 'GetPropertyAjax'
});
```

In the `getProp` method in the previous code, you'll notice that we're calling `this.getParameter()`. This is a method specific to the `AbstractAjaxProcessor` class, which we're **extending**. That means that all methods of the `AbstractAjaxProcessor` class are now also member methods of the `GetPropertyAjax` class we've created; so when we access methods of the `this` object inside our class, we're able to access those methods as well. This method in particular, retrieves the value of the `sysparm` we'll be sending over when we call this GlideAjax script include from our client-side script.

Speaking of our client-side script, let's build that out. For starters, we need to instantiate an instance of the `GlideAjax` class on the client, passing the GlideAjax script include name into the client-side constructor; after which, we need to use the `addParam()` method to specify two parameters: `sysparm_name`, and `sysparm_prop_name`. Here's what that might look like:

```
var ga = new GlideAjax('GetPropertyAjax');
ga.addParam('sysparm_name', 'getProp');
ga.addParam('sysparm_prop_name', 'glide.servlet.uri');
```

The `sysparm_name` parameter is mandatory whenever we use GlideAjax from the client: it tells the GlideAjax script on the server which method we want to run. The `sysparm_prop_name` parameter however, we've custom-defined. It's just the name of a parameter that we agree to expect on the server-side script include, and provide from the client-side script; just like a function parameter variable name, except that we have to manually retrieve it using `this.getParameter()` on the server.

There's more, though; when a GlideAjax script returns a value, it doesn't return it like a normal function. You can't for example, just do something like the following:

```
//The following will not work!
var answer = new GlideAjax('MyGlideAjax').myMethod();
```

Instead, after specifying all of the necessary parameters, we call another method of the `GlideAjax` class in our client-side script: `getXMLAnswer()`. This method accepts one argument: a callback function, as you can see in the following code:

```
var ga = new GlideAjax('GetPropertyAjax'); //Pass in Script Include
name
ga.addParam('sysparm_name', 'getProp'); //Method name
ga.addParam('sysparm_prop_name', 'glide.servlet.uri'); //Name of the
property to retrieve
ga.getXMLAnswer(ajaxCallback);

function ajaxCallback(answer) {
    console.log('The base instance URI property is ' + answer);
}
```

In the preceding example, we're passing in a reference to the `ajaxCallback` function to the `getXMLAnswer()` method. After completion, the `ajaxCallback` function is called. The callback function is called on the client with one argument: the value that was returned from the method specified in the `sysparm_name` parameter, cast to a string. If an object is returned, then the argument passed into the callback function will be a JSON-formatted string. You could then use `JSON.parse()` to parse the string back into a JSON object.

One more thing to be aware of, is that the `getXMLWait()` method runs asynchronously. What this means, is that you cannot be certain of the order of execution (that is, when it will run with respect to the rest of your code). Consider the following example:

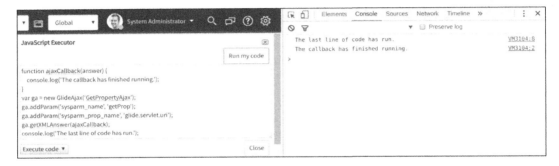

As you can see in the previous screenshot, the last line of code executes before the `console.log()` line in the callback function at the top.

GlideForm (g_form)

The GlideForm API is exposed within client-side scripts as the object variable `g_form`. This API provides methods for interacting with forms and fields, adding messages for the user, adding and removing options from a drop-down field, and more.

Below, we'll discuss some of the more commonly used and useful methods of the GlideForm API, and see how they can be put to use.

Setting/clearing messages on the form and fields

There are multiple methods for setting and clearing messages within forms, both at the top of the user interface (similar to the behavior of the server-side APIs: gs.addInfoMessage() and gs.addErrorMessage()), and against specific fields.

These methods are: showFieldMsg(), hideFieldMsg(), showErrorBox(), and hideErrorBox().

These methods of the g_form API are extremely useful for communicating information to the user from client scripts or UI policies, such as whether or not a field meets certain validation criteria.

One such set of field-level methods of the GlideForm (g_form) API, are showFieldMsg() and hideFieldMsg(), and the nearly-identical showErrorBox() and hideErrorBox(). These APIs are great for use inside of onChange client scripts, such as the following example:

```
var now = new Date();
now.setHours(0, 0, 0, 0); //beginning of today
var closedDate = new Date(g_form.getValue('closed_at'));
if (closedDate > now) {
    g_form.hideFieldMsg('closed_at', true);
    g_form.showFieldMsg('closed_at', 'Are you a time traveler?');
} else {
    g_form.hideFieldMsg('closed_at', true);
}
```

In the preceding example, we first declare a new JavaScript Date object, which automatically initializes to the date and time right now.

Next, we declare a new Date object, and initialize it with the current value of the closed_at field. We then call the setHours() method and pass in 0, 0, 0, 0, which sets the closedDate variable to 12:00 AM (00:00 hours) on the day selected so that on line 4, we can compare the two declared Date objects. If the value of the closed_at field is later than today, we then clear any other field messages (to avoid duplicate messages) and show a field message that asks the user if they're a time traveler. Otherwise, we clear out any existing field messages.

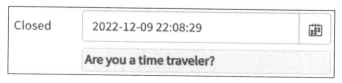

Notice that on line 5, we call `hideFieldMsg` (another `g_form` API) before adding our field message. This is because otherwise, if the user modifies the field over and over, they'll get more and more field messages stacked on top of one another.

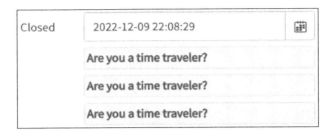

The `showFieldMsg()` and `showErrorBox()` methods both accept two arguments by default: a field name, and a message to display. A third argument can be passed into the `showErrorBox()` method: a Boolean (`true`/`false`). This argument indicates whether to scroll the form to display the field, if it's not in view when the script runs. The `showFieldMsg()` method has similar functionality, but requires four arguments instead of three: The field name, the message to display, the type of message (either `'info'` or `'error'`), and fourth: the Boolean indicating whether to scroll the field into view.

In the preceding example, we also use the `hideFieldMsg()` method of the `g_form` API. This method accepts one mandatory argument: the field name, as well as one optional argument: a Boolean indicating whether or not to clear all messages on the field. If false (or no value) is specified, only the last field message added will be removed.

The `hideErrorBox()` method, similar to `hideFieldMsg()`, accepts two arguments: the field name, and a Boolean indicating whether to clear all error boxes or not.

None of these methods return a value.

Dealing with drop-down list fields

Drop-down fields in forms, similar to reference fields, can have both a value, and a display value. For example, the **State** field on tasks-based table forms (such as the Incident form) has a set of **State** options with names like **New**, **In Progress**, and **Resolved**.

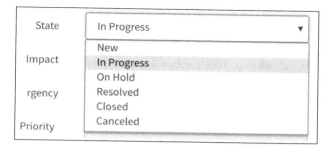

However, the actual value associated with these selection labels is an integer. In fact, the **State** field is specifically a number type field. This means that despite the label/display value that's displayed in the drop-down, if we call g_form. getValue('state'), we'll get a numerical value rather than the label we see in the form.

You can see the list of possible choices, and their corresponding values by right-clicking the field label and clicking on **Show choice list** (as an admin user, of course).

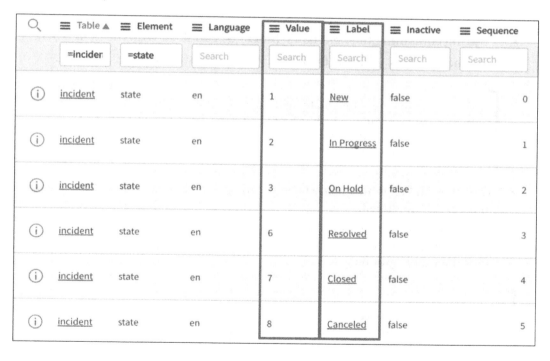

	Table ▲	Element	Language	Value	Label	Inactive	Sequence
	=incider	=state	Search	Search	Search	Search	Search
ⓘ	incident	state	en	1	New	false	0
ⓘ	incident	state	en	2	In Progress	false	1
ⓘ	incident	state	en	3	On Hold	false	2
ⓘ	incident	state	en	6	Resolved	false	3
ⓘ	incident	state	en	7	Closed	false	4
ⓘ	incident	state	en	8	Canceled	false	5

Whenever you create a new selectable value for a drop-down field, it's always good to leave some numerical space between the one you create, and the previous one. This applies to both the order field, as well as the value if it's a number field. For example, if the highest numbered value is 10, consider making your new option's value 15 or even 20.

There is virtually no limit on the value that can go in the order or value number fields, so It's perfectly fine to leave gaps of about 10 or even 100 between values. For example, the first item I want to show in a list might have an order of 10, the second an order of 20, and so on.

There are multiple GlideForm (g_form) methods for dealing with drop-down list fields: addOption(), removeOption(), and clearOptions().

The addOption() method can be called with three arguments, and a fourth optional one:

- A string containing the field name (not to be confused with the field label).
- The choice value, which is the actual value to be stored in the database.

In the preceding **State** field example , this would be the integer value actually stored in the database, not the choice label, which would be the name of the state presented to the user in the drop-down.

- The choice label, which is the label for the option to be displayed to the user in the drop-down list.
- The choice index [Optional], which indicates the order of the choice in the list. If this is not specified, the new list option will simply show up at the end, after the other options.

Note that this choice index is not the same as the order, which determines how the fields show up initially on load.

The `removeOption()` method on the other hand, only takes two arguments:

- A string containing the field name
- The choice value (not to be confused with the label) to be removed

Let's have a look at the following example, which combines the usage of the preceding two methods. Here, we've got the **Impact** field, with the three default options:

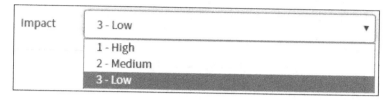

By looking at the `sys_choice` field, and filtering to show the **Incident** table, and the **Impact** field only, I can see that the option labeled **1 - High** corresponds to the value 1, **2 - Medium** corresponds to the value 2, and **3 - Low** corresponds to the value 3.

Let's imagine that under certain circumstances, we want to make it so the value 1 corresponds with the label `CRITICAL`, in order to make it more clear that users should not select this option unless it truly is a critical-level impact; but we don't want to alter the actual value of the selection, since certain business logic may pivot off that value.

To accomplish this, we might use a client script that runs code like this:

```
if (/*Condition to check*/) {
    g_form.removeOption('impact', '1');
    g_form.addOption('impact', '1', 'CRITICAL', 0);
}
```

We can test this by navigating to our form, pressing *Ctrl + Shift + J* to open the client-side JavaScript executor window, pasting in lines 2 and 3, and clicking **Run my code**:

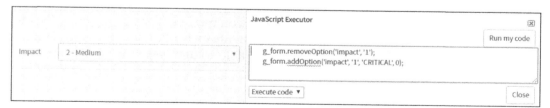

This code would result in the following options in the **Impact** field:

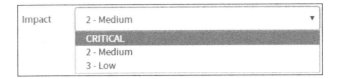

Because we gave the same choice value to the **CRITICAL** option, as the **1 - High** option had, and since the choice value is the only thing that's actually stored in the database, selecting the **CRITICAL** option in this form will result in the exact same value in the database, and upon reload (assuming our client script that changes this value doesn't run), it will show up again as **1 - High**.

We can also call `g_form.clearOptions('impact')` (which accepts only one argument: the field name) to clear all of the options from the **Impact** field rather than just one, and then we can populate the field with only the options we'd like to have there.

Getting and setting values on the form

Getting and setting values from a client script running on a form can be accomplished using a few different methods of the `g_form` class, each of which serves a different purpose:

The `getValue()` method accepts one argument: the `name` (not to be confused with the label) of the field. It simply returns the value that the field contains. If the field is a reference field, the value will be a `sys_id`. If it's an integer drop-down list like the **State** field, you'll get the number corresponding to the currently selected choice returned, always cast to a string.

Example:

```
g_form.getValue('assigned_to'); //returns the sys_id of the assigned
user
```

The `setValue()` method of the `g_form` class, as you might expect, is just the opposite of the `getValue()` method. It accepts two arguments instead of one (the field name, followed by the new field value), and it sets the field to that new value in the form.

Example:

```
g_form.setValue('state', '7'); //set the state field to closed
```

Note that while this change is immediately visible to the user, it does not update the record on the server until the user saves or submits the form.

Finally, we have `getReference()`, which is one of those special methods that accepts a callback function, which we discussed at the beginning of this chapter.

The `getReference()` method accepts the name of a reference field and a reference to a callback function. After sending an AJAX query to the server to retrieve the record details, it returns a GlideRecord object corresponding to the record referenced within the reference field.

This AJAX query, if done synchronously, would lock up the user's browser momentarily and result in a poor user experience. Luckily though, the fact that the `getReference()` method accepts a callback function means that this can be done asynchronously. In the following example, we specify an anonymous inline callback function rather than referencing one we've declared elsewhere, but the behavior is identical.

```
g_form.getReference('cmdb_ci', function(grCI) {
    var category = g_form.getValue('category');
    var grClass = grCI.getValue('sys_class_name');
    if (grClass == 'cmdb_ci_server' && category !== 'hardware') {
        g_form.setValue('category', 'hardware');
    }
});
```

In the preceding example, we get the referenced record from the `cmdb_ci` field. We then get the category for the record in this form, and the `sys_class_name` from the referenced CI.

Finally, we check if the CI is a server. If it is, but the category selected on the form isn't hardware, we make sure to set it to that. This way, you have to have hardware selected as the category if the CI you've selected is a server. A script like this would be most effective in something like an on change client script which runs whenever the `cmdb_ci` field is updated.

Controlling field visibility

There are many reasons you may want to control the visibility of a field or section in a form. Perhaps a given field is only applicable when a certain value is selected in another field; for example, many companies have a **Close notes** field, which would only be applicable when the **State** field is set to one of the closed values.

It is, however, important to be judicious when deciding whether to create a form view with many fields and rely on client-side logic to hide them, versus simply using different views for different situations. This is because each field, even when hidden by client-side logic, must load with the form. This increases the load on the user's network, and browser. For a few fields, this is virtually unnoticeable. However, if you were to have 40 fields load with a form only to be hidden in all but a few circumstances, this might be bad practice.

There are two methods of the g_form API on client-side scripts in ServiceNow that we'll discuss in this chapter: setVisibile(), and setDisplay().

The setVisible() method of the g_form object accepts two arguments: the field name, followed by a Boolean value which indicates whether or not the field should be visible. If the second argument is true, the field becomes or remains visible. If false, it becomes or remains invisible. Once invisible, the block where the field once resided remains empty, leaving a gap in the form.

Have a look at this **Configuration item** [cmdb_ci] field flanked by the **Business service** and **Parent Incident** fields:

Business service		Q
Configuration item		Q
Parent Incident		Q

Now let's press *Ctrl + Shift + J*, and execute the following script:

```
g_form.setVisible('cmdb_ci', false); //make the field invisible
```

The result is a gap where the field used to be:

Business service		Q
Parent Incident		Q

I suppose there may be some situations where this is desirable, but I imagine that typically you wouldn't want a big blank space in your form.

The `setDisplay()` method works in exactly the same way, but instead of leaving a gap, it sets the `display` CSS property of the element containing the field, to `none`. This means that it doesn't leave a blank area, and it re-flows the field layout around it, so that there is no gap:

```
g_form.setDisplay('cmdb_ci', false); //hide the field and block
completely
```

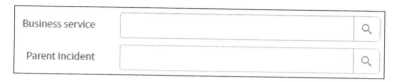

Field visibility can be controlled from client scripts and UI policies. That said, whenever possible, it's a good idea to use a UI policy to control field visibility, rather than a client script. This is because UI policies have a slightly lower and more optimized impact on performance.

Setting fields mandatory and read-only

Controlling whether a user can modify a field value, as well as whether a field value is required, can be accomplished using two methods of the GlideForm (`g_form`) API, respectively: `setReadOnly()`, and `setMandatory()`. Just as with field visibility,

Both `setReadOnly()` and `setMandatory()` accept two arguments: The field name, and a boolean value indicating whether the field should be mandatory/read-only.

In the following example, we set the business service field to read-only, and the configuration item field to mandatory:

```
g_form.setReadOnly('business_service', true);
g_form.setMandatory('cmdb_ci', true);
```

 By default, when a reference field on a form is made read-only, the reference icon disappears. This behavior can be reversed though, by modifying the system property: `glide.ui.reference.readonly.clickthrough`.

Neither of these methods return a value.

Submitting a client-side form

Form-based client-side scripts can submit the form (and any changes contained within it at the time) using one of two GlideForm (g_form) methods: save(), and submit().

The save() method will save the record as it exists in the form. It accepts no arguments, and returns no value. After saving, the user will be redirected back to the same form they were just viewing, with the same new or updated record loaded into it.

The submit() method of the client side GlideForm (g_form) object works in exactly the same way, except that it will redirect the user back to the previous page that they were on, rather than reloading the record in the form after saving it. You can control which page the user is redirected to, by using action.setRedirectUrl() inside a UI action script or client script.

 Remember that even if fields are not visible, they can still contain a value. When saved or submitted, the values of hidden fields are also submitted! For this reason, it's often a good idea to clear a field in the same script you use to hide it.

Disabling checking for mandatory fields

The g_form object has a lot of useful methods, but since they're largely similar to the GlideRecord API, we'll avoid going over each and every one. There's getValue(), setValue(), and so on. However, one of the unique methods it provides, allows you to disable mandatory fields on a form.

While this is rarely used in production code, this is an excellent tool for troubleshooting when you need to generate or save a record for testing, but it has complex and annoying rules around what fields need to be filled out before a record can be saved or progressed (I'm looking at you, change requests!)

This property is very simple, you simply write g_form.checkMandatory = false;.

GlideUser (g_user)

The GlideUser object is available to client scripts as the g_user object, which is initialized to the current user that's signed in.

The GlideUser client-side API gives you easy access to determining certain details about the user, including the user's name, roles, `sys_id`, and a method for getting access to client data set via the `putClientData()` API on the server.

The GlideUser (`g_user`) API is particularly useful because it eliminates the need to execute client-side GlideRecord queries to retrieve this information, which are costly in terms of performance or slow in terms of execution time.

Getting user details

A fair amount of the user's profile details can be gleaned from the GlideUser (`g_user`) API, as they are cached when the page is loaded.

There is a method to access the user's full name: `getFullName()`. This method accepts no arguments, but returns a string containing the current user's full name.

The user's first and last name are available via properties of the `g_user` object. Properties can be access directly without calling a method. For example:

```
var userFirstName = g_user.firstName;
```

Other properties directly accessible through the `g_user` object include the user's last name (`lastName`), sys_id (`userID`), and the user's username (`userName`). Any of these properties can be accessed directly from the `g_user` object.

Checking user permissions

A user's permissions are generally determined by the roles assigned to them, and ServiceNow provides several methods of the `g_user` object for determining if a user has a specified role or set of roles.

To determine if a user has a specific role, such as the `itil` role, you can call the `hasRole()` method. This method accepts one argument: the name of the role you're checking. It returns a Boolean value indicating whether the user has the role or not.

```
if (g_user.hasRole('itil')) {
    //do something
}
```

If the user has the `admin` role, this check will always return true (except potentially when checking for the `security_admin` role). However, there is a way to check if the user has the role while ignoring the admin override functionality: the `hasRoleExactly()` method of the `g_user` object. This method will only return `true` if the user has the exact role specified, rather than checking if the user has that role or the admin role.

```
if (g_user.hasRoleExactly('itil')) {
    //do something
} else if (g_user.hasRole('admin')) {
    //do something different
}
```

These methods are useful but checking a long list of roles would be inconvenient to do one at a time. Luckily, there is a method for checking multiple roles at once, from a comma-separated list: `g_user.hasRoleFromList()`. Note that this method only accepts a comma-separated string, and not an array. You can declare an array of roles, but you must use `.join(',')` to combine them into a comma-separated string like so:

```
var rolesList = [
    'catalog_admin',
    'catalog_editor',
    'catalog_item_designer',
    'catalog_manager'
];
if (g_user.hasRoleFromList(rolesList.join(','))) {
    //Do something catalog-related
}
```

Getting client data

As we learned in the previous chapter, server-side scripts can use the `putClientData()` method of the `GlideSession` API (which is accessible by using `gs.getSession()`) to associate a value with the user's session, so that the data can be accessed from client scripts using `g_user.getClientData()`. This method accepts one argument: the key (which must match the key of some data associated with a user's session from a business rule or other server-side code that ran prior to the current page loading). `getClientData()` returns the string value associated with that key.

```
var clientDataValue = g_user.getClientData('key');
```

GlideRecord

Just like the server-side version, GlideRecord is used to perform database operations on records within ServiceNow, such as querying, modifying, and creating records. The client-side version of the GlideRecord API only contains a subset of the methods available on the server, but it does enable one important new piece of functionality: callback functions.

The `query()` method of the client-side GlideRecord, as well as `insert()`, and `deleteRecord()`, all accept callback functions. In fact, each of these methods should never be called from a client-side script without a callback function.

The full list of documented methods in the client-side GlideRecord API is:

- `addOrderBy()`
- `addQuery()`
- `deleteRecord()`
- `get()`
- `getEncodedQuery()`
- `getLimit()`
- `getTableName()`
- `hasNext()`
- `insert()`
- `next()`
- `orderBy()`
- `query()`
- `setLimit()`

In this section, we'll learn about a few of these methods which are commonly used, and which differ from their server-side cousins. This means that we won't be re-hashing methods such as `addQuery()`, which behave pretty much identically to the way they do in server-side scripts.

Querying for one or more records

The `get()` method of the GlideRecord class in a client-side script only accepts one argument: a `sys_id`. Unlike the server-side equivalent, you cannot specify a field-value pair, or query; only a `sys_id`.

Interestingly, though the `get()` method does perform an Ajax query to the database, it can only be done synchronously; it accepts no callback function. This can have performance implications, but since only a single value is returned by `get()`, it's probably fair to say that the impact would be minimal. Still though, if you're interested in maximizing client-side user experience and performance, it may be best to do a regular `GlideRecordquery()`, and simply call the `setLimit()` method, passing in the number 1.

Here is an example of client-side usage of the `get()` method:

```
var gr = new GlideRecord('incident');
var recordSid = 'ef43c6d40a0a0b5700c77f9bf387afe3';
gr.get(recordSid); //Get the GlideRecord SYNCHRONOUSLY
if (gr.getValue('active') == 'true') {
    console.log('do something');
}
```

And here is an example of an asynchronous query to get a single record:

```
var gr = new GlideRecord('incident');
gr.addQuery('sys_id', 'ef43c6d40a0a0b5700c77f9bf387afe3');
gr.setLimit(1);
gr.query(function(grIncident) {
    if (grIncident.next() && grIncident.getValue('active') == 'true')
{
        //Do something with the Incident GlideRecord
    }
});
```

As you can see in the latter example, because we're using the `query()` method, we're able to run the query asynchronously, which is why the sole argument is a nameless (also known as anonymous) function.

The `get()` method has no such capacity for running asynchronously. As such, we strongly recommend against using it in almost any scenario. Instead, use the syntax from the preceding second snippet to retrieve a single record from the server asynchronously, using a callback function.

You might have also noticed that there is no `addEncodedQuery()` method of the client-side GlideRecord object. Not to worry though, you can still use encoded queries. Simply pass in an encoded query string as the sole argument to the `addQuery()` method, and it will function the same as the server-side `addEncodedQuery()` method.

Deleting a record asynchronously

As in the preceding section, the primary difference between server-side and client-side GlideRecords, is that client-side GlideRecord objects support callback functions. Of course, only certain methods of the GlideRecord class support callback functions; these are the methods which interact with the database.

In addition to the query() method, which retrieves records from the database, there are other methods which interact with the database.

The insert() and deleteRecord() methods work just the same as their server-side counterparts, except that they also accept callback functions. Using a callback function makes the operation asynchronous. For example, see the following code:

```
var gr = new GlideRecord('incident');
gr.addQuery(/*Your query*/);
gr.query(queryCallback);
function queryCallback(cb1) {
    cb1.next();
    cb1.deleteRecord(function(cb2) {
        console.log(cb2.getValue('number'));
    });
}
```

In this example, we're using two different callback functions in two different ways. First, on line 3, we're passing in a reference to the callback function queryCallback. This is different from calling the function (which you can tell because we don't include the parentheses after the function name). In the second example, on line 6, rather than passing in a reference to a function for our callback function, we define it inside of the parentheses, as an argument to the deleteRecord() method. This function is not stored in a variable like other functions in JavaScript; it's declared inline, and thus referred to as an anonymous function. It's not completely necessary to call a callback function from within another callback function, but this demonstrates the functionality and syntax for both types of callback functions.

Summary

In this chapter, we've learned a lot about the client-side API, including how to prevent major performance degradation due to client-side scripts looking up data on the server synchronously. Instead, we learned how and when to use GlideAjax and asynchronous lookups; and when not to use them (such as in onSubmit client scripts)! We also learned about how to interact with forms using the GlideForm (g_form), and the user object using the GlideUser (g_user) object.

11
Server-Side Scripting

Server-side scripting in ServiceNow might seem easier than client-side scripting, because you don't have to worry about AJAX, asynchronicity, or large performance impacts for seemingly optimized queries. However, due to the expanded and slightly modified functionality of server-side JavaScript, there are a few additional pitfalls to be mindful of!

Scripts that run on the server, and the server-side APIs, provide a great deal of power and control to the developer that's equipped to use them properly; however, they can also put great strain on the server if used improperly. Infinite loops and poorly optimized queries in server-side scripts can be far more difficult to troubleshoot and resolve than client-side issues. They can also have much more far-reaching impact.

A client-side script error might just make a form a bit more difficult to use, but a server-side error might slow down the whole system or make large segments of functionality unavailable. It's best to always be mindful of this fact when writing server-side scripts, but that doesn't mean that you should be afraid to write server-side code. When used properly, server-side code can be much more efficient then client-side, so as long as you're sure to test your code thoroughly, you'll have nothing to worry about!

One way to test your server-side code is by using background scripts. This provides a script window that allows you to execute server-side scripts, similar to the client-side JavaScript executor. If you have the High Security Settings plugin enabled and are on an older version of ServiceNow, you may need to elevate to the security admin role to see it as described in an earlier chapter, but you can access it by navigating to **System Definition | Scripts - Background** in the application navigator.

In this chapter, we'll learn about several new topics, including the following:

- Business rules
- `g_scratchpad`
- Reference qualifiers
- Query filters
- Script includes
- GlideAjax
- Condition scripts
- Default and calculated field scripts

Mozilla Rhino is an open-source implementation of JavaScript, written entirely in Java. Despite the similar-sounding names, Java and JavaScript are **vastly different** languages. You'll hear people make this mistake often. Recruiters, project managers, and just about anyone who doesn't deal with this kind of thing on a daily basis might be forgiven for making this mistake, but it's important for ServiceNow administrators and developers to know the difference.

You **do not need to know Java** to be effective as a ServiceNow developer, but you **do** need to know JavaScript. It does help however, to understand the class-based nature of languages like Java. This is because in server-side scripts, some class-based functionality is available in ServiceNow; specifically in the form of script includes. In fact, the default scaffolding of a new script include defines it as a class with the same name as the script includes itself.

 Note that in version ES6 and later, JavaScript does contain classes, but server-side JavaScript only runs with ES5 syntax. Classes in script includes in the Now platform use a custom class implementation.

JavaScript, the language used to both define and access code in script includes (and most other code used in the ServiceNow Now platform), is an object-oriented language, but it is not a class-based one. Instead, JavaScript is a **prototypal** object-oriented language. This means that you can declare a class in JavaScript (which is actually a function), and then extend the prototype of that class by adding *member functions* (otherwise known as **methods**) or *member variables* (otherwise known as **properties**).

Typically, JavaScript classes are defined and extended using the following syntax:

```
function MyClass(msg) {
    this.msg = msg;
}
MyClass.prototype.displayMessage = function() {
    if (this.msg && typeof this.msg === 'string') {
        console.log(this.msg);
    } else {
        console.log('No message defined in constructor.');
    }
}
```

This is written in what we call vanilla JavaScript: JavaScript without using API suites and libraries like jQuery, Angular, or the Glide API, so this is different from how we've seen classes implemented in script includes.

On lines 1-3 of the preceding script, we declare the class itself. I know, it looks like a function; that's because it is! In JavaScript, functions are just objects, and objects with with extended prototypes are classes. This first function is effectively the constructor of the `MyClass` class. On lines 4-10, we extend the class prototype by declaring a new member method: `displayMessage()`. Though the `msg` variable is not declared in the context of this method, we are able to access it as a property of the object in which it was initialized, using the `this` keyword.

Now that the `MyClass` class is defined, we can declare an instance of it by calling the constructor method using the `new` keyword, and access methods of the object like so:

```
var mc = new MyClass('This is a test string.');
mc.displayMessage();
```

This would result in a message being logged to the console: `This is a test string.`

This prototypal object extension is accessible in server-side scripts as well, but ServiceNow also exposes some Java-esque class description functionality, using `Class.create()` in script includes.

This isn't the only functionality that's added or changed in ServiceNow's server-side JavaScript. For example, the version of Mozilla Rhino that powers the Now platform, only supports up to JavaScript ES5. Until recently in fact, only up to ES3 was supported (in instance versions prior to Helsinki). In addition to the APIs provided server-side, there are occasionally overridden API methods. For example, until Helsinki came along and introduced the new scripting engine, many of the methods in the default JavaScript array class were overridden, such as the `indexOf()` method.

Because ServiceNow's server-side scripts execute in the context of Mozilla Rhino, you can access certain Java features, and this has a few advantages. For example, let's say you have a text file that's an attachment to a record, and you have a need to get the text out of that attachment. Consider the following script:

```
var gsa = new GlideSysAttachment();
var fileBytes = gsa.getBytes("incident",
"46e8219ba9fe1981013806b6e04fed06");
gs.info(fileBytes);
```

This gets the contents of the file, but since the file is interpreted on the server in Java, the output of this script looks something like this:

```
[B@f93b6c
```

Calling `toString()` on this object still doesn't give us anything different, but if we call a Java package directly to convert the data object to a string in Java, before it's passed back to JavaScript, we can extract the text contents of the file to a string:

```
var gsa = new GlideSysAttachment();
var fileBytes = gsa.getBytes("incident",
"46e8219ba9fe1981013806b6e04fed06");
fileBytes = Packages.java.lang.String(fileBytes);
gs.info(fileBytes);
```

The situations where you might need to use a package call like this are extremely rare, but it's important to understand the nature of the interaction between the underlying framework of ServiceNow (Rhino, which is Java-based), the higher-level APIs, and the language that you commonly interact with.

Dot-walking and GlideElement

As we learned in a previous chapter, dot-walking allows you to access fields on related records via a reference field (a type of field which contains a reference to another record), by chaining field names separated by dots. For example, to get the email address of the person to whom an incident is assigned from a business rule on the **Incident** table, you might use the following code:

```
var assigneeEmail = current.assigned_to.email.toString();
```

You might notice that we also used the `toString()` method in the preceding snippet. This is because, as we saw in the server-side Glide API documentation, fields accessed from server-side `GlideRecords` return `GlideElement` objects; not just values. JavaScript will generally coerce (sometimes referred to as casting) values to whatever datatype you're trying to use it as, but it is always best to explicitly convert values derived from `GlideElement` objects. Otherwise, you risk getting the wrong data type. Since GlideElement objects are... *objects*, you'll probably end up with a reference to that object, which can result in unexpected and extremely difficult-to-troubleshoot issues.

When not dot-walking, you can explicitly get a string value from a field by using the `getValue()` method, as in the following line:

```
var assigneeSysId = current.getValue('assigned_to');
```

Dot-walking can be **chained**, which means that by dot-walking to a reference field, you can continue to dot-walk through it to access fields on the table referenced in that field as well. For example, to get the email address of the **manager** of the person assigned to an incident from a business rule, we could use the following code:

```
Var managerEmail = current.assigned_to.manager.email.toString();
```

The maximum recommended number of steps in a dot-walk chain, is three, as seen above. To dot-walk further, consider using the `.getRefRecord()` API to get the GlideRecord object corresponding to the referenced record. For example:

```
var grAssignee = current.assigned_to.getRefRecord();
var grAssigneeManager = grAssignee.manager.getRefRecord();
var managerEmail = grAssigneeManager.getValue('email');
```

For three or fewer dot-walk steps, it may be less efficient to use `getRefRecord()`, as it returns the entire record, but for longer dot-walks, it can be quite useful.

Dot-walking isn't just for getting child-record field values in business rules and script includes though; it can also be useful for building queries, both in scripts, and in the condition builder!

To illustrate the dot-walking visually, navigate to the **Incident** table, open the query builder at the top of the list.

In List v2, you may need to first open the column drop-down, and select **Show Related Fields**; after which, reference fields in the list are followed by a dot-walkable reference.

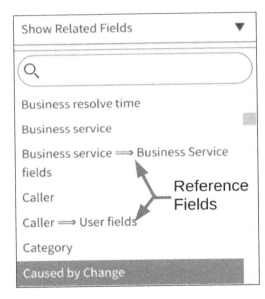

In list v3 though, dot-walking within the query builder is even simpler, and provides an even clearer illustration of how dot-walking can be used in queries. Simply click the dot-walk arrow to the right of a reference field name, and you'll be shown a list of fields on the table referenced by that reference field.

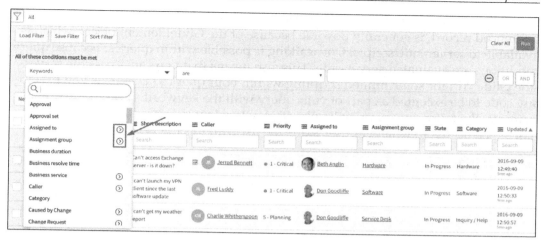

For example, the **Assigned** [assigned_to] field references the **Users** [sys_user] table. Clicking on the dot-walk arrow in the query builder here, allows us to select the value of a field in the referenced table, on which to filter.

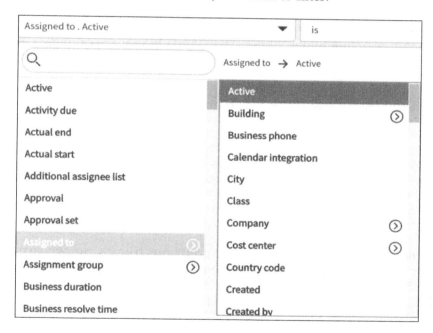

Dot-walking through reference fields in scripts, in order to access values on a referenced record, is generally possible because of the GlideElement object, which is available to server-side scripts. Dot-walking is possible within queries, because query conditions are evaluated server-side. This also means that you can access the server-side Glide API for some limited scripting within your queries (as long as you preface any code to be executed as part of your query with the keyword `javascript:`. For example, the following query will only display Incident tickets assigned to you—or more specifically, to whatever user loads the list with this query:

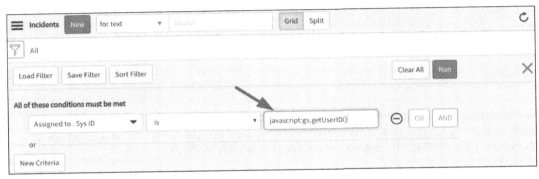

This is possible even though the GlideSystem (`gs`) object we're calling is a server-side API, because the script is actually evaluated on the server, just before the query is applied.

If we were to utilize the same filter as part of a scripted `GlideRecord` query, it would look something like this:

```
var gr = new GlideRecord('incident');
gr.addQuery('assigned_to.sys_id', gs.getUserID());
gr.query();
while (gr.next()) {
    //do something
}
```

As we discussed, dot-walking is possible in pretty much any script which executes server-side; this includes mail scripts, reference qualifiers, and query filters! However, it's important to be aware that in order to dot-walk successfully, the user must have access to the target table and field (the one being dot-walked into) via security rules.

Script includes

Script includes are the server-side equivalent of UI scripts (which we'll learn more about in the next chapter) in that they are effectively ever-present blocks of code that exist on the server in a given application scope.

Each script include defines a class or function in ServiceNow, that's accessible from any server-side script in its scope. The name of the script include record itself must match the name of a function or class in the `Script` field of the record, as this will also be the API name.

Script includes can be found in the application navigator, under **System Definition | Script Includes**.

The default structure of a script include looks like this:

```
var ExampleScriptInclude = Class.create();
ExampleScriptInclude.prototype = {
    initialize: function() {
        //Constructor
    },
    aMethod: function() {
        //Do some stuff
    },
    anotherMethod: function() {
        //Do some other stuff
    },
    type: 'ExampleScriptInclude'
};
```

When you type a value into the `Name` field of a new **Script Include** record, the **Script** field will be auto-populated with a basic scaffolding defining a script include class with the name you specified, and an initialize function. An initialize function is a constructor method which is automatically called when a new object is initialized by using the `new` keyword, as in the following example:

```
var esi = new ExampleScriptInclude();
```

If we accept parameters in the `initialize()` method, we make it possible to specify arguments when constructing an object. For example, we can alter the initialize function description to look like this:

```
initialize: function(constructorArg) {
    this.constructorArg = constructorArg;
}
```

Now, when instantiating an object from this class, we can specify a constructor argument like so:

```
var esi = new ExampleScriptInclude('arg value');
```

With the preceding code, the local variable `constructorArg` would be set to `'arg value'`, and would be available to any other function in the class as `this.constructorArg`.

Whenever possible, don't modify out-of-the-box ServiceNow script includes. Instead, create a copy and include your changes there. To add functionality rather than modifying it, you may also extend an existing script include, by changing the declaration similar to the highlighted portion of the code below, which extends the OOB (out-of-the-box) `Cart` script include:

```
var test = Class.create();
test.prototype = Object.extendsObject(Cart, {
customMethod: function() {
//Your code here
},
    type: 'test'
});
```

It's best to avoid making changes not only to OOB script includes, but any OOB record, if it can be helped. Sometimes it can't be helped, and that's fine, but the reason it's best to be careful when doing so is twofold:

- Modifying OOB records means that future upgrades will not be able to update them. For example, if you upgrade your instance from Helsinki to Istanbul, it may change some of the functionality of the cart API. However, if the cart script include has been modified by someone in your instance rather than being extended, the upgrade process will fail to modify that script include, and you'll have an upgrade error to resolve manually.

> Upgrade errors, also referred to as collisions, are a common place during the upgrade process, and aren't a big deal—but you want to avoid them whenever possible. They add up over time, and can add significant time and effort to the upgrade process.

- Any other scripts which reference or make use of the OOB script includes may break, if the existing record is modified to alter the functionality that's referenced.

Server-side GlideAjax

All script includes execute only on the server. However, there is a way to call certain script includes (specifically GlideAjax script includes) from client-side scripts. We already went over the client-side GlideAjax API, but here we'll learn how to write a server-side script that's intended to be accessible from the client using GlideAjax.

There are many reasons that a client-side script may need to access server-side functionality. One of the best reasons to use GlideAjax is because it runs asynchronously on the client, meaning that it doesn't lock up or negatively impact the user's client-side performance. It can also do some processing server-side, and return only the data you need, as opposed to returning large amounts of data and doing that processing client-side.

GlideRecord queries are another great example of when you might want to use a client-callable/GlideAjax script include, but there's already a way to perform queries asynchronously using the client-side GlideRecord API. GlideAjax would be more efficient but instead, let's consider the following example involving properties.

Imagine that another team has requested that under certain circumstances in the client (such as when the user selects a specific value from a drop-down field), the system should display an alert containing a message stored in a custom system property: `company.situational.message`. Unfortunately, there is no built-in way to access a system property from a client-side script, but luckily GlideAjax is here to save the day!

Let's create a client-callable script include to retrieve and return the value of a system property. Rather than simply returning the value of the specific system property the user requested for this functionality, let's do the clever thing and make it return the value of any property we specify, so we can re-use it in the future. This script include will be used as an example in the next chapter, so be sure to follow along with the steps below in your own developer instance.

1. To get started, navigate to **System Definition | Script Includes**. On that table, click **New**.

2. Give the script include a name. I went with `GetPropertyAjax`. I used `Ajax` in the name, to indicate that it's a client-callable GlideAjax script include, but you don't have to. After giving the Script Include a name, the **Script** field should auto-populate with the scaffolding for a typical script include:

```
var GetPropertyAjax = Class.create();
GetPropertyAjax.prototype = {
    initialize: function() {
    },

    type: 'GetPropertyAjax'
};
```

3. Click the **Client callable** tick-box, and the **Script** field should again be automatically updated to extend `AbstractAjaxProcessor`, and remove the `constructor` (`initialize`) method. The Script field should now look like this:

```
var GetPropertyAjax = Class.create();
GetPropertyAjax.prototype = Object.extendsObject(AbstractA
jaxProcessor, {

  type: 'GetPropertyAjax'
});
```

4. Now we just have to add our own method(s) into the script include on the blank line. To do so, start by declaring your method just like you normally would inside of a class/object in JavaScript, and complete the function to return the value we want to send to the client like so:

```
var GetPropertyAjax = Class.create();
GetPropertyAjax.prototype = Object.extendsObject(AbstractA
jaxProcessor, {
  getProp: function() {
    var propName = this.getParameter('sysparm_prop_name');
    return(gs.getProperty(propName));
  },
    type: 'GetPropertyAjax'
});
```

5. As you can see, we declare a function called `getProp()` which takes no arguments. This is because when using GlideAjax, relevant information is not passed into the called method/function as arguments, but rather as parameters. In this case, that parameter is called `sysparm_prop_name`. The client-side code will need to know this parameter name, as it'll have to call a method of the client-side GlideAjax API (`addParam()`) to set it.

6. We retrieve the value of the `sysparm_prop_name` parameter on line 4, and then pass that property name into the server-side GlideSystem API method: `gs.getProperty()` on line 5, returning the result.

Congratulations, you've just defined a client-callable GlideAjax Script Include! We'll learn how to make use of this in the next chapter.

Business rules

Business rules execute on the server, so the usual server-side APIs are available to any scripts that might need to be run. Also available in business rules, are the `current` and `previous` objects, though `previous` isn't available when the business rule runs asynchronously.

Business rules have an added level of granularity as to when they can be run. An administrator can choose to have a business rule run either before, or after a record or update has been saved to the database.

Let's say for example, that I'm looking at an incident ticket, and I change the **State** field to **Closed**. After saving the record, that record update is sent on its way to the database; but if we have a business rule with the **When** field set to **before**, then any scripts in it will be executed on that record prior to the record being saved to the database. This is important to note, because it gives you another means by which to reject an update before it hits the database using the `setAbortAction()` method of the `current` object:

```
current.setAbortAction(true);
```

Aborting an update in a before business rule also prevents other business rules from running against the record, since no database action is performed (no record is inserted/updated) once it's been aborted. The **When** field determines at what stage a business rule runs, but within that stage, the **Order** field determines the order in which they run. It's important to remember that fact when potentially aborting a database action. For example, if another business rule runs first and updates another record, aborting the database action in a business rule that runs later won't undo the changes made by the previous business rule with a lower **Order** field value.

There is however, another way to prevent other business rules from running when a record is updated. There is a method of the GlideRecord API called `setWorkflow()`, which takes a Boolean (`true`/`false`)value as an argument. When the subsequent database action is performed, no business rules will run. Here's a usage example:

```
var gr = new GlideRecord('incident');
gr.get('176baa97c0a80169011360192b738ebf');
gr.setValue('active', 'true');
gr.setWorkflow(false);
gr.update();
```

The above code will prevent any automatic business logic from running as a result of our update to the selected record.

You can also call this method on the `current` GlideRecord object in a business rule, using `current.setAbortAction(true)`. This will prevent any further business rules from running, whether it's used in a before or after business rule.

business rules come in various types, which execute at different times. In this section, we'll learn about each of them and what they're used for.

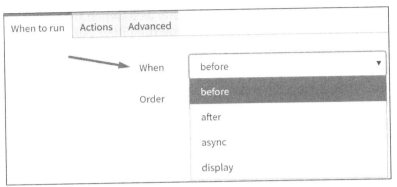

After business rules

Aside from before business rules, we also alluded to after business rules, which execute, as you might expect, after a database action is completed. Since before business rules execute before the record is saved to the database, any changes made to the `current` object in the context of the business rule's script or actions are automatically saved to the database. Here's an example of that:

```
if (current.getValue('state') == '5') {
    current.setValue('active', 'false');
}
```

Notice that we did not do anything to submit the record to the database for insert/update. When using a *before* business rule, there's no need to call the `update()` method on the `current` object, because it's about to be saved to the database anyway! However, with *after* business rules, you'll need to call `update()` to submit the new data in the current object like so:

```
if (current.getValue('state') == '5') {
    current.setValue('active', 'false');
    current.update();
}
```

Asynchronous business rules

Asynchronous business rules execute after the *after* business rules. However, the server returns a response to the client after the *after* business rules, which means that when the form reloads, the results of any *after* business rules will be shown, but not the results of *asynchronous* business rules. Asynchronous rules will be run on the server at a later time; usually only a few seconds later, when the server has resources available to run it.

Asynchronous business rules are generally the best way to update records that are not the current record, and which don't need to be displayed when the form reloads. It would be possible to accomplish that using *after* business rules, but that would not be the most performance-effective way to accomplish that task. The primary exception though, is when you need to have access to the `previous` object, which is only available in *before* and *after* business rules.

Display business rules and g_scratchpad

Display business rules execute on the server when a request is made to display a record in a form, but before the data is sent from the server to the client. The `current` object is available to *display* business rules, but any changes to the field values, while they are sent to the client and displayed in the form, are not permanent unless the user saves the record with the new values. Think of any changes made in a *display* business rule as modifying the data in-flight to the client, not in the database.

The most common usage of a *display* business rule is to set values on the `g_scratchpad` object. This object is passed to the client, along with the rest of the data about the record, which means that it's also accessible on the client. Thus, *display* business rules can be used to retrieve data from the server and send it to the client. This can be an extremely efficient and effective alternative to situationally using asynchronous queries or GlideAjax calls, since the data is available on the client on-load rather than having to wait for an asynchronous AJAX response.

Setting a variable using `g_scratchpad` in an asynchronous business rule is as easy as: `g_scratchpad.propName = propVal;`. Similarly, retrieving that value in a client script is as simple as: `var propVal = g_scratchpad.propName;`. As you can see, the `g_scratchpad` variable is just an object, the values of the properties of which can be set and retrieved just like any other object.

One excellent example of when to use a *display* business rule, is when you need to compare a field in a form with the value of that same field on the server. Here's an example of how that might be accomplished:

```
(function executeRule(current, previous /*null when async*/) {
    g_scratchpad.originalStateVal = current.getValue('state');
})(current, previous);
```

Best practice dictates that *before* business rules be used to update the `current` object, *after* business rules be used to update related records such as those in reference fields and related lists which might need to be displayed when the record loads, *async* business rules should be used to update records and perform actions that don't need to be displayed or loaded after the form reloads, and *display* business rules should be used to retrieve and provide server-side information to client-side scripts on load.

Default versus calculated field values

It is an easy mistake to make, to think that giving a table column (AKA field) a default value, and giving it a calculated value, have effectively the same result. However, this is not the case. Default and calculated values behave quite differently, and should be used for quite different purposes.

In this section, we'll explore what each are (and are not) meant to be used for, and the difference in behavior between them. We'll also discuss field calculation scripts, and best practices regarding default and calculated fields.

Default values

Default field values can be quite simple: a string, an integer, or whatever data-type matches the field's type.

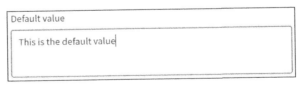

You can get a fair bit more advanced with it though, by using the `javascript:` keyword in the beginning of your value similar to the way we can run scripts in the condition builder. Any code after the `javascript:` would be executed on the server when the form loads, or when a record is inserted into the database (but not when updated) without a value in that field.

Default value scripts will have access to the current object, but remember that on a new record form, the default value is calculated on the server, before/while the form is loaded. At that time, there is no data in the current object.

If there is no value in the field when it is inserted into the database, then the default value will be applied. However, if any value exists in the field when the record is created, the default value is not calculated or used.

Given that, in addition to on insert (as long as the field is blank on insert), the default value is also calculated in order to be displayed in the new record form, consider the following code:

```
javascript:'Record created by ' + gs.getUser().getDisplayName() + ' on ' + current.getValue('sys_created_on') + '.';
```

By using the current object in the above code in the Default value field, when the form loads, we're getting a blank value for the sys_created_on field, but the rest of our code still executes. Thus, on the new record form, we'll see a default value like this:

```
Record created by John Smith on .
```

Note the lack of the expected creation date in the default value string.

If we were to erase this value on the new record form or leave it blank by creating the record in a way that doesn't use the form (such as via a script or through list editing), then the default value would be re-evaluated on insert, at which point there would be a current object for it to reference, so we would get the expected output. However, if we load the form, get the value with the missing creation date, and then save it, then the incorrect value will be saved to the database. The default value will not be re-evaluated on insert, because the field would now have a value in it!

Pro Tip

When creating a new record from the form, the default value will be pre-populated in the field to which it applied (as we learned above). However, you can prevent this from happening so that the default value only puts data into the field on insert (and not on the new record form) by checking if the current object is populated. Here is an example using the same code as above, but wrapped in a conditional block that should cause it to only populate the default value if the record is being inserted into the database (when the current object is available):

```
javascript:if (!current.sys_created_on.nil()) { 'This record was created by ' + gs.getUser().getDisplayName() + ' on ' + current.getValue('sys_created_on'); }
```

This behavior is what fundamentally separates the default value functionality from the calculated field functionality.

Calculated values

While default values apply only on form load or on insert, and are not re-evaluated if the field is updated later or if the value changes, calculated fields always apply, and are re-evaluated whenever the record is updated. Also, while a field's default value may be scripted using the `javascript:` keyword, calculated fields are always scripted.

To enable setting a field as calculated, begin by loading the **Advanced view** of the field dictionary record by clicking on the **Advanced view** UI Action:

Next, go to the **Calculated Value** form section, and check the **Calculated** checkbox. This will enable the field calculation script editor:

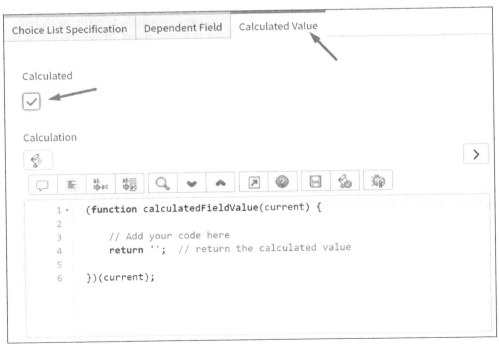

Calculated field values do have access to the `current` object (just like default value scripts), but since they are re-evaluated whenever the record is updated, it's less of an issue that the `current` object is empty when loading the new record form.

Even though it would be changed once submitted, it's best to avoid a user seeing null in a calculated field on the new record form. It's often a good idea to put in some filler text to be displayed if the `current` object is empty, or even leave the field blank before it's submitted, as you can see in the following example script:

```
(function calculatedFieldValue(current) {

    var userName, updatedDate;
    if (current.sys_created_on.nil()) {
        return '';
    }
    var grUser = new GlideRecord('sys_user');
    if (grUser.get(gs.getUserID())) {
        userName = grUser.getDisplayValue();
        updatedDate = current.getValue('sys_updated_on');
        return 'Record updated by ' + userName + ' on ' + updatedDate +
'.';
    }

})(current);
```

Summary

In this chapter, we learned about the scripting back-end of ServiceNow. We learned about Mozilla Rhino, and the Java underbelly of ServiceNow, as well as how to interact with it through JavaScript. We also learned about default vs. calculated fields, dot-walking in GlideElement objects, and server-side asynchronicity in ServiceNow; both examples of server-side scripts in ServiceNow. On the topic of Script Includes, we discussed the server-side component of GlideAjax scripts which we touched on briefly in a previous chapter.

12
Client-Side Scripting

Whenever we say that something executes or happens client-side, or on the client, it's important to understand that we're referring to the user's web browser.

While it is important to understand the underlying architecture on which ServiceNow runs for server-side scripting, client-side scripting grants you access to a whole new set of non-ServiceNow APIs: The **Document Object Model** (**DOM**), and ServiceNow APIs which, grant you the ability to directly modify what the user sees and how they interact with the presentation layer of the system, without modifying any back-end logic or data. You can change field labels, choice list options, flash or highlight a field, throw an alert or confirm dialog, request input from the user, and more.

ServiceNow recommends against *directly* accessing or modifying webpage elements in the DOM, but luckily most of what you might want to be able to do can be accomplished using client-side APIs provided by the Now platform!

In this chapter, we'll learn about:

- Security
- Compatibility
- Building for performance
- UI scripts
- Best practices

Client scripts

Client scripts are not the only example of client-side scripting, but they're probably the most ubiquitous (hence the name). A client script is a snippet of JavaScript that's sent from the server to the user's browser, to be executed client-side.

Keep in mind that any time a UI policy can effectively reproduce the desired functionality that you might otherwise use a client script for, it is best to use the UI policy. However, more advanced functionality often requires the use of more advanced conditions or functionality. That is where client scripts come in!

As a general rule, a well-written client script will return control of the browser to the user very quickly, and perform any server lookups **asynchronously**. This includes looking up properties from the server, performing GlideRecord queries, and handling time-zones.

Pro tip

We've written a script specifically for handling time-zones in ServiceNow, both from server-side and client-side scripts! You can find this free tool at http://tz.snprotips.com/.

One exception to the rule that any server lookups must be done asynchronously, is when executing onSubmit scripts. This is a type of client script which executes when the user clicks on the **Save**, **Update**, or **Submit** buttons on a form. onSubmit client scripts are the exception here because, as we saw in the chapter detailing client API documentation, asynchronous operations are performed asynchronously. This means that the browser doesn't wait around for them to be completed. When the form submits, the page reloads, so the form could submit before the callback function is ever called! For this reason, onSubmit client scripts should only be run synchronously. All other client scripts that need to communicate with the server, as a general rule, should run **asynchronously**.

Client scripts, like UI policies and catalog client scripts, execute only within forms (with the exception of onCellEdit scripts, which also execute on the list view). This means that if you're using a client-side method of controlling data such as a client script or UI policy, you must use another means by which to protect that data from being modified in the list view. You may accomplish this by using ACLs (security rules), data policies, business rules (with the setAbortAction() method of the current object), or by disabling list editing altogether.

Pro tip

Just like in business rules and other server-side scripts, you can access variables on a form from within client-side scripts using the g_form client API, by dot-walking into it in the string argument like so: g_form.setValue('variables.var_name', 'var value'). The same applies to other g_form methods, such as setDisplay()/setVisible(), setReadOnly(), and setMandatory().

Client script types

There are multiple types of client-side scripts: UI actions (if configured to run client-side), UI policies and UI Policy actions, client scripts, and catalog client scripts (which are pretty much identical to client scripts, except that they run on catalog item forms rather than regular ServiceNow forms that display a record.

Client Scripts are a specific kind of client-side script, which execute on forms (or in the case of onCellEdit client scripts, on the list view) of a record. client scripts come in four basic types: onLoad, onChange, onSubmit, and onCellEdit. Each type runs under different conditions, and often has a different use than the others.

onLoad

onLoad Client Scripts execute as soon as the system loads the form, and can be used to perform actions such as controlling the options that show in a drop-down field based on the values in the record loaded from the database.

Pro Tip

An onLoad client script can provide onChange-like functionality, as it allows you to access the DOM, and directly interact with form components using standard JavaScript APIs, or the ServiceNow g_form.getElement() method. At that point, we can use the standard element.addEventListener() JavaScript API to monitor for keyboard, mouse, or other events. However, this is strongly recommended against whenever avoidable, and will **not** work in the Service Portal. Functionality that relies on DOM access should not be relied upon.

onChange

onChange client scripts execute whenever the selected field's value is modified. Additionally, when the form first loads, this technically constitutes a change event, insofar as it triggers onChange scripts (just like onLoad scripts, which we'll learn about shortly). However, by default, onChange client scripts include a condition block which returns to halt execution of the rest of the script if the variable isLoading is true (meaning that the change is the result of the form loading, not of a manual change), or if the new value for the selected field is blank.

```
if (isLoading || newValue === '') {
    return;
}
```

By simply removing the `isLoading` condition, we can cause an `onChange` script to execute as though it were both an `onLoad` script as well as `onChange`.

The other condition (if `newValue` is blank) also prevents execution. This is another scenario that the default client script behavior precludes, but which you may want to *un-preclude*, as it were. That is, you may want to perform some action when a field is changed to a blank value, in which case you might want to override that condition as well. You may not want to execute the exact same code if the field's new value is blank, but often you'll want to do something.

Consider an example where the business would like to employ some new functionality like so:

- Whenever an Incident is assigned to a group which has a manager, and the `assigned_to` field is empty, the manager of that group should be set as the assignee for the incident
- If the **Assignment group** field is cleared out, the **Assigned to** field should also be cleared out

For this, we might use an `onChange` client script like so:

- **Name**: Set assignee when assignment group changed
- **Table**: **Incident** [`incident`]
- **Type**: onChange
- **Field name**: Assignment group

 We set the field that triggers this client script to **Assignment group**, because that's the field which we'll be watching for a change (not the field that we'll be modifying).

```
function onChange(control, oldValue, newValue, isLoading,
isTemplate) {
    if (isLoading) {
        return; //Do nothing if we're just loading the form
    } else if (newValue == '') {
        //If assignment group blank, blank out assigned to
        g_form.setValue('assigned_to', '');
    }
    else {
        g_form.getReference('assignment_group',
assignmentGroupCallBack);
    }
}
function assignmentGroupCallBack(grAssignmentGroup) {
    g_form.setValue('assigned_to', grAssignmentGroup.
```

```
getValue('manager'));
}
```

On *line 2*, you might notice that we've removed the condition that would return if the new value is blank. This is because we want to perform an action (clearing out the **Assigned to** [assigned_to] field when the value is cleared out. Instead, we have the same condition on *line 6*, wherein instead of returning, we blank out the assigned_to field value.

Next, on *line 10*, we call the getReference() method, and pass in both the field name (assigned_to), and a reference to our callback function (declared on *line 13*). This causes the lookup from the server to run asynchronously, limiting the impact on client-side performance.

On *line 14*, inside our callback function, we then call the setValue() method of the g_form client-side API, and set the assigned_to field to the value of the manager field on the assignment group GlideRecord object that was passed into our callback function from the asynchronous query.

There is one way in which this could be improved from a client-side performance perspective. When we get the value of the **Manager** field in our callback function on *line 14*, we get a sys_id. We then use this to set the value of the **Assigned to** field. When we set this field with a sys_id, the system has to perform a lookup on the reference table to retrieve the display value. If we used something like a GlideAjax script and returned both the value and display value, we would maximize our efficiency. However, we could also use an asynchronous query to pull the display value of the **Manager** field, and then specify that as an additional parameter when setting the value using g_form.setValue(). That would prevent the reference field from having to retrieve the display value for the **Assigned to** field (the manager's name).

```
g_form.setValue('assigned_to', managerSysID, managerName);
```

onSubmit

onSubmit client scripts execute whenever the user saves the form, whether they click **Save**, **Submit**, or **Update** (or any other UI action for that matter).

It's important to understand that any asynchronous code in an onSubmit client script runs the risk of not executing, as the form may reload before it has a chance to receive a response from the server! Synchronous code runs in a serialized fashion, so it would prevent the form from refreshing before the code has finished running. For this reason, any necessary queries or other server requests should be performed synchronously in an onSubmit script. This is nearly the only situation in which you should intentionally run queries synchronously in a client-side script.

Additionally, `onSubmit` client scripts have the benefit of being able to tacitly allow or prevent submission before the data is sent to the server, by simply returning a Boolean `true` or `false`. Because of this facet, `onSubmit` client scripts are an excellent way to validate data on the form, or even call the `confirm()` function to confirm some intention with the user.

onCellEdit

`onCellEdit` client scripts are highly similar to `onChange` client scripts, except that they execute on lists rather than on forms. It's also possible to *Shift + click* and select multiple values for editing in a list view (as you can see in the following screenshot). This highlights multiple fields (actually, one field across multiple records), so that when you double-click on one of them and edit the value, it edits the value across all fields in the selected records.

In the preceding screenshot, the second, third, fourth, and sixth records' assigned to values are selected. By double-clicking one of them, we'll see the following input box:

 Note the indication at the bottom that reads: **4 records will be updated.**

Because of this multi-edit functionality, there are different parameters available as arguments to onCellEdit scripts versus, for example, onChange scripts. onCellEdit scripts have the following arguments available in the function scope:

- **sysIDs**: An array of the sys_ids for each record you've selected. If the user only selected one, this will be an array with only one element.
- **table**: The name of the table containing the records being modified.
- **oldValues**: An array of the old values (prior to any changes) for each of the cells being modified.
- **newValue**: The new value to be placed in the cells being edited. This will be the same value for each cell, as onCellEdit scripts execute once per change (that is, per field to be updated), whether it's a bulk change or one-off. This is the value the user entered to update each of the fields to.
- **callback**: This is a tricky one. callback is the callback function to be executed upon completion of this script. If true is passed into this callback, then any additional onCellEdit client scripts will continue to run (or, if none are left to run, the change will be committed to the database). However, if false is passed into this callback, any further scripts are not executed and the change is aborted.

Security

The browser of the user who is loading the page and requesting the content is the literal **client** that's performing the action. It's also responsible for executing any client scripts, UI scripts, client-side UI actions, processing the UI policies and applying UI policy actions. This includes controlling whether fields are mandatory, read-only, or indeed visible at all.

This can seem like an effective means of protecting content; for example, by hiding a field if the user doesn't have the appropriate permissions, or even setting it as **read-only** using a client script or UI policy. However, it's important to realize that any client-side measures can be overridden by the user!

Anything which really needs to be secured so the user can't see or modify it should be secured using ACLs (security rules). Data policies are another option, and can be used as UI policies on the client as well. This way, data policies can back up their client-side component, making them more secure and effective. However, ACLs work client-side as well, and data policies cannot be scripted like ACLs can, so complex conditions are more difficult to implement.

As a general rule, you should use ACLs to secure tables and fields for specific roles, and use UI/data policies to secure them against specific **conditions**. For example, if only users with the ITIL role should be able to modify a given field, then you should use an ACL. However, if users should only be able to modify the **State** field when the **Active** field is set to `true`, then you might want to use a data policy.

Compatibility

ServiceNow itself runs on a ServiceNow server somewhere out there on the internet, and doesn't require much in the way of compatibility. It can be accessed from just about any system with a modern standards-compliant web browser and an active internet connection. However, every browser has subtle nuances and hitches to how it executes client-side code. For this reason, most web applications (such as ServiceNow's Now platform) recommend a particular web browser which renders the application most effectively, and most closely adheres to modern web standards. In the case of ServiceNow (as with most web apps), the recommended web browser is Google Chrome.

While there was a time when Internet Explorer was required for many web applications, there are few good reasons to use it nowadays, unless your web app requires some proprietary and potentially insecure plugin such as ActiveX. Because Chrome is the recommended browser for ServiceNow, try loading the site/page in Chrome or Firefox if you notice any rendering errors while on another browser (especially Internet Explorer). Once you know the source of the issue, you can either troubleshoot or report the issue to ServiceNow. While ServiceNow does recommend Chrome, they do earnestly want the platform to work well in every modern browser.

> For troubleshooting issues with compatibility with Internet Explorer, you may try disabling any browser add-ons, which can be accomplished by running the command `iexplore -extoff`. You could also try enabling or disabling Internet Explorer's compatibility mode. Chrome's incognito mode allows you to run the browser without most extensions as well, which can be similarly helpful for troubleshooting compatibility issues.

Compatibility is also another good reason to avoid using direct **Document Object Model (DOM)** manipulation of the webpage in your client scripts. The client-side Glide API tries to handle any discrepancies in how each browser interprets your code in order to handle any compatibility issues automatically.

Build for performance

Client-side performance is just as important as server-side performance, but it's even easier to negatively impact client-side performance, since any server lookups have the potential to lock up the user's browser for a couple of seconds (a lifetime to an end-user!). Even scripted actions which you might not think would result in server lookups, such as updating a reference field value, can result in a synchronous server lookup, which can negatively impact a user's browser performance.

> As we learned earlier in this chapter, specifying a third argument (the display value of the record) when setting a reference field, prevents the server lookup, improving performance!

It's important to understand which actions may result in performance-impacting server lookups. It's equally important to understand how (and when) to mitigate that performance impact using asynchronous callback functions, or by combining lookups into one big request and providing all of the information that would otherwise need to be looked up from the server when a field is populated, as with reference fields. This technique of combining multiple lookups into a single request can be a major performance-saver, because it eliminates the most costly part of the lookup: The transit time (sending the request from the client to the server).

Reference fields

As we alluded to above, reference fields have a unique property that in order to populate them manually (that is, not from a script), it requires up to two separate server lookups. The first lookup occurs when you type something into the field, so that it can provide suggestions, as you can see in the following screenshot:

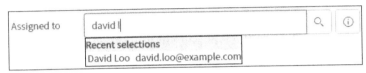

The second lookup happens if a value is pasted in (or if a script populates the field with a `sys_id` as a value), and functions to retrieve the display value of the record being referenced.

As we learned earlier, the first lookup doesn't happen when populating the value from a script, but the second can be avoided by passing in an additional argument to the `setValue()` method of the `g_form` API, as in the following example:

```
g_form.setValue('assigned_to', assigneeSysID, assigneeName);
```

There is also an opportunity for asynchronous callback functions to improve client performance when getting a GlideRecord value from a reference field. The `getReference()` method of the `g_form` API sends a request to the server, but by passing in a reference to a function (a callback function) as the second parameter to this method, we can ensure that this server lookup happens asynchronously, and thus has minimal impact on the user experience.

GlideAjax and asynchronous GlideRecord

We've learned that an asynchronous GlideAjax call is usually the best way to get the server-side data that we might need for a client-side script. However, GlideAjax is complex and requires creation of both a server-side and client-side script, so in many cases it's just fine to use another asynchronous method (such as GlideRecord) to retrieve data from the server, when we need to access related records in a client script, UI policy script, or other client-side script. However, as we learned earlier in this chapter, it's best to avoid asynchronous calls when dealing with onSubmit client scripts; otherwise, the form may submit before the callback function has a chance to be called!

g_scratchpad

Another means by which to improve client-side performance, is by making certain information available on the client as the data is sent along with the rest of the data about the record from the server. This can be accomplished using g_scratchpad, a shared object available both to display business rules, and client-side scripts.

Display business rules, executing as they do on the server, have access to the current object, and the server-side API. This is an incredible resource for performance optimization on the client, because you can prevent nearly all server lookups from client-side scripts, if you can predict them in advance!

For example, consider a scenario in which you need to display the manager of the assignment group in a field message like so:

You might need to have an onChange client script that'll use GlideAjax or an asynchronous GlideRecord query to get the group manager's name, but what about when the form initially loads? There is an even more efficient way to retrieve that information!

To display the group manager in a field message on load, we would just need to create a display business rule that'll run on the records to which this applies, with the following code:

```
g_scratchpad.assignGrpMgrName =     current.assignment_group.manager.
getDisplayValue();
```

Then, all you need is an `onLoad` client script that uses that same property of the `g_scratchpad` object like so:

```
g_scratchpad.assignGrpMgrName =     current.assignment_group.manager.
getDisplayValue();
```

This limits the total number of client-side server lookups, to zero!

UI scripts

UI scripts are quite similar to script includes. While script includes are blocks of server-side code, accessible to any server-side script, UI scripts are blocks of code that are available to any client-side script on a page on which they load.

Global UI scripts are relatively simple. They are available on any form in the system, as they are sent from the server to the browser along with all of the other relevant information (the record data, client scripts, and other data). When the UI script is set to **Global**, any other client-side script can access the code within it. For example, imagine that we have a UI script with the following code in it:

```
function sayHello() {
    alert('Hello!');
}
```

If we mark this UI script as global, then on any client script or UI policy script, we can call `sayHello()`, and the user will see an alert message that says `Hello!`, even though the function that does that action isn't defined anywhere in the script that calls it.

Furthermore, if we don't wrap the code in a function (or if, in the UI policy, we call the function as you can see in the following code snippet), then that code will execute on every page on which the UI script loads.

```
function sayHello() {
    alert('Hello!');
}
sayHello();
```

Non-global UI scripts are a little different though, as they don't load on every form in the system. Instead, you have to tell the system when to load them up along with the rest of the page. This is often done by creating a new UI macro and formatter.

Creating a new UI macro can be done from **System UI | UI Macros**. Give the macro a name, then in-between the `<j:jelly>` and `</j:jelly>` tags, enter the following line:

```
<g:requires name="ui_script_name.jsdbx" />
```

This is written in Jelly, a form of executable XML. ServiceNow is moving away from the use of Jelly, but one of the remnants where it still exists, is in UI macros. The only thing to be aware of here, is that we're telling the system that the UI formatter we're about to create which will use this UI macro, is going to use the UI script we define. In this case, `ui_script_name`. Replace this with your UI script's name followed by the `.jsdbx` extension, and the UI macro will cause the UI script to load on the page that it's on. Save the record.

Once the UI macro is defined, you'll need to create a formatter to place the UI macro within a form. You can create a new formatter from **System UI | Formatters** in the application navigator. Give it a name, tell it what table to run on (we'll use **Incident** [incident] as an example), and enter the name of the UI macro you defined in the formatter field. Make sure that the **Type** field is set to **Formatter**. Save that record too.

Finally, go to the form (by opening a record) on the table you selected. Open the form designer (**Configure | Form Design**). Find the newly created formatter at the bottom of the list on the left.

Drag the new formatter anywhere on the form, save the new layout, and the next time you load that form, your UI macro will execute and you'll see the alert! As mentioned above, you can do this exact same thing without all the trouble of a UI macro by making the UI script global, but then you don't get to control when it loads, which can potentially impact performance.

Running only necessary scripts

Just as with UI scripts, it's best only to send those script files from the server to the client, that you intend to execute.

Sending data from the server to the client is *expensive* in terms of performance on-load. For this reason, it's best not to simply put all of your reusable code into a UI script, and call arbitrary functions as needed. Instead, think carefully about when and where your scripts will load, and whether there's a way you might be able to load it only under certain conditions which indicate when it might be needed. Going back to our example of UI scripts, this might take the form of having a specific view to which certain users are redirected using view rules, then you can add the necessary formatter only on that particular view.

Scripts from the server

One of the main themes over the last couple of chapters, has been performance. That's not an accident. Whether you're sending AJAX requests to the client from the server, or sending script files from the server to the client—whether you're executing synchronously, or asynchronously—it's important to always consider *"what impact will this have on the user experience, can I improve that, and (if not), is it worth it?"*

Often, a few-millisecond delay in processing is well worth the added or improved functionality that a given script might add, but even so, it's important to consider whether there is a more efficient way to accomplish the same end-goal. Lag, or non-responsiveness, is a cumulative frustration. Below are a few things to avoid in order to maintain a positive user experience. These are not strict rules that must always be followed, but they are general guidelines that, if you go against, you should carefully consider the reason and whether there is an alternative.

- Don't send more data from the server to the client than you have to. This includes script files, unnecessarily large AJAX responses and just about any other Server/Client communication.

- Don't send more data from the client to the server than you need to.

Since bandwidth is most commonly asymmetrical, upload has a higher impact and lower speed than download, which means that client/server communication can be even slower than server/client communication. Keep your datasets to a minimum.

- Except in certain circumstances, such as `onSubmit` client script, execute all requests to the server from the client asynchronously. This will prevent the user from having to wait around until your request has finished, before it returns control of their browser or tab back to them.
- Try not to alert or confirm anything on submission of the form, if you can think of a better way to accomplish your goal.

 Alerts and confirmation dialogues are generally not the best user-experience and pull the user out of the ServiceNow interface and flow. Imagine an example where, if a user changes a certain field to a particular value, you want to confirm that they meant to select that. Instead of an **alert** on submission, try informing the user tacitly as it's selected. For example, use `g_form.showFieldMsg('field_name', 'message text here', 'info', true);`. This `g_form` method can accept either *info* or *error* as its third argument as a string, and the fourth (optional) argument specifies whether to scroll the field into the user's viewport (if it isn't already).

If your code ever contains a nested loop, carefully consider whether there is a better way to do what you want to do. Nested loops can be very performance-intensive. For example, consider the following code:

```
var gr1 = new GlideRecord('table_name');
gr1.query();
var gr2;
var result = [];
/* OUTER LOOP */
while (gr1.next()) {
    gr2 = new GlideRecord('other_table_name');
    gr2.addQuery('field', gr1.getValue('field_name'));
    gr2.query();
    /* INNER LOOP */
    while (gr2.next()) {
        results.push(gr2.getValue('other_field_name'));
    }
}
```

This loops through every single record in `gr1`, and then compares one field from `gr1` with a similar field in `gr2` in a query. All results returned from that query are then pushed into an array. A much more efficient way of doing this would be to get all the values from `gr1` in an array, and then change the `gr2` query to check whether the validating field is one of the values specified like so:

```
/* FIRST QUERY */
var gr1 = new GlideRecord('table_name');
gr1.query();
var valuesForQuery = [];
while (gr1.next()) {
valuesForQuery.push(gr1.getValue('field_name'));
}
/* SECOND QUERY */
var gr2 = new GlideRecord('other_table_name');
gr2.addQuery('field', 'IN', valuesForQuery);
gr2.query();
var results = [];
while (gr2.next()) {
    results.push(gr2.getValue('other_field_name'));
}
```

Summary

This chapter taught us all about client scripts, including the different types, and when each runs. We also learned about potential security and compatibility concerns, including how to avoid them! We also discovered and reinforced some ways to ensure that we're building with performance in mind, including how to talk to the server in various ways and circumstances, without negatively impacting the user experience.

Service Portal Scripting

In this chapter, we're going to learn about scripting in ServiceNow's service portal: a relatively new addition to ServiceNow, which provides a user-friendly UI. The service portal consists of a front-end, as well as a builder. Rather than **UI macros** and **Jelly**, the service portal uses widgets and the Angular JavaScript library. We touched on service portal configuration in *Chapter 3, UI Customization*, but in this chapter we're going to learn more about scripting in the service portal by building a user-friendly front-end page for meetings that tie into our Virtual War Room application.

While the rest of the scripting section of this book assumes a basic understanding of JavaScript, this chapter assumes at least a passing familiarity with the Angular JavaScript library. This is required for any advanced service portal widget scripting.

In this chapter, we'll learn about:

- URLs in the service portal
- Creating and configuring widgets
- The widget editor
- Angular scripting
- Client and server-side widget scripts
- Option schema

Author's note

Special thanks to Kim W. for her massive contributions to the knowledge contained within this chapter. Without her, this chapter would either not exist, or be woefully inadequate.

Setting up appointments

We'll start by setting up functionality in our Virtual War Room application that allows us to set up meetings related to Virtual War Rooms. Luckily, ServiceNow has some OOB functionality for this: we're going to be using the **Appointment** [itil_appointment] table to track meeting details for our Virtual War Rooms.

Navigate to a **Virtual War Room** record, right-click the header, and go to **Configure | Related Lists**. Select the **Appointment->Task** option, and click **Save**.

We can now see the appointment related list on the **Virtual War Room** record. Create around five new Appointment records related to the Virtual War Room by clicking the **New** button in the appointments related list. Once you've created one, you can just right-click in the header and use **Insert and stay** after making minor tweaks in order to create duplicate records. We just need a few records to use as examples for a later step.

Be sure to fill in the **Subject, Notes, Starts** and **Ends** fields for each record—we'll be using those fields later on. Vary the dates of the meetings so at least one is in the past, and at least one is in the future.

URLs in the service portal

Many widgets dynamically pull information from the portal URL. There is a generalized standard for URI parameter names, though you can change some of them depending on your needs. However, you cannot change the parameters that OOB (Out of the box / system default) widgets use without creating custom variations of those widgets.

The most common parameters used in service portal URIs are:

- id: The ID of the portal page
- table: The table related to what's being displayed. For example, the form page accepts a sys_id and table, which translates to a specific record.
- sys_id: The sys_id of a specific record.
- view: Which view (such as a form view) to display

Example: https://<instance>.service-now.com/sp?**id**=form&**table**=incident&**sys_id**=<sys_id>&**view**=sp

This link points to the portal with the URL suffix **sp**. Within that service portal it points to the `form` page, and loads a record on the `incident` table with the specified `sys_id`, and the service portal (`sp`) view. If you were to use this link, passing in an incident `sys_id` from your instance, you'd see the specified record in the form view `sp`.

Here's another example URL:

```
https://<instance>.service-now.com/sp?id=list&table=incident&view=ess
```

This link would show a list of Incidents in the self-service view (`ess`). By changing `view=`**ess** to `view=`**default**, the columns shown would change (depending on the differences between those views in your instance).

For our **Virtual War Room** page, our widgets will be looking for the `table` and `sys_id` in the URL. To construct the page URL, go to the **Virtual War Room** record we created the appointments on, and grab the `sys_id` of that record by right-clicking on the header of the form and clicking **Copy sys_id**.

Our link will end up look like this:

```
https://<instance>.service-now.com/sp?id=war&table=u_virtual_war_
room&sys_id=<sys_id>
```

Of course, first we'll have to build the **war** page which you can see we've used as the value for the `id` parameter.

Creating the meeting widget

Before we create our custom **Virtual War Room** page, let's create a **widget** that grabs meeting information, as well as a few other details from the Virtual War Room record.

Navigate to **Service Portal | Widgets** from the application navigator, to get to the widget list. Click the **New** button in the top-right corner to create a new widget record.

Let's name our widget `War Room Meeting Details`. Now that the widget's been created, scroll down to the **Related Links** section, and click **Open in Widget Editor**.

On the widget editor, let's start by adding a little HTML. In the **HTML Template** field, add:

```
<div>
  <div class="test">
    Hello, World!
  </div>
</div>
```

Now that we have some content, let's enable the widget preview. Click **Save** at the top right or hit *Ctrl + S*, and then click the hamburger menu next to the **Save** button.

Click the checkbox next to **Enable Preview**, and click the eye icon next to Save.

If the **Server Script** field is not currently visible on the widget editor page, check the boxes in the header and verify that **Server Script** is checked. Those checkboxes toggle the various fields that you can look at in the widget editor. It is easier to view all fields simultaneously using the widget record instead of the widget editor.

This widget is going to be dynamic, and will pull data from the URL to locate the correct record and appropriate data. We can do this using the $sp.getParameter() method in the server script. Since we're currently not on a page that has the correct data in the URL, we're going to comment out those lines, and add in some default values to use while we're in the widget editor.

Add the following script to the **Server Script** field:

```
(function() {
    // data.table = $sp.getParameter('table');
    // data.sys_id = $sp.getParameter('sys_id');

    /** testing defaults -
    these are values we'll use
    until we put the widget on the page.
    */
    data.table = 'u_virtual_war_room';
    data.sys_id = 'cd4fdd084f560300993533718110c7a7';

    // query for the current record
    var gr = new GlideRecord(data.table);
    gr.get(data.sys_id);

    data.number = gr.getValue('number');
})();
```

In the preceding script, we're grabbing some information using the `table` and `sys_id` of the current record, so make sure to update the value of `data.sys_id` to match the `sys_id` of a Virtual War Room record in your instance. This is just a static value pointing to any Virtual War Room record for testing purposes.

To display this data in the widget itself, we need to add a call to that dynamic variable. Edit the HTML to display this:

```
<div>
  <div class="test">
    Hello, World!
  </div>
  <div class="war-number">
    {{data.number}}
  </div>
</div>
```

By using `data.number` in the HTML above, we're accessing the `number` property of the `data` object, which is transferred to and from the server, with data related to our request.

With the above configuration, we're grabbing information from the server to display in our widget using Angular. Congratulations!

We need more information though—we specifically want to grab meeting information from the **Appointment** table for our Virtual War Room.

In the server script, we need to query the **Appointment** table and retrieve the appointments where the **Task** field matches the current Virtual War Room (the one whose sys_id we passed in via the URL), and grab dynamic values from each of them. Since there can be multiple appointments, we want to order the list by the **Starts** field.

Add the getAppointments() function to your server script like so:

```
(function() {

    // data.table = $sp.getParameter('table');
    // data.sys_id = $sp.getParameter('sys_id');

    /** testing defaults -
    these are values we'll use
    until we put the widget on the page.
    */
    data.table = 'u_virtual_war_room';
    data.sys_id = 'cd4fdd084f560300993533718110c7a7';

    // query for the current record
    var gr = new GlideRecord(data.table);
    gr.get(data.sys_id);

    data.number = gr.getValue('number');
    data.appointments = getAppointments(data.sys_id);

    // get meeting information from Appointment table
    function getAppointments(id) {
        var appointment = {};
        var appointments = [];
        var grAppt = new GlideRecord('itil_appointment');
        grAppt.addQuery('task', id);
        grAppt.orderBy('starts');
        grAppt.query();
```

```
    while (grAppt.next()) {
        /** for each appointment found,
        construct an object with the
        values for that appointment
        */
        appointment = {};
        appointment.subject = grAppt.getValue('subject');
        appointment.startValue = grAppt.getValue('starts');
        appointment.starts = grAppt.getDisplayValue('starts');
        appointment.ends = grAppt.getDisplayValue('ends');
        appointment.notes = grAppt.getValue('notes');
        // push each object to the array.
        appointments.push(appointment);
    }
    return appointments;
}

})();
```

Next, we'll want to change the HTML to display the information we've gathered from each appointment. Rather than write a block of HTML for each of the potential meetings, we're going to iterate over the data.appointments array using the ng-repeat angular attribute:

```
<div>
  <div class="war-number">
    {{data.number}}
  </div>
  <div class="meeting-info" ng-repeat="appointment in data.
appointments">
    <h4>
      {{appointment.subject}}
    </h4>
    <div class="meeting-date">
      Scheduled: {{appointment.starts}} - {{appointment.ends}}
    </div>
    <div class="meeting-notes">
      {{appointment.notes}}
    </div>
  </div>
</div>
```

We now have a widget that displays the appropriate meeting information! It's time to edit our Virtual War Room page, and include the meeting information as part of it. Now that we're done testing without the context of the page, comment out the test data values for `data.table` and `data.sys_id`, and uncomment the proper values. The beginning of our server script should now look like this:

```
(function() {

    data.table = $sp.getParameter('table');
    data.sys_id = $sp.getParameter('sys_id');

    /** testing defaults -
    these are values we'll use
    until we put the widget on the page.
    */
    // data.table = 'u_virtual_war_room';
    // data.sys_id = 'cd4fdd084f560300993533718110c7a7';

    // query for the current record
    var gr = new GlideRecord(data.table);
    gr.get(data.sys_id);

    data.number = gr.getValue('number');
    data.appointments = getAppointments(data.sys_id);

    // get meeting information from Appointment table
    function getAppointments(id) {
        var appointment = {};
        var appointments = [];
        var grAppt = new GlideRecord('itil_appointment');
        grAppt.addQuery('task', id);
        grAppt.orderBy('starts');
        grAppt.query();

        while (grAppt.next()) {
            /** for each appointment found,
            construct an object with the
            values for that appointment
            */
            appointment = {};
            appointment.subject = grAppt.getValue('subject');
            appointment.startValue = grAppt.getValue('starts');
            appointment.starts = grAppt.getDisplayValue('starts');
```

```
                appointment.ends = grAppt.getDisplayValue('ends');
                appointment.notes = grAppt.getValue('notes');
                // push each object to the array.
                appointments.push(appointment);
            }
            return appointments;
        }
    })();
```

Go to `https://<instance>.service-now.com/`**`sp?id=war&table= u_`**
`virtual_war_room&sys_id=<sys_id>`. Remember to replace `<sys_id>` with
the `sys_id` of the war room, and of course, `<instance>` with your instance name.
While on that page, *Ctrl* + right click the **Form** widget to bring up the widget
context menu, and select **Page in Designer**.

 The *Ctrl* + right click shortcut does not currently work in all browsers,
and does not work if no widgets are visible on the page. If it isn't working,
go to the page record (**Service Portal | Pages**) and click the **Open in
Designer** link under **Related Links**.

We currently have a **Form** widget in the middle of the size 12 column in one
container. Instead of this, we want our *War Room Meeting Detail* widget in the size
12 column in the top container, and we want to add another container with two
size 6 columns below.

Inside the new columns, add the **Ticket Conversations** widget to the left column, and add/move the **Form** widget to the right column of the second container. Refresh the portal page to see the new layout and content. It should look like this when you're all finished:

 Sometimes, the page layouts can be very persistent. If this occurs, remove the offending containers/widgets, and re-add them to the page.

Aesthetic changes

Our widget displays the proper information, but it looks a bit out of place on this page, and the style isn't consistent with everything else. Let's make a few changes to help standardize the view.

Using the **Widget Context Menu** (*Ctrl* + right click on the widget), select **Widget in Form Modal**.

If you cannot access the **Widget Context Menu**, you can either make edits by navigating to the widget record, or open the widget in the **Widget Editor**. However, since we've commented out the defaults, no data will show in the widget preview when using the editor.

By using predefined bootstrap class names, we can make some modifications easily. Alter the body HTML template to look like this:

```
<div class="panel panel-default">
  <div class="war-number panel-heading">
    {{data.number}}
  </div>
  <div class="panel-body list-group">
      <div class="meeting-info list-group-item" ng-repeat="appointment
  in data.appointments">
      <h4>
        {{appointment.subject}}
      </h4>
      <div class="pull-right meeting-date">
        Scheduled: {{appointment.starts}} - {{appointment.ends}}
      </div>
      <div class="meeting-notes">
        {{appointment.notes}}
      </div>
    </div>
  </div>
</div>
```

Save the record by clicking the **Save** button at the bottom of the modal, or by hitting *Ctrl + S*. Refresh the page, and the widget should look like this:

This is much better, but what if there are no meetings scheduled for a Virtual War Room? We can determine which HTML shows up by using the `ng-if` Angular attribute, which evaluates whether the condition is true, and displays or hides segments accordingly. Alter the HTML to the following:

```
<div class="panel panel-default">
  <div class="war-number panel-heading">
    {{data.number}}
  </div>
  <div class="panel-body list-group" ng-if="data.appointments.length >
0">
    <div class="meeting-info list-group-item" ng-repeat="appointment
in data.appointments">
      <h4>
        {{appointment.subject}}
      </h4>
      <div class="pull-right meeting-date">
        Scheduled: {{appointment.starts}} - {{appointment.ends}}
      </div>
      <div class="meeting-notes">
        {{appointment.notes}}
      </div>
    </div>
  </div>
  <div class="panel-body none-found" ng-if="data.appointments.length <
1">
    <p>
      No meetings have been scheduled.
    </p>
  </div>
</div>
```

Option schema

When we were going over the **Cool Clocks** in *Chapter 3*, *UI Customization*, one of the configurations we made involved setting a time zone for each instance of the Cool Clock. The variable responsible for determining the time zone in the Cool Clock widget is part of the **Option Schema** for that widget.

Widget options are incredibly useful for making widgets reusable. They allow each instance of a widget to have slightly different results, or display in different ways without having to create a new widget each time.

Let's add some options to our meeting widget! Open the **War Room Meeting Details** widget in the **Widget editor**. Using the hamburger menu, select **Edit option schema**.

Use the **+** at the top right of the modal window to add new option schema. We're going to create two options: one will be to limit the total number of meetings we can list, and the other will remove meetings that have already occurred. The option schema should look like this:

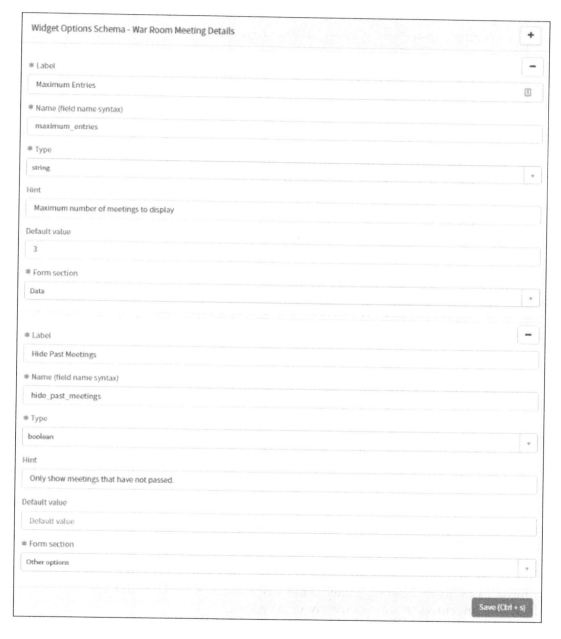

Option schema details are stored in the widget as a JSON object. If you are unable to use the widget editor to add options, put this in the **Option Schema** field on the widget record:

```
[
    {
        "hint":"Maximum number of meetings to display",
        "name":"maximum_entries",
        "section":"Data",
        "default_value":"3",
        "label":"Maximum Entries",
        "type":"string"
    },
    {
        "hint":"Only show meetings that have not passed.",
        "name":"hide_past_meetings",
        "section":"other",
        "label":"Hide Past Meetings",
        "type":"boolean"
    }
]
```

Now that we've set up the options, we need to configure the server script to respond to those options. Option values are stored in a pre-defined `options` object—in order to access the option values, we use `options.<name>`. Make the following alterations to the server script GlideRecord query in the `getAppointments()` function:

```
var grAppt = new GlideRecord('itil_appointment');
grAppt.addQuery('task', id);
grAppt.orderBy('starts');
if (options.hide_past_meetings == 'true') {
    grAppt.addQuery('ends', '>', gs.now());
}
if (options.maximum_entries) {
    grAppt.setLimit(options.maximum_entries);
}
grAppt.query();
```

In our revised query, we're looking to see if the option `hide_past_meetings` is `true`, and to limit the number of results to the option for maximum entries. In our **Option Schema**, we've set the `maximum_entries` default value to 3 — if no other value is entered for that option, the value will be set to 3, and the query will return 3 records at most. `hide_past_meetings` causes the script to check the `ends` date, so we can show only meetings that are currently in progress.

Now that we've defined our **Option Schema**, let's put it to the test. Navigate back to the Virtual War Room test page (`https://<instance>.service-now.com/sp?id=war&table= u_virtual_war_room&sys_id=<sys_id>`), and open up the **Widget Context Menu** (*Ctrl* + right click). Click the first item on the list: **Instance Options**. The following modal window should pop up:

 If options exist, but no option values exist, sometimes the **Instance Options** item in the **Widget Context Menu** will not be clickable. If you are unable to use the **Widget Context Menu** to configure **Instance Options**, or if that item is not clickable, open the page in the **Page Designer**, and click on the **pencil** icon at the top-left of the widget.

By changing the values of our options, we can change the number and types of meetings that appear in this widget instance!

This functionality allows us to create modular widgets that can be reused, instead of creating new widgets. We could, for example, put another copy of this widget on this page and have one display all meetings, and one display upcoming meetings. In a rush, it is a lot easier to change an option value than it is to create an entirely new widget, and too many single-use widgets can become cumbersome to maintain in an instance.

 Certain option names are used to access fields in the **instance of widget** record itself, and should be used with caution in custom option schema. As examples, the **Title** field of the widget instance can be accessed with `options.title`, and the Bootstrap color can be accessed with `options.colors`. If you need to create a custom title option, use a different name in the **Option Schema**.

Troubleshooting widgets

There are a few different methods of troubleshooting a widget, depending on the information you're looking for. In the server script, we can use `gs.log()` or `gs.info()` to log data from the server. In the client controller and the body HTML template, we can use `console.log()` or `console.warn()`, and use the browser's console to debug certain issues.

[Technically we can use `alert()`, but generally, logging in the console is better.]

The **Widget Context Menu** is also helpful for troubleshooting. In particular, the last two items can be incredibly helpful:

'War Room Meeting Details' generated in : 0.004

Instance Options
Instance in Page Editor ✎
Page in Designer ✎

Edit Container Background

Widget Options Schema
Widget in Form Modal
Widget in Editor ✎

Log to console: $scope.data
Log to console: $scope

Let's briefly go over what they each do:

- **Log to console: $scope**: This prints out the widget instance object, with all the parameters/values associated with that widget instance.

- **Log to console: $scope.data**: This is generally used more often. Instead of printing the entire scope, it prints the data object contained in that scope. The data object is the predefined object we built in the server script of our widget. If a widget is having issues displaying the correct information, this option can help narrow down where the problem might be.

Summary

In this chapter, we learned how to build widgets with custom and default option schema, build an aesthetically pleasant UI, and troubleshoot widgets in the service portal. We also learned a little about scripting in the service portal using the Angular JavaScript library.

14

Debugging

ServiceNow is a vast and potentially very complex system, which means that the need to debug your code now and then is not only inevitable, but perfectly normal. The key is to write detailed test scripts, and test thoroughly so that any bugs are discovered prior to reaching your production instance.

In this chapter, we're going to learn about the various tools and methods used in troubleshooting and debugging your code in ServiceNow, including the following topics:

- Debug message logging
- Client-side debugging
- Server-side debugging
- Debugging security and ACLs
- Server-side JavaScript debugger

Logging

 While there is a feature called **session debug logging**, this section is about the system log and how to use logging within scripts effectively for troubleshooting your code.

Logging is something that you can employ both server-side, and client-side. There are several useful logging API methods that can be employed for various purposes, and in different situations: `info()`, `warn()`, and `error()`, each with respectively higher levels of significance. These three types of logging methods are available both from the GlideSystem API (available within server-side scripts as the `gs` object) on the server, and from the console API on the client (For example, `console.warn('message')`).

An informational message (using `gs.info()` on the server, or `console.info()` on the client), is meant to inform a curious admin perusing the logs, of some important state information, or perhaps about successful execution and final state of a particularly complex script. This is especially useful when no other state information is necessarily printed out, such as within a scripted REST API which, since it is executed by a service account, does not present any informational messages and is not conducive to debugging. Imagine an example where a scheduled job runs each night to clean up some records or perform some other activity:

```
var sj = new MyScheduledJobHandler();
var result = sj.performJob();
gs.info('The scheduled job MyScheduledJob completed on ' + gs.now() +
' with a result of ' + result + '.');
```

This job is handled entirely by calling the `performJob` method contained within the `MyScheduledJobHandler` script include class. Assuming that we'll log any errors or warnings inside the script include itself, this script logs the results returned from the `performJob` method. If there is some problem with this scheduled job in the future, an admin can simply search the logs for instances of its name, which is logged along with the status message, to find out whether anything's wrong or not. This can also be useful, because it tells you exactly when the job executed, so you can filter the logs for other entries made within a few seconds or minutes of that time-frame, and check for more serious errors or warnings.

As you might guess, *warning* log messages should be paid more attention to. While they don't necessarily indicate that something has *broken*, they might contain information about aberrant behavior or data that could *lead* to an error, or which is otherwise unexpected. For example, imagine you've written a business rule or script include, and you want to have some information logged to the system log table every time a certain logical path is executed; such as if that path is an exception that may lead to errors elsewhere and thus should be noted, but would not *necessarily* halt or prevent the rest of the script from running. Consider the following code example:

```
function lookAtWidgets(widget) {
    if (widget >= 5) {
        lookatThem(10);
    } else if (widget < 5) {
        dontLook(0);
    } else {
        //How did we get here?
        gs.warn('Unexpected value passed into lookAtWidgets function:
' + widget + '. ')
    }
}
```

This function expects an integer value. It has one logical path for if the value passed in is greater than or equal to 5, and another logical path for if it's less than 5. However, if it's neither (such as if the value passed in was not an integer), then the function logs a warning.

Errors are another thing altogether, and usually indicate that something has gone rather terribly wrong. An error often, but not always, indicates that execution needs to halt for one reason or another. If an error is passed into the `gs.error()` method after the message (such as when generated from a `catch()` block), the details of the error are also logged.

Client-side scripts on the other hand, can talk directly to the browser, so they can either log messages to the browser's console (using `console.log()`, `console.warn()`, and `console.error()`), or in the event of a more significant error, they can alert or log a message within the ServiceNow interface using the `g_form` client-side API.

The browser console will often display `info()`, `warn()`, and `error()` messages differently. For example, Chrome's console will display them each like so:

In the absence of a proper debugger with break points and the like, logging can be the best way to check the value of a given variable at various points throughout the code's progression.

Consider an example where you have to call a script include to perform some action on a record stored in a GlideRecord object, but the script is failing. Perhaps you're not sure at what point it is failing. It might make sense to print out the results of the query to the log, such as the `sys_id` of the record returned. If the value is undefined, then the query has failed or returned no records. It can also be helpful to log the values of various variables at various points throughout the progression of your function, if you're not sure where the fault or unexpected behavior is happening. In this case, it can be helpful to initialize a `logMessage` variable at the beginning of your code, to a blank string: `var logMessage = '';`. This way, you can append useful information to it (`logMessage += 'varName on line 12 = ' + varName + '\n';`), and generate only one log message at the end.

Logging information, whether it's on the client or the server, is an extremely useful tool for development debugging, but consider the impact that it can have on your instance if each log message you created remains in your code when it's pushed to production. Consider also that some companies have been using, and will continue to use ServiceNow for many years, and they'll be developing more and more as time goes on. Each new piece of code introduced with unnecessary log messages, increases database throughput and log table size. This can adversely impact system performance as well as increasing the backup/restore, and save/retrieve times in your instance. It also makes it more difficult for other developers/admins to find logs generated by their own code.

> If your log tables have a high throughput, making it difficult to find logs from your own code, try beginning your logs with a string unique to your script. For example, begin the log message with the function or class name followed by a colon; then, add that as a *starts with...* query when filtering the logs table.

Heavy-usage tables such as **Task** [task], or even child-tables such as **Incident** [incident] or **Request** [sc_request], can cause business rules and related script includes or client scripts to be called hundreds, if not thousands of times per day, so be mindful of what you're logging, and when.

Client-side debugging

Logging is an effective means of assisting with debugging by providing visibility into variable values at various points throughout your code, and this applies whether you're working with client-side or server-side code.

There are some troubleshooting tools that straddle the line between client-side and server-side; one of which is the **JavaScript Log and Field Watcher**. You can enable this tool by clicking on the **System Settings** sprocket at the top-right of the ServiceNow interface, going to the **Developer** tab, and then clicking the toggle:

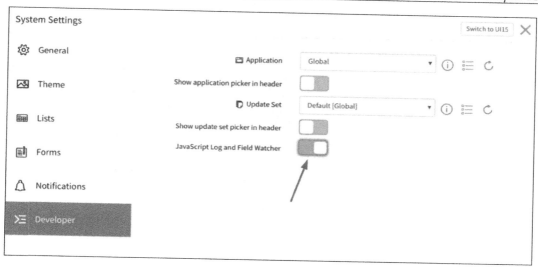

Once enabled, you may want to resize the JS Log and Field Watcher panel by clicking **Medium** or **Large** at the top-right of that panel.

When this is enabled, the JavaScript Log and Field Watcher will display at the bottom of the interface. Much of what you'll find in the JavaScript Log is what you would also find in your browser's console log, but the Field Watcher will display debugging information about a specific field you select. This can be extraordinarily useful for determining whether an ACL or business rule is impacting a given field.

By right-clicking on a field and choosing **Watch - 'fieldname'**, we tell the Field Watcher to pay specific attention to any operating performed on this field. As an example, let's watch the **Priority** field on the **Incident** form.

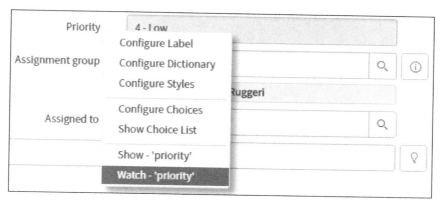

If we reload the form while watching the **Priority** field, we can then see some highly useful information in the **Field Watcher** tab, such as the name of the UI policy that's controlling whether the field is read only, as you can see in the following screenshot:

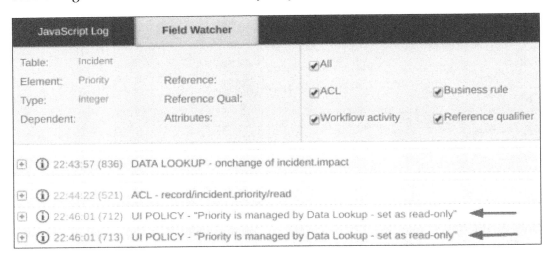

If you modify a field's value and save the form, you can even see things like the UI Policy that was triggered, the value in the watched field on submission, and so on.

Debugging field visibility

While *watching* a field and viewing the actions performed upon it in the **JavaScript Log** and **Field Watcher**, it can be difficult to watch a field if you can't right-click it because it's hidden from the form. Instead, you can grab the field name (attainable from the table dictionary) and open up the background scripts module, from **System Definition | Scripts - Background**.

 You may need to elevate to the security_admin role prior to performing some of the following steps.

In a background script, you can write the following, replacing fieldName with the hidden field's name:

```
gs.getSession().setWatchField('fieldName');
```

Once that's done, simply reload the form with the field in question, and assuming the field is actually on the form and on the view you're loading, the **Field Watcher** will tell you what UI policies, client scripts, ACLs, or other functionality might be acting on the field.

> Background scripts allow you to execute arbitrary server-side code, but be wary; arbitrary code execution is powerful, and if you aren't careful, you could cause serious harm to your instance.

Another way of debugging field visibility, as well as other field-level properties such as whether a field is mandatory or read-only, is to click on the **System Diagnostics | Session Debug | Debug UI Policies**. This will enable the `glide.ui.ui_policy_debug` session property. Once this is enabled, if you navigate back to the **Incident** form, and you'll see the results of any UI Policy Actions on the form, and when each UI Policy runs while it loads.

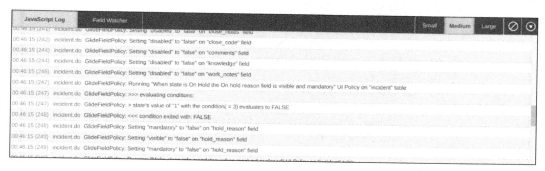

You can disable this debugging condition by either clicking the **System Diagnostics | Session Debug | Disable UI Policies Debug**, or to disable all debug conditions, **System Diagnostics | Session Debug | Disable All**

> Session debug conditions persist even when impersonating other users, but do not persist after logging out and back in. This allows you to debug in various permissions contexts!

Server-side debugging

Server-side debugging can consist of debugging server-side scripts and other behavior, as well as performance and security issues. Debugging server-side scripts can often be slightly more difficult, as the exact source of the undesired behavior is not necessarily logged or thrown as an error message visible on the client. Instead, you must search through the logs for thrown errors, and sometimes use trial-and-error and custom log messages to determine the exact source of the issue. For this reason, using `try/catch()` blocks in your server-side code can be a good idea. This is also true of client-side code in fact, but it is especially important with server-side code.

> While `try/catch()` blocks are a great way to build in error-handling behavior, it should not be relied upon to control the flow of your code. They should only be used when the catch block can handle the error in some sensible way. Otherwise, pass the error up the call stack and perhaps a higher-level function will be able to handle it more effectively. The following is an example of how **not** to use `try/catch()`:
>
> ```
> var gr = new GlideRecord('task');
> gr.addQuery(myEncodedQuery);
> gr.query();
> if (gr.next()) {
>     try {
>         var stateVal = gr.incident_state.toString();
>     } catch(ex) {
>         gs.info(gr.getValue('number') + ' is not an
> incident. Getting value from State field.');
>         var stateVal = gr.state.toString();
>     }
>     return stateVal;
> }
> return false;
> ```

Sometimes, strange behavior (or even poor performance) can result from bloated, corrupted, or stagnant instance cache. Issues can arise from changing field names or other dictionary data, altering schema information, or other major changes like that. These changes might not immediately have impact on cached server-side data, resulting in aberrant behavior, but this can often be easily remedied by clearing the instance cache. This can be done quite simply, by navigating to `/cache.do` on your instance.

Flushing your system cache can cause a slight performance degradation until the cache is repopulated, but if you suspect an issue, it is usually worth It to clear the cache as an added troubleshooting step.

Reference versus value

Another unique property of server-side code, is the structure of a GlideRecord. A GlideRecord consists of field-value pairs; the name of the GlideRecord object property corresponds to the field name (that is, `gr.number` refers to the `number` field of the corresponding record). However, on the client, these properties of the GlideRecord object are strings; whereas on the server, these properties refer to GlideElement objects.

Why is this important, you ask? To answer that question, we must first understand one of the quirks of JavaScript: **pass-by-reference**. In JavaScript, a variable can hold one of two types of values: a **primitive value**, or a **reference**. A primitive value might be a string, a number, a Boolean, `null` or `undefined`.

Primitive values are stored on the **stack**, and are accessed directly by the variable. You might say that they are contained within a variable. A reference value on the other hand, is merely a pointer (or, you might say, a **reference!**) to an object which is stored on the **heap**. The difference between the heap and stack isn't important here, but what is important is that they're different. A variable in JavaScript does not technically contain an object, but rather a reference to that object. Consider what might print out, if we run the following in a background script:

```
var parent = { prop1: 'val1' };
var child = parent;
child.prop1 = 'new value';
gs.print(parent.prop1);
```

In the preceding example, we declare an object: `parent`, with a property: `prop1`, set to a value: `val1`.

On line two, we then declare `child`, and set it as a reference to the same object as `parent`. In doing this, we might think that we are setting it to an `instance` of parent, but that is not the case!

On line three then, we set `prop1` in the `child` object to new value, and then finally on line four, we print out the same property of the `parent` object.

So, what prints out? Although one might expect the `prop1` property of the `parent` object to remain unchanged, due to the fact that both variables are references to the same object, modifying `child` also modified `parent`! Thus, on line four, we print out the new value, `new value`.

This applies just the same to GlideRecord objects on the server, since their properties are not a primitive value like a string (as they are on the client), but GlideElement objects. Consider the following code:

```
var num;
var gr = new GlideRecord('incident');
gr.setLimit(2);
gr.orderBy('number');
gr.query();
while (gr.next()) {
    if (gr.number == 'INC0000001') {
        num = gr.number;
    }
}
gs.print(num);
```

Above, we set a limit of 2 records to return, and order them by number. This should give us `INC0000001` and `INC0000002`. In this code, we've specifically set a condition so that we will only set the `num` value, if the number we get ends in 0001. However, the next time the loop is run, we change the value of the GlideElement object that resides at `gr.number`, which the variable `num` references. When we print the contents of `num`, we're *really* printing out the contents of `gr.number` at the moment we access it. Therefore, we print out `INC0000002` instead of the otherwise expected `INC0000001`.

Debugging security

Aside from UI policies and client scripts, we also alluded to ACLs being a potential cause for a field being read-only or hidden. ACLs are evaluated and execute server-side. While the JavaScript Log and Field Watcher *does* show you some information about when different ACLs execute on a given field, there is a great deal of additional information specific to ACLs that can be found by enabling the **System Diagnostics | Session Debug | Debug Security** module. This causes some information to display below the form/list for each ACL that's evaluated. These messages look like the following:

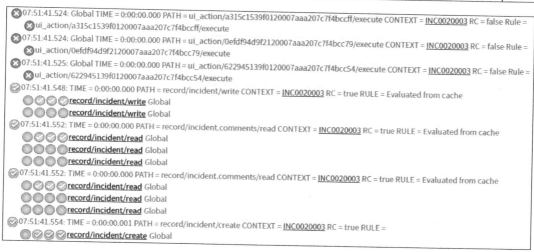

A blue circle indicates that it has been evaluated from the cache, whereas the green circle indicates that the ACL was evaluated based on data on the server, and passed. A red circle obviously means that the ACL check was not successful.

At least one ACL rule is checked and logged for each field on the form when it is loaded, as well as ones for the table and record itself. Whenever a user requests access to an object (a record, a field/value, or even a table), the system checks for any ACL rules matching that object. If a match is not found, the default security rule applies. When the High Security Settings plugin is enabled, this defaults to denying access. However (and more commonly), when a matching rule is found, the permissions of that rule are evaluated against the user. The user must then pass all three conditions of the ACL:

- Does the user have one of the required roles (if specified)?
- Is the condition true?
- Does the script (if specified) return true?

If any one of these checks fails, then the user is denied access to the requested object. If a user is denied access to read a specific field on a form for example, it will not be displayed on the form at all. If the user is denied write access on the other hand, the field is shown as read-only (the same as if it were set as read-only by a UI policy).

As we learned in a previous chapter, setting a field to read-only on the client alone is not a secure way to prevent users from writing to it. However, an ACL has a server-side component as well. Even if users bypass the read-only field on the form, they will not be able to set the field value on the server if an ACL does not allow it. This is similar to the behavior of a UI policy/data policy pair.

When you activate a server-side debugging module, it remains active until one of the following occurs:

- You activate the **Stop Debugging** module, located in system security
- You log out from the instance
- The session expires (for example, the session times out)
- You close the browser

JavaScript debugger

The JavaScript debugger is sort of a re-launch of a ServiceNow feature that was removed in the Fuji release. Since then, the feature has undergone a major overhaul before being reintroduced, resulting in the functionality that we now have access to in Istanbul and later versions of the Now platform.

The debugger can be opened by clicking on the JavaScript debugger button in the list of icons above any **Script** field, such as those above the Script field on a business rule.

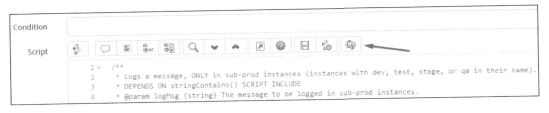

Nearly everything relating to debugging happens within a specific session, and the JavaScript debugger is no different. In order for the debugger to interact with a script's execution, it must be open in a browser window that's within the same `interactive session` (aka, user session) as the session in which the script is being executed on the server.

If you open an incognito window in Chrome or an equivalent private window in another browser, and log in to ServiceNow, this allows you to impersonate a user in one browser window, and remain as your Administrative account in the other. Since these are separate sessions, the JavaScript debugger will not work across them.

Of course, code execution will also only be debugged if at least one breakpoint is set, and if the JavaScript debugger is indeed open, and switched on. The debugger launches by default, in an **On** state. Clicking the small **pause** icon at the top-right of the debugger will turn it off, at which point you can click the I/O icon to turn it back on.

Debugger interface

The icons you'll notice at the top-right of the debugger are (from left to right):

1. Pause/resume debugging (*Shift + F2*)
2. Resume Script Execution (*F9*)
3. Step over the next line (*F8*)
4. Step into the next line (*F7*)
5. Step out of the current function

Resuming the script execution executes whatever line the breakpoint has halted execution on, and continues execution until the next breakpoint, or until all server scripts have finished running.

Clicking the **Step into** button in the JavaScript debugger after execution has paused on a given breakpoint will execute the line on which the debugger has paused, and then will pause execution on the *next* line. If the current line executes an external function, then the next line that's executed will be the first line of the external function, but by using **Step into**, the debugger will pause execution before executing that line. For example, if a business rule executes a Script Include, you can step into it and trace the execution of that script. If there are any breakpoints within that script include, it will automatically stop there either way.

Stepping over a line with a call to an external script (such as a script include) is very similar to stepping *into* it, except that stepping *over* executes that script as a unit and (unless there is a separate breakpoint within that external script) skips to the next line to be executed in the script you're looking at. The external script is executed, but it doesn't step you into it to watch that execution like step into would.

Finally, stepping out of the current function will execute any remaining lines of the function as a unit, and then returns to the calling function. Consider the example we used above, where a business rule calls a script include. In that example, if we have a breakpoint in the script include, and use the step out option after execution halts at that point, we can cause the rest of the script include to execute as a unit, and break on the next line of the `calling` function after the line which called to the function in the script include.

The interface of the debugger has several additional features while actually debugging a script. The panel on the right displays a list of local and global variables, and their contents. Even GlideRecord objects field contents will be displayed.

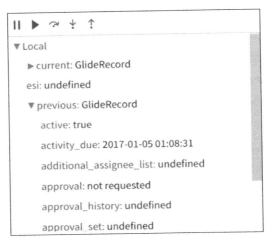

Not only that, but since global variables are also available, you can see things like the contents of the `g_scratchpad` object, the `answer` variable when it's applicable, and loads more.

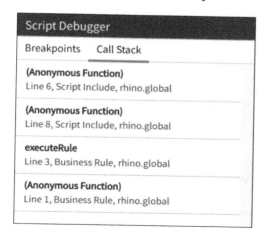

▼ Global

    answer: global.IncidentReasonSNC

    ▶ browser: Object

    cp: undefined

    ▶ current: GlideRecord

    gFormSecurityReadOnlyFields: undefined

    g_max_table_length: 80

    ▶ g_scratchpad: GlideFormScratchpad

    g_tz_offset: -28800000

    g_warn_time: 100.0

    glide.security.is.admin: true

    ▶ gr: GlideRecord

    ▶ gs: GlideSystem

    isBrowserSupported: allow

    isCmsPage: false

    names: undefined

    qc: undefined

On the left side of the debugger interface, we still have a tab containing our **Breakpoints** which we can jump between, but we also have the **Call Stack** tab. This shows the execution call stack from bottom to top:

Script Debugger

Breakpoints   Call Stack

(Anonymous Function)
Line 6, Script Include, rhino.global

(Anonymous Function)
Line 8, Script Include, rhino.global

executeRule
Line 3, Business Rule, rhino.global

(Anonymous Function)
Line 1, Business Rule, rhino.global

Here for example, we have the anonymous function wrapper around our business rule at the bottom, the `executeRule` function inside it (which contains the business rule code), the function inside the script include which is called by the business rule, and the function inside the second script include, which is called by the first.

Finally, we've got the **Transaction Details** on the left, below the **Call Stack**. This includes details about the transaction between the server and client which initiated the code which triggered the debugger. If this transaction was a post from a form submission for example, this would include the details of that update:

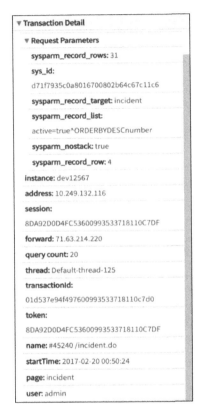

Breakpoints

Creating breakpoints in your code is as easy as opening up any record with a script editor field (business rule, UI policy, ACL, and so on.), and left-clicking in the margin (on the line number). This will add a blue arrow to indicate a breakpoint on the specified line, as you can see below. However, though you can add breakpoints to client-side script objects, these breakpoints will be ignored since the debugger only functions server-side.

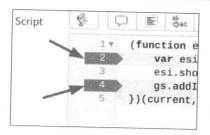

 Breakpoints are linked with the line number on which they're generated. If your script has 10 lines and you create a breakpoint on the 9th, but then remove three of the lines so that there are only 7, the breakpoint will not be visible in the script editor, but will show as a breakpoint on the last line of the script in the debugger. To fix this, you can add enough lines to your script in the script editor, to remove the errant breakpoint. You can then remove the extra lines.

Once a breakpoint is created within a script, it will show up on the left pane of the debugger window. All active breakpoints will show in the debugger window.

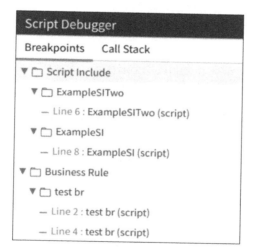

In the preceding screenshot, we have 3 scripts containing breakpoints: a business rule called `test br`, a script include called `ExampleSI`, and another script include called `ExampleSITwo`.

The business rule (`test br`) is a display business rule on the `incident` table, meaning that it executes whenever an **Incident** form is loaded. It contains the following script, which calls the `showMsg()` method of the `ExampleSI` script include, and then prints out an `InfoMessage` when it's done:

```
(function executeRule(current, previous /*null when async*/) {
var esi = new ExampleSI('This is the test message.');
esi.showMsg();
gs.addInfoMessage('Done!');
})(current, previous);
```

The highlighted lines indicate where the breakpoints are.

When this business rule is executed, it will stop on the breakpoint on line two. If we press *F9* to resume the script's execution, it will call out to the external script (a script include: *ExampleSI*). In order to demonstrate the call stack, this script include also calls to another external script include, as you can see below. Again, the highlighted lines indicate the break points:

```
var ExampleSI = Class.create();
ExampleSI.prototype = {
    initialize: function(msg) {
        this.msg = msg;
    },
    showMsg: function() {
        var esit = new ExampleSITwo();
        esit.showProvidedMessage(this.msg);
    },
    type: 'ExampleSI'
};
```

As mentioned above, the final script include (`ExampleSITwo`) is called from the preceding Script Include (`ExampleSI`), and it is the script which finally displays the message that the above two scripts have been passing along:

```
var ExampleSITwo = Class.create();
ExampleSITwo.prototype = {
    initialize: function() {
    },
    showProvidedMessage: function(msg) {
        gs.addInfoMessage(msg);
        return true;
    },
    type: 'ExampleSITwo'
};
```

With these scripts and break-points in place, let's go ahead and load an **Incident** record form with the script debugger loaded and enabled, and watch the execution.

The first thing that we notice, is that the form does not load. Instead, the script which runs on the server to retrieve the data and send it to the client is paused while the debugger runs. Our first breakpoint halts on line 2 of our business rule. Note that since the breakpoint is on the line which declares the esi variable, that variable will not be populated until we advance the execution by either stepping over/into the function, or by resuming execution, as you can see in the following screenshot:

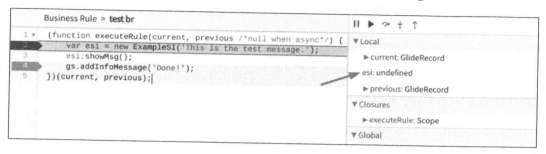

If we press *F9*, we'll advance to the next breakpoint in the execution flow, even though it is in an external script include: ExampleSI. This line (line 8 of the ExampleSI script include above) calls a method of the ExampleSITwo script include. If we then use *F7* to step into that function, we'll be able to advance line-by-line, through it, breaking on each line until we press *F7* again or use some other means to resume the script execution.

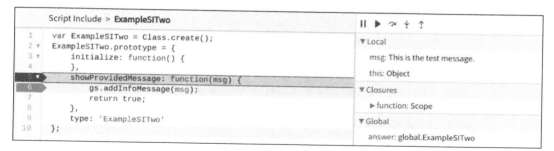

Using these features and tools within the script debugger, you can trace complicated webs of large and interconnected script execution paths, directly view variable states tacitly, mid-execution, and all without needing to modify existing scripts at all. These features also save you from having to add unnecessary log statements and search through your system logs just to find out what a given variable is set to at a given point during execution, or exactly what path a script's execution takes.

With the introduction of the script debugger, Istanbul heralded a whole new era of server-side script debugging. It is now available in every version of ServiceNow after Istanbul.

General debugging

In addition to what we've discussed in the preceding sections, some general debugging tips and principals should be applied in order to preserve the performance of your instance, and to make your debugging as efficient as possible.

One important principal of debugging, is of course to check whether your script even ran. If you have access to the script debugger, this is a simple matter of adding a breakpoint to the script and seeing if execution halts before or after the line with the breakpoint, then stepping through each line until you find the issue. If not, however, you may need to add an `infoMessage` or log statement to the script or code block which you want to know about. There is, however, another way, if you're checking the execution of a business rule. The **System Diagnostics | Session Debug | Debug Business Rule** module can be used. This will tell you when a given business rule loads, by preceding it with an arrow `==>`, and when it completes execution with an arrow pointing in the opposite direction `<==`.

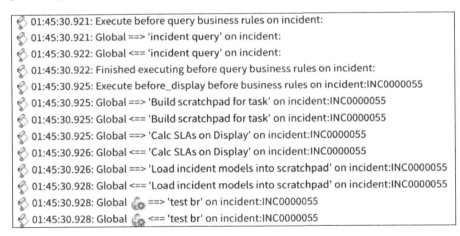

The small icon that looks like a person with a cog in front of them, indicates that the business rule is customized (meaning it's not a system/out-of-the-box business rule).

If you find that your business rule is not executing, the **Debug Business Rule** module will also display the reason that it was skipped.

```
09:43:21.42: Execute before query business rules on sys_user:
09:43:21.42: Global === Skipping 'user query' on sys_user:; condition not satisfied: Condition: gs.getSession().isInteractive() && !gs.hasRole("admin")
09:43:21.42: Finished executing before query business rules on sys_user:
```

But sometimes your issue is not merely that a script is or is not executing. Quite often, you might find yourself seeing the result of a script (for example, an error message, a notification, or some interaction with a field) that you want to stop or modify, but will have no idea what script it might be coming from. Is it a client-side, or server-side script? Is it a business rule, script include, client script, UI script, script field on a UI policy, or even a script executing within the **Condition** field of another script? The search can be frustrating!

A quick and easy way to perform a general search within all application files (including all scripts) is to navigate to the **Application Files** table (`sys_metadata`), and use the keyword search to search for text at the top of the list view, and include the name of the field that's being interacted with, the text of the message you're seeing, or the specific error message.

| ☰ | **Application Files** | New | **Search** | for text ▾ | Couldn't find the record |

Using the debugging techniques we've learned about in this chapter, you should be able to fly through any issues logged against the ServiceNow instance, and discover the source of any code-related problem you might face!

Summary

In this chapter, we begin to wrap things up by re-visiting some of the various ways that things can go wrong with our scripts and other changes, and then looking at some of the ways we can go about mitigating those issues. We learned how to write code so that it logs helpful, informative messages at the appropriate level, and how to go about resolving any bugs or potential issues that this exposes. In the next and final chapter, we're going to learn even more about how to build robust, error-free code, from other ServiceNow seasoned professionals!

15
Pro Tips

In our final chapter, we'd like to leave you with some **pro tips**. This chapter will contain an assortment of many of the best tips from elsewhere in this book, as well as many new tips from ServiceNow and IT Service Management industry experts.

In this chapter, we're going to learn about a great deal of topics, including:

- List personalization and customization
- Free tools to make you a more effective ServiceNow developer
- Unique and little-known APIs and scripting pro-tips
- Risks to be aware of and pitfalls to avoid
- Tips and tricks that the pros wish they knew when they were first starting out

While this chapter includes contributions from a myriad of industry experts, we could only fit so much into it. However, just before the second edition of this book was released, we released *The ServiceNow Handbook*: a compendium of pro-tips, guidelines, and best-practices every ServiceNow developer should know. The handbook is a good follow-up after finishing Learning ServiceNow, to raise your skills to the next level. You can find it at `http://handbook.sngeek.com/`.

Admin pro tips

This section will focus on ServiceNow administration tips and tricks, including lessons shared with us by industry professionals. We'll also highlight some pro-tips from throughout this book, and condense and re-cap them here.

List personalization

As a general (though not universal) rule, settings in ServiceNow can be either **personalized**, or **configured**. Personalizing a feature is generally a user-specific thing, whereas configuration is global and affects all users. One example of this, is with list columns. In **List v2**, most users can personalize list columns by clicking on the gear ⚙ icon. Clicking this icon will display a menu where one can select the columns that display on the selected list. Once personalized, the gear icon will display a small blue circle in the bottom-right corner ⚙ In **List v3**, this personalization option is available from the hamburger menu at the top-left of the list.

Configuring list columns on the other hand, by right-clicking the list column header and going to **Configure | List Layout** on **List v2** (or the same way on **List v3** from the hamburger menu), will change the columns displayed in the list view for all users. This also allows you to add fields to the list that you dot-walk to from reference fields on table records.

It's important to know though, that when a list layout is changed through configuration, only users without personalized list columns will see the change. In order to revert any personalization, open the **Personalize list columns** dialog again, and click on **Reset to column defaults**.

Update set selector

The **update set picker** in ServiceNow can be found in the **System Settings** cog-menu from the top-right of the ServiceNow interface in the banner frame. In the **Developer** tab of the **System Settings** menu, you can see the currently selected update set, as well as an option to display that same update set selector in the ServiceNow header. The same options apply for your selected **Application Scope**. However, whether you view the currently selected update set in this menu or in the header, it is a static field which only updates when you reload the page (not just the content frame , but the whole page), or update it manually by clicking the refresh icon to the right.

Before making changes in a development instance that you'd like to potentially move to production or other sub-prod instances, it's a good idea to double-check that you're in the correct update set. However, this drop-down field can lie. Since the field is displayed client-side, but the updates happen server-side, imagine the following scenario:

You have two tabs open. When you open them, you have a particular update set selected. However, in one of these tabs, you change to a different update set. In the first tab, the initial update set will continue to appear to be selected. Yet in either tab, updates you make will be stored within the **new** (most recently selected) update set; not necessarily the one that displays in the UI. To update the displayed update set so that it accurately shows the selected set from the server, you can click the refresh button from the **System Settings** panel, in the **Developer** tab, next to the update set selector.

Reference field background color

The background color within a reference field can change colors! For example, if an invalid value is entered, it may turn red. However, if a field is a **Dynamic Creation** field, this means that it accepts not only reference values. but if a new value is entered which doesn't map to a referenced record, it will create it! When such a value is entered, the field will turn green. This can have unintended consequences, so it's always best to be careful with this type of field, and make sure that this is indeed the type of field you intend to use whenever you use it. You can enable or disable this functionality on any reference field's dictionary record by checking or un-checking the **Dynamic creation** checkbox.

A similar concept applies to String field types, which allow you to specify choice options. Normally, choice options are used for drop-down fields, but for String fields, they can allow the user to select quick blurbs to fill out a field with commonly-used strings.

List v3 rendering

After enabling the **List v3** plugin (or when deploying a new instance if it's on a recent edition at launch), you may expect all lists to render in List v3 by default. However, embedded lists, list reports, some related lists, and any hierarchical lists will be shown in List v2 by default, as they don't support List v3. More and more types of lists are supporting List v3 in every new version of ServiceNow, but this is an important thing to keep in mind.

List, form, and new window shortcuts

Most admins know about the `.list`, `.form`, and `.config` shortcuts, but if you aren't familiar with the notion: entering a table name (such as `sc_req_item`) into the application navigator filter bar, followed by a dot and the word `list`, then pressing *Enter*, will automatically redirect you to that table's list view. Enter `.form` rather than `.list`, and you'll be directed instead to the `New record` form on that table. The `.config` shortcut will take you to the configuration options for that table.

What many don't know about the application navigator filter shortcuts, is that if you enter `FORM`, `LIST`, or `CONFIG` in all-caps (that is, `sc_request.LIST`) before pressing *Enter*, it will open the corresponding page in a new tab, rather than the current one.

Adding the ServiceNow frame by URL

Whether you use the `.LIST`/`.FORM`/`.CONFIG` shortcuts, middle-click, *Ctrl* + click, or right-click and click to **Open link in new tab**, doing so will open the content frame in a new tab or window without the ServiceNow application navigator and banner frame. In this case, the URL will look something like: `https://your_instance.service-now.com/table_name_list.do?sysparms=values`

To add the ServiceNow frame back, just make the following modification (in bold) to the URL:

`...service-now.com/nav_to.do?uri=table_name_list...`

Author's note

I've built an extension for the Google Chrome browser to automate this with the click of a button, which you can find by searching for `ServiceNow Framerizer` on the Google Chrome Web Store, or going to `http://framerizer.sngeek.com/`.

Impersonation simplification

Impersonating a user can get confusing, especially if you're like most developers/admins, and have multiple tabs open all the time. Impersonating a user in one tab, effectively impersonates the user within your entire session (all windows/tabs), even if you can't necessarily tell that until you refresh. The issue here is similar to what happens when you change update sets in one tab without refreshing the others. If you impersonate a user in one tab, that tab refreshes to show your impersonated user account in the top-right, but if you don't reload all other tabs, you might be confused as to why you don't see the content you'd expect there.

Instead, many admins/developers prefer to open a new in private or incognito window, log in there, and impersonate the other user only in that window, as that will not impact your other browser windows. This way, you can have two windows side-by-side, both with different user sessions logged in!

Derived field risks

When a field on a record's form, or in a table's list view, is derived from another table by dot-walking through a reference field, that's called a derived field. For example, if you have a field called **Requestor** on a task record, which is a reference to the `sys_user` table, you could also have a field called **Requestor Email**, which would contain the value of the `email` field from whatever user record is referenced in the `requestor` field. Assuming the obvious field names for **Requestor** and **Email**, the field name for this derived field would be `requestor.email` (It uses dot-walking!)

What's important to understand about derived fields, is that if you don't explicitly protect them with an ACL, UI Policy, or otherwise, users may be able to modify these fields, which actually modifies them on the source record! This means that modifying the **Requestor Email** field on this task, for example, would result in the Email field of the `sys_user` record being modified, since the Requestor email field is not actually a field on the record you're viewing!

Finding derived fields and other field data

Since derived fields can have some risk associated with them, it's a good idea to get a sense of which fields on a given form are derived. To tell whether a form on your field is derived or not, you can right-click the field label, and click `Show (field_name)`.

The bold path at the top of the dialog will show if the field is on another table. This dialog will also show you lots of useful information about the field, such as the reference qualifier, and field type:

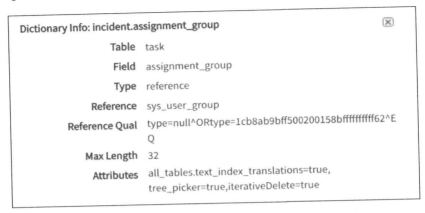

Dictionary overrides

A lot of new ServiceNow admins make the mistake of directly modifying a field's label, attributes, or other dictionary properties, on a base table that is extended by other tables. For example, you might choose to modify the **Short description** field on the **Incident** table so the label says **Issue description** instead, but if you do so from the **Form Designer**, or on the base table (**Task** [task] in this case), you'll be changing it for all tables which extend task! This includes, requests, change tickets, and many other task types. Instead, we can use **dictionary overrides** and custom labels from the field dictionary.

Scripting pro tips

The following Pro Tips will help you remember how to make the most of the ServiceNow/Glide APIs, as well as avoid scripting pitfalls. We'll learn what the pros wished they knew when they were starting out, as well as the reasons behind some of the more arcane pieces of the ServiceNow development puzzle.

Avoiding nested loops

Nested loops have their place in development, but if you aren't careful, they can lead to serious performance degradation due to the fact that the inner loop will run a certain number of times, multiplied by the number of times the outer loop runs.

It is often possible to avoid having to run a nested loop, in favor of running two separate loops (which means that each loop would only run a set number of times).

Consider the following code:

```
var innerGR;
var results = [];
var outerGR = new GlideRecord('table_name');
outerGR.query();
while (outerGR.next()) {
    innerGR = new GlideRecord('other_table_name');
    innerGR.addQuery('field', outerGR.getValue('something_to_
compare'));
    innerGR.query();
    while (innerGR.next()) {
        results.push(innerGR.getValue('some_field'));
    }
}
```

This code requires constructing a new GlideRecord object (innerGR), a new query, and iterating over each record—for every record found within outerGR. The only reason it's constructed this way, is because we want to get a value from records in innerGR that meet a query based on another value from outerGR, and push them into results. However, we can accomplish this much more efficiently by simply separating out these two queries, and creating a temporary array to store up the values from outerGR, that we're using in the query in innerGR like so:

```
var queryValues = [];
var results = [];

var outerGR = new GlideRecord('table_name');
outerGR.query();
while (outerGR.next()) {
    queryValues.push(outerGR.getValue('something_to_compare'));
}
innerGR = new GlideRecord('other_table_name');
innerGR.addQuery('field', 'IN', queryValues);
innerGR.query();
while (innerGR.next()) {
    results.push(innerGR.getValue('some_field'));
}
```

As you can see, by pushing the values we want to search on into an array, and then performing only one outer (though no longer outer, but stand-alone) query, we can dramatically improve performance of our script.

Limit logging

Writing values to the system info, warning, or error logs can be an excellent troubleshooting and debugging step during development. For example, if a server-side script is not executing as expected, you might use gs.info() or gs.log() to log the values of some variables to the system logs, or log some messages to help you trace the execution path. However, often developers forget to go back through all of the scripts they modified once the issue is resolved, and remove their log statements. This can clutter the production logs, and increase the size of the log file which impacts performance and makes detecting issues in production by monitoring the logs, more difficult.

A good way to resolve this issue, would be to create a new script include that, rather than containing a class, contains a directly accessible function. This function would check whether the user was in a production instance or not, and log only if not. We've written a script include that should accomplish this for most cases, below:

```
/**
 * Logs a message, ONLY in sub-prod instances (instances with dev,
test, stage, or qa in their name).
 * DEPENDS ON stringContains() SCRIPT INCLUDE
 * @param logMsg {string} The message to be logged in sub-prod
instances.
 * @param [level="info"] {string} The log level of the message to be
logged in subprod instances. info, warn, error, or log.
 * @param [subProdKeywords=['dev', 'test', 'stage', 'qa']] {array} The
 */
function subProdLog(logMsg, level, subProdKeywords) {
    //If level isn't specified, blank it out so the default case below
will run.
    if (level === undefined) {
        var level = '';
    }
        if (subProdKeywords === undefined || !(subProdKeywords.length
> 0)) {
        var subProdKeywords = ['dev', 'test', 'stage', 'qa'];
    } else if (typeof subProdKeywords == 'string') {
        subProdKeywords = subProdKeywords.split(',');
    }
```

```
        if (stringContains(gs.getProperty('glide.servlet.uri'),
    subProdKeywords).answer) {
            switch (level) {
                case 'info':
                    gs.info(logMsg);
                    return true;
                case 'warn':
                    gs.warn(logMsg);
                    return true;
                case 'error':
                    gs.error(logMsg);
                    return true;
                case 'log':
                    gs.log(logMsg);
                    return true;
                default:
                    gs.info(logMsg);
                    return false;
            }
        }
        return false;
    }
```

This script accepts one mandatory argument (logMsg: the message to be logged), and two optional arguments (level: the log level; info, warn, error, or log - and subProdKeywords: The list of keywords to look for in the instance name, to check whether the instance is sub-prod or not). In most cases, the default value of subProdKeywords (dev, test, stage, and qa) is sufficient. However, if you have more sub-prod instances, you can either add those keywords into this script, or just pass in a custom value for this list. You should also consider whether your production instance would include any of these values. For example, if your production instance name (usually your company name) is prodevnerds, then you might want to change the value it searches for in your dev instance, from dev to the full instance name prodevnerdsdev.

By using this script to log your test and debugging messages, you can avoid having to add in logging messages manually each time you test or debug something in a sub-prod instance, and you don't have to worry about overloading the production log files with unnecessary messages. You can use the standard gs.info/warn/error APIs only for messages that should actually be logged in production, such as when a problem occurs.

Always use getters and setters

Server-side GlideRecord objects contain an element for each field on the record. These elements are not primitive values (strings, numbers, Booleans), but Objects. The type of object is GlideElement, and the usual GlideElement API is available. However, since JavaScript is a loosely typed language, you can reassign a variable of one data-type (such as an `Object`) to another type (such as a `string`). Thus, setting a GlideRecord (`gr`) element's value to a string will overwrite the reference to the GlideElement object itself. This bad-practice example would look like:

```
gr.short_description = 'New short desc.';
```

This would replace the GlideElement object with a string. This is not good.

Technically, Rhino (the server-side implementation of JavaScript that ServiceNow uses) handles this on the server so we can't overwrite the GlideElement object with a string like this, but it's still best practice not to write our code like this.

Instead, using `gr.setValue('short_description', 'New short desc.');` sets the value of the GlideElement object. This is the proper way to make this change.

By the same token, failing to use a getter method (`.getValue()`) has risks as well. The following code sets the value of the `sDesc` variable to a reference to the GlideElement object in the `short_description` property:

```
var sDesc = gr.short_description;
```

If we then change the value of the Object at the location `gr.short_description` (for example, by calling `gr.next()`), then we've changed the value of `sDesc` as well! This is because of a feature of JavaScript, called **pass-by-reference**. To avoid unexpected results like this, always use `.getValue()`, and `.setValue()`. There are a couple of exceptions to this rule: setting journal fields, which are not actually stored on the record itself, but are referenced from the `sys_journal_field` table—and getting or setting **variables** (though you should still use `.toString()` with variables to ensure you get a primitive value).

What the pros wish they knew

We asked the ServiceNow admin and developer community: **What do you wish you'd known, when you were first starting out with ServiceNow?** We've compiled their responses here, along with our own insights and recommendations. This section is for those real life-saving tips, that many developers or admins learn the hard way, or after doing things the hard way for a long time!

Field case

Object labels and names have their own capitalization standards in ServiceNow. Table labels for example, get a capital letter in the beginning of each word in the label. *Requested Items*, for example; or *Local Update Sets*. **Field labels** on the other hand, get a capital letter, but only for the first word (aka sentence case). For example: *Short description*, or *Business service*.

Field and table **names** on the other hand (not to be confused with labels), always use lower-case.

Understanding this, you can ensure that your custom table and field labels adhere to the typical ServiceNow capitalization standards, which is important because changing these things can have broad impact if your tables are extended. Worst case scenario would be if you had to completely relabel a field or table, so that the label no longer matches the name (as the name cannot be changed without data loss), since this may make the field name unintuitive.

Generating encoded query strings

Here's a Pro Tip recommended by Vinitha Vijay, on the ServiceNow Community (`community.servicenow.com`):

Building GlideRecord queries by chaining `.addQuery()` and `.addOrCondition()` method calls in scripts can be complicated, and difficult to troubleshoot unless you execute your query (such as in a background script) and print out all the results to check that they're what you expect.

Instead, simply navigate to the table you're running your query on, and build the query there using the condition builder. You can run the query at any time, to validate that the records returned are exactly the type you expect. Once the query is perfect, you can simply right-click the last component of the query breadcrumbs just above the query builder, and click **Copy query**:

This set of query builder conditions, results in the following encoded query:

```
priorityIN1,2^state!=3^active=true^assigned_to=javascript:gs.
getUserID()
```

You can inject JavaScript into these queries, as in the preceding example, and you can also use a variable to populate some component of it using string concatenation. For example, consider the following:

```
var priorityList = ['1', '2'];
var encodedQuery = 'priorityIN' + priorityList +
'^state!=3^active=true^assigned_to=javascript:gs.getUserID()';
gr.addEncodedQuery(encodedQuery);
```

How to modify OOB scripts

Certified ServiceNow Application Developer and Implementation Specialist Rob Pickering, has another tip for us. The advice Rob wishes he'd had as a ServiceNow developer just starting out, was to follow best-practices more closely. For example, Rob says:

> *If you wish to modify an out-of-box Business Rule, you should copy it, set the original to inactive, and then make your modifications to the copy. This will preserve the original business rule and it will upgrade properly, giving you an opportunity to evaluate if your changes should be deprecated in a new release.*

Other technical best practices

While the ServiceNow Wiki has been replaced by the docs pages (which can be found at `https://docs.servicenow.com/`) and Developer site (`https://developer.servicenow.com/`), it was an excellent source of relevant information. Most of the contents of the Wiki has since been migrated to the docs site.

ServiceNow Platform Architect, Chuck Tomasi, has written many Technical Best Practice articles on the Wiki pages (which can be found by searching for the term **Technical Best Practices**).

Some of our favorite technical best practice articles (which we'll mention but not repeat here), are:

- Coding best practices
- Commenting your work
- Upgrades best practices
- Exporting and Importing XML files

Summary

ServiceNow is a powerful IT Service Management platform, but it is also a very open platform. There's little you *can't* do, with ServiceNow; but with this great development power, comes great developer responsibility—and risk! This is what best practices and your development instance, are for. By looking for best practice advice from industry pros on ServiceNow community posts, blogs, and articles online—and by trying out new techniques on your development instance first—you can be more confident in your ServiceNow development and administration decisions.

As you learn more about the platform and how it works, these best-practices will become intuitive and second-nature to you. Keep reading, researching, and learning, and soon you'll be writing technical best practice documentation of your own.

To that end, we recommend another book by the same author as this one: The ServiceNow Development Handbook. This is a short (<100 page) densely-packed compendium of best-practices, pro-tips, and important conventions, as well as explanations of why they're important. You can find this book at http://handbook.sngeek.com/.

We hope you've enjoyed this book, and that you feel you've learned something valuable from it. Thank you for reading and learning with us!

Index

A

Access Control Lists (ACLs)
  High Security Settings plugin 179
  security rules 175-177
  versus data policies 151-153
ACL process order 178
addActiveQuery() method, GlideRecord 214
addErrorMessage() method, GlideSystem
  about 236
  example usage 236
addInfoMessage() method, GlideSystem
  about 236
  example usage 236
addNotNullQuery() method, GlideRecord
  about 214
  example usage 214
addNullQuery() method, GlideRecord
  about 214
  example usage 214
addQuery() method, GlideRecord
  about 211, 212
  example usage 213
  query operators 212, 213
admin pro tips
  about 343
  derived field risks 347
  derived fields, finding 347
  dictionary overrides 348
  field data, finding 347
  form shortcut 346
  impersonation simplification 347
  list personalization 344
  list shortcut 346
  List v3 rendering 345

  new window shortcut 346
  reference field background color 345
  ServiceNow frame, adding by URL 346
  update set selector 344
Angular 75
API class
  structure 208
application menus 20, 21
application navigator
  about 15, 16
  favorites, adding 17-20
  filter text box 16, 17
appointments
  setting up 304
approvals 133
assignment 134
asynchronous business rules 279

B

background scripts 265
banner frame
  about 3
  Connect chat conversations 12
  global text search 12, 13
  Help icon 11
  Profile link 14
  system settings 4-10
base table 101
Bootstrap 75
breakpoints
  creating 336, 337
build for performance
  about 293
  asynchronous GlideRecord 295

H

hasNext() method, GlideRecord
about 219
example usage 219
hasRole() method, GlideSystem
about 239
example usage 239
hasRole() method, GlideUser
example usage 241
High Security Settings plugin 265

I

initialize() method, GlideRecord
about 210, 220
example usage 210, 220
insert() method, GlideRecord
about 220
example usage 221
instance
branding 61
Integrated development
environment 196-198
isMemberOf() method, GlideUser
about 241
example usage 241

J

JavaScript 267
JavaScript debugger
about 332, 333
breakpoints 336-339
interface 333-336
JavaScript Log 324
Jelly 75

L

legacy APIs 185
linting 196
list personalization 344
lists 27, 30
List v2 plugin
versus List v3 plugin 28-30

List v3 rendering 345
list view 44
logging 321, 322

M

M2M table
creating 83-86
many-to-many relationships 83, 87
meeting widget
aesthetic changes 312, 313
creating 305-311
option schema 314-317
method 208
modules 20, 21
Mozilla Rhino 183, 210, 266

N

next() method, GlideRecord
about 221
example usage 222
nil() method, GlideElement
about 233
example usage 233
non-global UI scripts 297
notification devices 170, 171
notifications
about 164
demo 165-169

O

object 208
onCellEdit client scripts
about 290
arguments 291
onChange client scripts 287-289
one-to-many relationships 79-82
one-to-one relationships
enforcing 88-93
onLoad client scripts 287
onSubmit client scripts 289, 290
OOB scripts
modifying 355

Made in the USA
Coppell, TX
07 April 2021